FREEDOM'S STRUGGLE

The Fugitive Slave's Request

Flying from the greatest danger,
  Save my child! In mercy save!
Hear my cry, thou gentle stranger,
  Pity a poor, fainting slave!

Hunted, with the bloodhounds
baying,
  Rushing in our dreary track,
And no voice of mercy, staying
  Those who fly to bring us back.

Oh! The chain, the lash, the halter!
  Mem'ry tears my throbbing breast.
Can my steps a moment falter?
  Can my feet a moment rest?

Long I tread the weary distance,
  And in desert places crouch,
Pressing on with no assistance,
  And the ground my only couch.

Oft, the night-winds coldly gather
  Round my precious babe and me,
But we'll live upon the heather
  If we only may be free.

Better die with Freedom's banner
  Waving o'er my lowly grave,
Than possess the noblest manor,
  And my name be still a slave!

Take, oh take me to thy dwelling,
  Give a flying captive rest!
Is the tide of gentle feeling
  Swelling in a white man's breast?

Did I cheer her weary sadness?
  Did I shield her fainting form?
Did I shelter her with gladness?
  Does she find with us a home?

FREEDOM'S STRUGGLE

A Response to Slavery from the
Ohio Borderlands

by

GARY L. KNEPP

LITTLE MIAMI PUBLISHING CO.
MILFORD, OHIO
2008

Little Miami Publishing Co.
P.O. Box 588
Milford, Ohio 45150-0588
www.littlemiamibooks.com

Copies of this book can be obtained by contacting the publisher.

Printed in the United States of America

Hardcover first printed 2008
ISBN-13: 978-1-932250-60-2
ISBN-10: 1-932250-60-3

Paperback first printed 2009
ISBN-13: 978-1-932250-71-8
ISBN-10: 1-932250-71-9

Library of Congress Control Number: 2007943024

Contents

Preface

WHY HAS THE STORY OF THE UNDERGROUND RAILROAD captured our collective imaginations in recent years? Perhaps the answer should be—why shouldn't it. It is a story that plays out in our churches, along moonlit pathways, in courtrooms, and in dozens of darkened cellars and attics. It is a story that envelops the human condition—altruism and greed, faith, betrayal, compassion, and courage. And it is just a darn good story—the stuff of Hollywood: mystery, intrigue, violence, clandestine activities, and hairbreadth escapes.

As significant as it was, the Underground Railroad was merely the most dramatic expression of the antislavery movement. Those who engaged in the "enterprise" were a small minority. They were committed radicals who were willing to leap across the socially acceptable line into criminality; facing, if caught, six months in jail, a one thousand dollar fine, confiscation of property used in the activity, and civil penalties to compensate slaveowners for their losses. These people, both black and white, many of whom will remain forever anonymous, risked much in the name of freedom.

There were many more people, although unwilling to cross the divide, who worked in the antislavery movement. They spoke against slavery from the pulpits. They became antislavery activists in their community, signing antislavery petitions. They participated in lawsuits. Some condemned slavery in the legislature. Others voted for Liberty Party candidates at the ballot box. Through their efforts slavery had become, by the mid-nineteenth century, the most critical issue in the country.

Veteran *Cincinnati Enquirer* reporter, Walt Schaeffer, has written about the Underground Railroad in southwest Ohio for years. In 1999, he described Clermont County as "the hole in the map." He meant that

Clermont County's Underground Railroad story was largely untold.

The Clermont County Underground Railroad Research Project, created to celebrate Clermont County's bicentennial, was designed to fill in that "hole." Due to the success of the project, it was continued several years to design the Clermont County Freedom Trail. The Freedom Trail is a self-directed driving tour which visits many of the sites in the county associated with both the Underground Railroad and the abolitionist movement. We are very proud that the National Park Service has designated nineteen of our sites and my Public Education Program and guided bus tour within its Network to Freedom Program—the most in the country. You may obtain a copy of the Freedom Trail brochure by contacting the Clermont County Convention and Visitors Bureau at (513) 732-3600, or by consulting their Web site at www.clermontcvb-ohio.com.

As you read through *Freedom's Struggle*, you will see what a prominent role the people of this county played in this most important episode in our nation's history.

Gary Knepp
Milford, Ohio
January 2008

Acknowledgements

An undertaking of this sort is always a team project. As usual, I want to first thank my family. My parents, Bill and Nancy Knepp, have always supported my efforts. My daughter, Mariah, has shown remarkable patience and understanding and has often helped me locate an illusive grave marker of an Underground Railroad conductor. My wife, Hilda, has provided another set of eyes reading through the manuscript, saving me from an embarrassment of typos.

June Creager, Executive Director of the Clermont County Convention and Visitor's Bureau, saw the potential of Clermont County's story and initiated the Underground Railroad research project. She secured the financial support of the Clermont County Commissioners and has always cheerfully supported me in the research and later in seeking recognition from the Network to Freedom Program of the National Park Service. Without June, this book would not have been possible.

The Clermont County Board of Commissioners, especially Martha Dorsey, Richard Martin, Robert Proud, and Mary Walker, have always been strong supporters and deserve a lot of credit for the success of the research project and Freedom Trail.

Oloye Adeyemon of the African American Taskforce, former Midwest Regional Director of the Network to Freedom Program and independent researcher, was my mentor. He pointed me in the right direction, alerted me to the nuances of the topic and enthusiastically welcomed the latest uncovered tidbit of history. But most importantly, he showed me that the abolition movement and the Underground Railroad, an era of unequalled racial cooperation, could be a model for racial reconciliation. This field has often been co-opted by activists with a political agenda. They could do well to emulate Oloye's approach.

Librarians are special people. After all, I married one. The librarians from the Clermont County Public Library were terrific. They tracked down obscure books and documents from libraries and archives all over the country. This book is richer because of their efforts. I especially want to thank Beth Eicher, Leslie Jacobs, Sue Riggs, Patsy Shively, Hilda Knepp, and Mary Ann Yannessa, herself a biographer of Levi Coffin. Alison Gibson of the Ripley, Ohio, library was also very helpful.

Thanks to Anne Hagedorn, author of *Beyond the River*, for sharing her research with me and for providing an invaluable resource for readers and researchers alike.

There were historians in every community who helped me dig out the stories of their towns and churches. Edna Burns of Historic New Richmond was always eager to help and found a number of obscure sources with fascinating accounts that I would have never found. Cathy Barre was very generous in sharing information about her home in Moscow. Greg Roberts is enthusiastically preserving the history of the Parker Academy. Don Larrison opened many doors for me in Felicity. Cliff Hughes was a great help with the history of the Lindale Baptist Church. Walt Carter provided me with very important and groundbreaking information regarding the Bethel Baptist Church. Aileen Whitt's work, especially in Clermont County's black history, was invaluable. Herm Fagely's early morning e-mails helped me untangle the county's family connections which were vitally important in tracing our networks. Izella Cadwallader was an unending source of information about Williamsburg. Caroline Miller of Augusta, Kentucky, compiler extraordinaire, supplied me with an incredible store of valuable information about Northern Kentucky history, enabling me to provide several important connections to Clermont's story. Richard Crawford was always willing to share his knowledge of Clermont County.

Rick Riggs, thank you again, for your inspired cover design. You have designed the covers for all my books. I cannot ask for more. And thanks to Mike Stretch for his creative interpretation of the book for this softcover edition.

Thanks to Patricia Bradford and Tiffany Ranly. Patty first suggested, as she likes to often remind me, that I take the research position, teased out the locations of Underground Railroad sites from property records, and typed every one of the many applications to the Network to Freedom program. Tiffany typed each page of the manuscript through each of the many revisions, demonstrating a real talent for deciphering my handwriting and understanding my often convoluted directions.

Thank you Barbara Gargiulo, publisher, for your gentle and steady hand. You have made this a better book. And to Kimberly Peet for her hours of editing.

Former U.S. Congressman Rob Portman must be recognized for drafting legislation which created the National Park Service Network to Freedom Program. It has done much to focus academic attention to the topic and has spawned a boom in tourist activities throughout the country.

Jim Cliff, aka "Sparky," went on a photo expedition throughout Clermont County with me, took a number of photographs in the book, and is always ready to be helpful.

Dr. James Westhieder, a colleague from Clermont College, read through the manuscript and made helpful suggestions.

And lastly, thank you to our community ancestors, both black and white. You risked much in helping your fellow Americans to freedom.

The Fugitive's Song

This boasted land, so free and brave,
    Has robbed me of my all!
Pronounces me a chattel, slave,
    And holds my limbs in thrall!

They stole away my noble crown
    My Maker gave to me,
And buried me from my manhood down,
    Among the beasts to be.

Upon my mind, the iron hand
    Of tyranny was laid,
And crushed me with a cruel band
    Which Slavery has made.

They would not let my mind arise,
    Aspiring to be free,
Lest I should learn the boon to prize,
    Of glorious liberty.

They veiled my soul's immortal light
    With shadows dark and drear,
And bade me, in a cheerless night,
    Drag out each weary year.

Should I, because God gave to me
    A skin of darker hue,
To a frail mortal bend the knee,
    And for his favor sue?

On, no! I spurn the very thought;
    I can not be a slave!
I can not be at auction bought!
    I'd rather find my grave.

And I have left the sunny land
    Where bitter waters flow,
And here before you now I stand,
    My griefs to let you know.

(From the *True Wesleyan,* January 4, 1850)

Part One

The Antislavery Movement

Introduction

SLAVERY WAS THE GREAT, PREGNANT UNRESOLVED ISSUE at the American Constitutional Convention. Some Northern delegates wanted to abolish the institution. Many Southerners, but not all, were adamant that slavery be protected. They threatened disunion if their demands were not met. A compromise, called an "Agreement with Hell" by William Lloyd Garrison, left slavery largely a state issue. Thus, the Union was preserved.

Opposition to slavery was a complex, multifaceted, decades-long struggle. People opposed slavery for a number of reasons. For evangelical Christians it was a matter of faith. Others opposed slavery on humanitarian grounds. The "politicos" did so because of the threat to our political institutions posed by an arrogant, overreaching "slaveocracy."

Just as they disagreed over the reasons for opposing slavery, opponents differed on how to end the institution. Abolitionists wanted to end slavery immediately, whether through moral suasion, political influence, or, if necessary, war. The radical "immediatists" were not willing to wait. They felt compelled to obey God's law, not man's. And so, despite the risks, they became involved in the Underground Railroad, fighting the system one human being at a time. Emancipationists wanted to end slavery gradually, giving slaves time to acclimate to freedom and slaveowners time to adjust to a free labor system. They believed that the Constitution limited the national government's authority to abolish slavery. Congress could, however, restrict the expansion of slavery into the new territories. Once contained, they thought slavery would die a natural death.

In 1800 slavery was of marginal interest to the nation. America was preoccupied with external threats, building the economy, and cementing the Union. In time, the nation spread westward and slavery with it. Voices of dissent were raised in the North. These voices were met by Southerners who loudly defended the "peculiar institution." By the onset of the Civil War, slavery had enveloped every major institution of American antebellum society.

Evangelical Christians emerged from the Second Great Awakening with a social conscience. God wanted them, they believed, to combat the ills of society. Chief among these was slavery. Great debates were held in churches to determine whether the Bible sanctioned slavery. Proponents of each side quoted passages in the Holy Book that they believed supported their position. Antislavery ministers, such as John Rankin, published tracts condemning slavery. Slavery's apologists issued their responses. Eventually, the great Protestant denominations—Presbyterian, Baptist, and Methodist—split over the issue.

Two community-based organizations battled over the issue. The American Colonization Society's answer was to send free blacks to Africa. The American Antislavery Society was formed to free the slaves. Agents for both organizations sallied forth into the community—raising money, forming chapters, and proselytizing.

The courts were not immune to the controversy. The law was a conservative institution, dedicated to upholding the rights of property owners. Antislavery advocates frequently lost cases. But often the horrors and basic unfairness of slavery were unmasked in the course of a trial. Abolitionists were spectacularly successful in capitalizing on the excesses of slavery and turning them into public relations bonanzas. A new breed of lawyer surfaced, shifting the focus from property rights to human rights. Gradually, the balance began to tip toward freedom.

Abolitionists, dissatisfied with the glacial progress of "moral suasion," decided to enter politics. They formed the Liberty Party—dedicated to the immediate end of slavery. Because of the dominance of economic issues, the rock-solid allegiance to traditional parties, and poor organizational skills, the new party had little impact. With the spread of slavery to the new territories, antislavery dissidents left their old political homes. They formed several transitional parties before coalescing into the Republican Party in 1854.

All the while, thousands of Americans, not content with the slow progress toward freedom, decided to break the law. They harbored fugitive slaves in darkened cellars and barn lofts. They hurried the freedom seekers along moonlit pathways from one station to the next on the Underground Railroad.

Freedom's Struggle tells the story of the people of Clermont County, Ohio, and their struggle with slavery. Twenty-one miles of Clermont County's border was formed by the Ohio River. Across the river lay slaveholding Kentucky. Location alone guaranteed that her people would become intimately exposed to slavery. Clermonters saw slaves working boats tied up to the county's riverports. Kentuckians leased slaves to work in Clermont tobacco fields. Hundreds of slaves fled across the Ohio River en route to Canada.

Opposition to slavery in Clermont County was deep-seated. The county was settled by antislavery Southerners who came here to escape what one immigrant called the "baneful" effects of the institution. The descendants of these early settlers intermarried, inculcating the next generation with their antislavery ethos.

Not everyone here was opposed to slavery. Some businessmen supported slavery because they profited from trade with the South. Some poor whites favored slavery because they feared competition from slaves who would work for less. Racists believed blacks were designed by the Almighty to be slaves forever. And there were many who were simply ambivalent about the subject.

Clermont County's story is, in many ways, representative of the nation's story. We can trace the development of the struggle for freedom in its many guises and see how slavery came to dominate the public debate. It is ultimately, however, the story of one community's struggle for freedom.

CHAPTER 1

In The Beginning

THE ORIGINS OF SLAVERY IN THE WESTERN WORLD can be traced to the Portuguese, who learned about the institution while establishing trading posts in Africa. They imported African slaves to work the sugar fields of the Madeira and Azore islands in the mid-fifteenth century and introduced the practice to the New World. The Portuguese soon internationalized the trade.[1]

Africans were first seen in the American colonies on August 20, 1619, when a Dutch ship brought "20 negars to Jamestown, Virginia." The Africans came as indentured servants, not slaves. Unlike slaves, they were bonded to service for a specified number of years, at which point they became free. Most were sent to the tobacco fields of the colony. It was not until the eighteenth century that large numbers of Africans came to North America as chattel slaves.[2]

Slavery spread throughout the American colonies, but found greater success in the South where conditions for large-scale commercial agriculture were more suitable. Southern slaves grew sugar, tobacco, rice, indigo, and cotton. In the North, slaves generally served as skilled craftsmen, day laborers, and house servants. One exception to this general rule was in New York, where slaves grew wheat along the banks of the Hudson River. There, slaves counted for as much as 20 percent of the total population. The institution came under attack in the North during the latter third of the eighteenth century, prompting laws providing for gradual emancipation.[3]

By 1790, the slave population in the United States had grown to 697,897, or nearly 18 percent of the total population. Ninety-eight percent of the slave population was concentrated in the South.[4] Slavery had, by this time, become firmly entrenched in the Southern economy and social structure. Many Southern delegates, particularly from Geor-

gia and South Carolina, came to the Constitutional Convention in Philadelphia in the summer of 1787 firmly committed to protecting slavery.

Support for the institution was not unanimous. Benjamin Franklin,
himself a former slaveowner, urged the convention to draft a statement
condemning slavery. John Adams and Alexander Hamilton also
opposed slavery. George Washington vowed never to buy another slave,
and hoped the convention would adopt an emancipation scheme. James
Madison believed that slavery was a "deep rooted abuse." But, like
lesser known antislavery delegates, these founding fathers believed that
pushing the issue would lead to the collapse of the convention and the
imminent implosion of the new republic. Madison guided the delegates
through the treacherous waters, preserving the republic at the expense
of nearly seven hundred thousand slaves.[5]

The Constitution, while sanctioning and protecting slavery, did not
use the terms "slavery" or "slave." Instead, code words such as "other
persons," "persons held to service or labour," and "such persons" were
used to assuage the sensibilities of Northern delegates.[6]

There were several provisions of the Constitution that spoke
directly to slavery. Among them were the protection of the international slave trade until 1808;[7] the counting of slaves as three-fifths of a
person for congressional representation;[8] states were prohibited from
emancipating a "person held to service of labour" in another state;[9]
and Congress was forbidden from enacting any amendment to the
Constitution outlawing the slave trade before 1808, but were given permission to tax the imports of slaves.[10]

The most controversial and far-reaching clause of the Constitution,
directly related to slavery, was known variously as the "Three-fifths
Rule" or the "Three-fifths Clause." This clause counted slaves, or these
"other persons," as three-fifths of a person for purposes of Congressional representation. Southerners feared that if only whites were
counted, the North would gain an unacceptable margin of control in
the House of Representatives and in the Electoral College. Northerners
objected. Elbridge Gerry of Massachusetts suggested that since slaves,
as property, had as many political rights as did horses or cattle in the
North, Northern livestock should be counted as well.[11] After several
months of unresolved debate, Southern delegates bluntly addressed the
issue: Northerners must give the South significant representation to
their slaves or they would oppose ratification of the Constitution.
Finally, the Northern delegates conceded the point. Slaves were

counted as three-fifths of a person for the purpose of Congressional representation.[12]

This compromise had far-reaching consequences in antebellum politics. According to historian Richard H. Brown, "from the inauguration of Washington until the Civil War, the South was in the saddle of National politics."[13] The South had one-third more seats in the House of Representatives than it would have had otherwise. Slaveholders occupied the presidency for much of our early history. Southerners held the position of Speaker of the House for a comparable period of time. And eighteen of the thirty-one Supreme Court justices during the same period were slaveholders. Similar margins of Southern representation were found in the federal bureaucracy.[14]

Garry Wills argues that the ratio was also a determining factor in the outcome of a number of important federal laws. He claims that Missouri would have entered the Union as a free state, that President Jackson's Indian removal policy would have been defeated, that David Wilmot's proviso banning slavery in territories gained from the War with Mexico would have passed, and that the Kansas-Nebraska Bill would have failed to pass Congress, had only whites been counted for representation.[15]

Clearly, the Constitution not only protected slavery, but guaranteed its protection by giving the South a margin of control in the federal government far beyond its actual strength. Further, it clearly did not "secure the blessings of liberty" to seven hundred thousand black slaves. All of this led abolitionist William Lloyd Garrison to proclaim that the Constitution was "a covenant with Death" and "an agreement with Hell."[16]

While the delegates debated the Constitution, the Confederation Congress passed the Northwest Ordinance. The ordinance, called the "Third Great Chapter" by Franklin D. Roosevelt, established a territorial government in the lands north and west of the Ohio River. Further, it provided for due process and freedom of religious expression, created public schools, and outlined a process for creating new states in these lands.[17]

Article VI of the ordinance spoke directly to the issue of slavery.

There shall be neither slavery nor involuntary servitude in said territory, otherwise than in the punishment of crimes, whereof the party shall have been duly convicted: Provided, always, That person escaping into the same, from whom labour or service is lawfully claimed in any one of the Original states, such fugitive may be lawfully reclaimed, and conveyed to the person claiming his or her labour or service as aforesaid.[18]

For many holding antislavery views, in both the North and South, Article VI made these lands attractive for settlement. However, much of the Ohio Territory was still occupied by the Shawnee, a fierce tribe determined to defend their homeland from white incursion. This obstacle was removed in 1795 when the Shawnee ceded their land in Ohio through the Treaty of Greenville.

Dozens of families immigrated to what is now Clermont County shortly after the signing of that treaty. Among them were families with pronounced antislavery sentiments including the Gatches, Fees, Sargents, Burkes, and Denhams. Unfortunately, most of these families left little written record of their thoughts of slavery. Rev. Philip Gatch was the exception.

Fig. 1.1. *The burial markers of the Reverend Philip and Elizabeth Smith Gatch in the Gatch family plot in Milford, Ohio's Greenlawn Cemetery. Reverend Gatch was an antislavery delegate to Ohio's first constitutional convention in 1802.*

Reverend Gatch was born in Baltimore on March 7, 1751. At age twenty-one, he "converted" to Methodism and, soon thereafter, became an ordained minister. One man, upset over what he thought was Gatch's undue influence over his wife, organized a gang to rough up the young minister. Gatch was tarred and feathered. The brush splashed hot tar into one of his eyes, blinding him in that eye. After recovering from his ordeal, Gatch was assigned to a more congenial circuit in Powhatten County, Virginia. Here he met his future wife, Elizabeth Smith, the daughter of a slaveowner.[19]

Gatch's father-in-law gave him and his daughter a farm and lent him several slaves to work it. Reverend Gatch was not comfortable having slaves work for him. He wrote,

I was never in the spirit of slave holding . . . the consequences are so pernicious to both black and white . . . we are born with a disposition of freedom in us, and it is contrary to our nature to feel comfortable under the yoke of oppression.[20]

Reverend Gatch became a slaveowner several years later when his father-in-law bequeathed nine slaves to him. On December 18, 1788, Gatch appeared before the Powhatten County, Virginia, court to free his slaves. The manumission paper states, "I Philip Gatch of Powhatten County do believe that all men are by nature equally free; and from a clear conviction of the justice of depriving my fellow Creatures of their natural Right do hereby emancipate or set free the following persons."[21] In 1790 Gatch joined the Virginia Society for Promoting the Abolition of Slavery. This organization presented one of the earliest memorials to Congress requesting the abolition of slavery in the District of Columbia.[22]

In 1798, Gatch decided to leave his prosperous thousand-acre farm in Buckingham County, Virginia, for the wilds of the Northwest Territory. He felt that he had no other choice but to leave his home in order to escape the evils of slavery, which he called "that bane of true godliness." He was, he wrote, "unwilling to lay bones there and leave my children whom I tenderly loved in a land of slavery not knowing the evils thereof would amount to in their time."[23] Gatch purchased nine hundred acres of land at the forks of the Little Miami River and established a homestead with his wife, children, and several of his former slaves.[24]

Obed Denham, a native of New Jersey, was another antislavery man who moved to Clermont County. In 1796, he purchased fifteen hundred acres of land in what has become Tate Township. Denham platted out a village in 1798 that he called Plainfield, after his hometown. The name of the village was soon changed to Denhamstown and then to Bethel in 1802.[25]

Denham made a practical statement of his antislavery sentiments when he gave lots 80 and 108 in the Village of Bethel "for the use of the Regular Baptist Church who do not hold slaves nor commune at the Lord's Table with those that do practice such tyranny over their fellow creatures."[26] According to historian Byron Williams, Denham's gift established "the first legally organized practical emancipation society west of the Alleghenies."[27] Benjamin Morris wrote that "Obed Denham was not alone in his anti-slavery principles. He ought rather to be considered the representative of a very large class that lived in his day. His untiring energy and zeal in the course of human freedom made him prominent."[28]

The Ohio Territory stood on the cusp of statehood in late 1801. Local "correspondence societies," of which Denham was a member, were formed to determine the advisability of seeking statehood. The Federalists and the Democratic-Republicans, the dominant political parties of the day, began to agitate over the issue of whether Ohio should legalize slavery. The Federalists opposed any further extension of the institution. The Democrats, who were primarily from Virginia, supported legalization. The Federalists accused the Democrats of pushing for statehood in order to legalize slavery. Tempers flared as the debate raged. Men like Obed Denham were very uneasy about the status of slavery in their adopted home.[29]

A constitutional convention, to consist of thirty-five delegates elected by the organized counties, was called to convene on November 1, 1802, at the territorial capital of Chillicothe. Denham actively supported Philip Gatch and James Sargent for Clermont's delegates. Both men were originally from Maryland. Both were Methodist ministers. Both were former slaveowners. Denham could count on both to oppose any efforts to legalize slavery in the state.[30] Gatch accepted the nomination because "much depended on the constitution that might be formed."[31] Both Gatch and Sargent were easily elected in the October 12, 1801, election. Gatch was chosen to serve on the preamble committee and the committee to draft the Constitution's first three articles. Sargent's participation at the convention was unrecorded.[32]

The questions of slavery and black rights provoked, according to delegate Jacob Burnett, "warmth of feeling" sufficient to rip the convention apart. Controversy erupted when a letter attributed to President Thomas Jefferson was read by a delegate. The letter promoted legalization of slavery in Ohio for black males up to age thirty-five and

Fig. 1.2. *The burial marker of Bethel founder Obed Denham in the Old Settlers Cemetery in Bethel, Ohio.*

females up to twenty-five. He argued that legalization of slavery in Ohio would defuse the institution and, therefore, hasten its demise.[33] The logic of this proposal is illusive. The president was duplicitous. Due to the decades-long depression in the tobacco market, Virginia had a surplus in slaves. Jefferson was most likely trying to curry favor with wealthy slaveowners by opening a new market for their "produce."

This debate stoked Clermonters' sensitivity about slavery.[34] They sent to Gatch and Sargent a petition that was introduced to the convention on November 19, 1802. The petition prayed "that those privileges which are the absolute right of all men, may be secured to them." The petition was tabled.[35] The vote on the issue was finally called. The legalization of slavery failed by one vote. The delegates inserted the following into Ohio's Constitution: "There shall be neither slavery nor involuntary servitude in this state."[36]

Once the slavery issue was resolved, the delegates turned their attention to the issue of civil rights for the estimated one to two hundred free blacks in the state. Blacks were, at first, given the right to vote. A motion to reconsider was offered. The vote on this motion resulted in a 17–17 tie. Gatch and the entire southwest Ohio delegation voted for the original motion. Edward Tiffin, the president of the convention, broke the tie by voting for the motion to reconsider, thereby denying blacks basic civil rights guaranteed to the white citizens of the state.[37]

Gatch left the convention with mixed feelings. He was pleased that slavery had been banned, but he was not happy that free blacks had been denied the right to vote. He did, however, believe that blacks had "a right to claim the protection of the laws of the state and had to be treated with justice and humanity."[38]

Clermont County's antislavery heritage was firmly rooted from the very beginning.

Notes

1. Paul Johnson, *A History of the American People* (New York: HarperCollins, 1998), 4–7.
2. Ibid., 27–28.
3. Peter Kolchin, *American Slavery, 1619–1877* (New York: Hill and Wang, 1993), 24–27.
4. Ibid., app. 10, 242, table 3.
5. Joseph J. Ellis, *Founding Brothers: The Revolutionary Generation* (New York: Alfred A. Knopf, 2000), 110–115.
6. Paul Finkelman, *Slavery and the Founders* (Armork, N.Y.: M. E. Sharpe, 1996) 3.
7. U.S. Constitution, art. 1, sec. 9, cl. 1.
8. Ibid., art. 1, sec. 4, cl. 4.
9. Ibid., art. 4, sec. 2, cl. 3.
10. Ibid., art. 5.
11. Finkelman, *Slavery*, 9.
12. Ibid., 13–15.
13. Richard H. Brown, as quoted in Garry Wills, *Negro President: Jefferson and the Slave Power* (Boston: Houghton Mifflin, 2003), 5.
14. Wills, *Negro President*, 6–7.
15. Ibid., 5.
16. William Lloyd Garrison as quoted in Finkelman, *Slavery*, ix.
17. FDR quoted in William Donohue Ellis, *The Ordinance of 1787, The Nation Begins* (Dayton, Ohio: Landfall Press, 1987), intro.; Finkelman, *Slavery*, 34. Eventually, the

states of Ohio, Indiana, Illinois, Michigan, and Wisconsin were created from the Northwest Territory.

18. Ellis, "The Northwest Ordinance of 1787," *The Ordinance of 1787*, art. 6, 128.

19. G. L. Knepp, *Nine Who Made a Difference* (Batavia, Ohio: Cragburn Press, 2000), 5–6.

20. Elizabeth Conner, *Methodist Trail Blazer, Philip Gatch, 1751–1834, His Life in Maryland, Virginia and Ohio* (Rutland, Vt.: Academy Books, 1970), 145.

21. Ibid., 150.

22. Ibid., 152–53.

23. Ibid., 176.

24. Ibid., 7. The area is now known as Milford, Ohio.

25. Louise Abbott Fisher, *Cincinnati Times Star*, April 25, 1940; J. L. Rockey and R. J. Bancroft, *The History of Clermont County, Ohio: with Illustrations and Biographical Sketches of its Prominent Men and Pioneers* (Philadelphia: Louis H. Everts, 1880), 324.

26. Ibid., 24.

27. Byron Williams, *The History of Clermont and Brown Counties, Ohio: from the Earliest Historical Times Down to the Present* (Milford, Ohio: Hobart Publishing Co., 1913) 1: 214.

28. Benjamin Morris, "Incidents in the Early History of Clermont County," *Clermont Courier,* June 28, 1860.

29. Ibid.; Donald J. Ratcliffe, *Party Spirit in a Frontier Republic: Democratic Politics in Ohio, 1793–1821* (Columbus, Ohio: Ohio State Univ. Press, c1998), 66.

30. Gary L. Knepp, "Clermont: Present at the Creation of Ohio," *Community Press,* September 9, 2003.

31. Conner, *Methodist Trail Blazer*, 205.

32. Ibid.

33. Ratcliffe, *Party Spirit in a Frontier Republic*, 70–71.

34. Morris, "Incidents in the Early History of Clermont County," *Clermont Courier,* June 28, 1860.

35. Conner, *Methodist Trail Blazer*, 206–209; *Journal of the Convention of the Territory of the United States Northwest of the Ohio . . . ,"* (Chillicothe, Ohio: printed by N. Willis, 1802) 23.

36. Ohio Constitution of 1802, art. 8, sec. 2.

37. Ratcliffe, *Party Spirit in a Frontier Republic*, 71; Conner, *Methodist Trail Blazer*, 207.

38. Conner, *Methodist Trail Blazer*, 207.

CHAPTER 2

God and Slavery

A FIRESTORM OF REVIVALISM swept through the United States in the early years of the nineteenth century. At times this exuberant, emotional, and personal brand of Christianity enveloped whole families and even entire communities. Thousands gathered at "camp meetings" to experience this tumultuous form of expression. The most famous of these camp meetings was held in the summer of 1801 at Cane Ridge, Kentucky, with the Rev. Barton Stone leading the estimated ten to twenty-five thousand congregants in worship. James Finley described the scene as follows:

A vast crowd, supposed by some to have amounted to twenty-five thousand, was collected together. The noise was like the roar of Niagara. The vast sea of human beings seemed to be agitated as if by a storm. I counted seven ministers, all preaching at one time. . . . Some of the people were praying, some crying for mercy in the most piteous accents, while others were shouting vociferously.

Finley was physically affected by what he saw about him: "My heart beat tumultuously, my knees trembled, my lip quivered, and I felt as though I must fall to the ground."[1]

Winthrop Hudson attributed the strong emotional experience of the camp meeting to the compression of the traditional process of salvation involving "guilt, despair, hope and assurance" into a short period of time lasting days or even hours. This emotionally cathartic event led to orgasms of jerking, barking, crying, laughing, dancing, and rolling on the ground.[2] These revivals moved northward across the Ohio River the next year. This phenomenon lasted for nearly two generations.[3]

Historians have called this period of intense revivalism the Second

Great Awakening. These evangelic Christians believed that the country was infected by social ills, especially slavery. They felt that they had to move out into the greater community to oppose and eventually eradicate it. Southerners, and their Northern apologists, would have none of it. Not only did they deny that slavery was a sin, but they argued that God had actually sanctified the institution. They quoted the Old Testament as their ultimate authority for their argument.

Most of these passages merely report the existence of slavery as proof of God's approval, as can be found in Leviticus 25:44: "As for your male and female slaves whom you may have, you may buy male and female slaves from among the nations that are round about you."

The argument follows that since the Bible flowed from the mind of God to the hand of man, the mere existence of slavery must have the approval of God. One of the most interesting and misapplied passages in the Bible used not only to justify slavery but to rationalize black inferiority can be found in Genesis 9:25–27. The story, often referred to as the curse of Ham, finds Noah drunk. His son, Ham, comes into his father's tent and not only finds his father drunk but naked as well. An angry Noah becomes aware of his son's intrusion. He curses Canaan, Ham's son, and condemns him to be "a slave of slaves shall he be to his brothers." Another of Ham's son's, Cush, is identified as the traditional Father of the Cushites or Ethiopians—a tribe of blacks. As twisted as the logic of this story may be, it was grasped by Americans who were eager to justify their racist attitudes.

Abolitionists responded in kind by quoting general passages in the New Testament. One of their favorites was Acts 17:26: "And God hath made of one blood all nations of men." The theme is the brotherhood of man. Since God made men "of one blood" none could be slaves.

The most powerful weapon in the abolitionists' biblical arsenal was found in Matthew 7:12: "So whatever you wish that men do to you, do so to them; for this is the law and the prophets." The logic of the so-called Golden Rule is obvious. No one would want to be a slave and so no one should enslave another.

Activists published a deluge of pamphlets attacking the proslavery, biblically based argument. Perhaps the most influential author was John Rankin. Rankin was a Tennessee-born Presbyterian minister who moved to Ripley, Ohio, in 1822. He became a nationally known abolitionist and Underground Railroad conductor.

Rankin received a letter on December 2, 1823, informing him that his brother Thomas had purchased a slave. Reverend Rankin was horrified. He responded by writing his brother a series of letters arguing against slavery. He never sent the letters to Thomas, but instead published them in the *Castigator* newspaper of Georgetown, Ohio. The first letter appeared on August 17, 1824.

He opened the letter with this strong condemnation.

I consider involuntary slavery a never failing fountain of the grossest immorality, and one of the deepest sources of human misery; it hangs like the mantle of night over our republic, and shrouds its rising glories.[4]

Rankin, throughout the next twenty letters, attacked slavery on a broad front. He reserved his Biblical arguments for the last three letters.

He debunked the curse of Ham by arguing that the curse applied only against the descendants of Ham, the Canaanite. Africans were not related genealogically to Ham and were, therefore, not affected by the curse.[5] Another proslavery argument held out that since Abraham owned slaves,[6] God must have approved. Not so, argued Rankin. Abraham had servants, who were at times armed, not slaves.[7] Leviticus 25 sanctioned slavery, according to its supporters. Rankin differentiated the slavery of the

Fig. 2.1. *Rev. John Rankin of Ripley, Ohio, was Clermont County's agent of the American Antislavery Society and a well-known Underground Railroad conductor.*

Old Testament and the modern American variety. Moses, he wrote, recognized slavery of non-Jews because they practiced idolatry. Many Africans became committed Christians. Were they not to taste the fruits of the Jubilee, or Freedom?[8]

Rankin, in his last letter, warned of an impending apocalypse if America did not abolish slavery. He reminded his readers that God condemned Egypt for enslaving the Hebrews and said, "I will bring judgment on the nation which they serve."[9] And did not God promise "to loose the bonds of wickedness, to undo the thongs of the yoke, to let the oppressed go free"?[10]

He asked his brother this question: "Could the most malignant hatred do worse than hold a man in abject slavery for life? Thus it is most evident that the slaveholder does violate the law and the prophets."[11]

Rankin's letters were bound and distributed throughout Kentucky and Ohio. Alexander Rankin, his brother, who later became the pastor at the Felicity, Ohio, Presbyterian Church, sold copies of the tract in Kentucky and Tennessee. Perhaps as many as twenty separate editions of his book, known as *Letters on American Slavery*, were issued between 1833 and 1850.[12] Rankin took great personal satisfaction from this exercise when his brother Thomas brought his slaves to Ohio and freed them.

The issue of whether the Bible condoned slavery was frequently debated in churches throughout the first half of the nineteenth century as this account relates. A formal debate was scheduled at the Williamsburg, Ohio, Methodist Church. The question was framed: "Does the Bible Justify Slavery?" Judges were elected to decide the issue. Each debater was given one hour and twenty minutes to present their case.

The man supporting the proposition went first. He pointed out that Abraham had servants, which were held to be the equivalent of slaves. Joseph's brothers sold Joseph as a slave. He also emphasized examples in the New Testament where slavery was accepted. He concluded his argument by stating that slaves "were an article of merchandize, with which a person had the right to do as he pleased."[13]

His opponent conceded that slavery reduced men, whom God made in his own image, to property. "Yes! An article of property; on whose neck an inhuman tyrant could place a yoke, and on whose rights he could innocently place his foot." He argued that the Bible, taken as a whole, condemned slavery "as an outrage against the creation of the universe, but that common sense and every feeling of humanity classes the accursed traffic in human flesh, among the damning sins of a revolted world." He closed his argument by quoting Christ: "In as much as ye have done it unto one of those the least of my brethren, ye have done it unto me."[14]

The judges returned their verdict: The Bible does justify slavery. The correspondent reminded the reader that the majority of the audience disagreed with the conclusion. "The truth is powerful," he wrote, and "will prevail." Man's conscience will not let him believe that the "Gospel of peace and goodwill to men justifies the sin of slavery,"[15] he concluded.

Fig. 2.2. *The Williamsburg Methodist Church, located at 330 Gray Street in Williamsburg, Ohio, as it appears today.*

Methodists, Presbyterians, and Baptists were prominent among the early settlers of Clermont County. Nationally, each of these denominations denounced slavery as a sin in the latter days of the eighteenth century. By the 1830s the widespread use of the cotton gin, with its reliance upon slave labor, eventually prompted Southern Christians to back away from their earlier condemnation of the institution.[16] Peter Cartwright, a Methodist circuit rider, described the evolution of this change. He wrote that Methodist ministers were poor in the beginning, but as their personal wealth grew many became slaveholders. At first these ministers "preached loudly against it. Then, they began to apologize for the evil; then to justify it on legal principles; then on Biblical principles, till lo and behold! It is not an evil but a good! It is not a curse but a blessing!"[17]

Each of these Protestant denominations wrestled over slavery for nearly fifty years before they split apart over the question.

The Methodists

In 1780 the Methodist Conference in Baltimore, Maryland, condemned slavery as "contrary to the laws of God and Nature." Four years later, the same conference voted to suspend ministers who refused to free their personal slaves.[18] For the next sixty years, Methodists waged an increasingly divisive war over the issue. By 1845 the church had split into three factions: the Northern Methodists were generally antislavery; the Southern Methodists favored the institution; and a radical band of abolitionists formed a new church known as the Wesleyan Methodist Church in 1843.[19]

Most Methodists in Clermont County were generally, though not exclusively, antislavery. For the most part, however, they remained disengaged from the abolitionist movement. There were groups of Methodists whose radically exuberant abolitionist viewpoints prompted them to bolt from the mother church and to form Wesleyan enclaves in various locales around the county. Many of the members of these churches became active participants in the Underground Railroad.

The Presbyterians

The Presbyterian Church began cleaving in the mid-1830s over several doctrinal issues, resulting in the formation of two distinct assemblies known popularly as the "Old School" and the "New School."[20] The

Cincinnati Journal and Luminary underscored the centrality of slavery in the dispute: "The question is not between the new and the old in relation to doctrinal errors; but it is slavery and antislavery. It is not the standards which were to be protected, but the system of slavery."[21]

One of the seminal events in the antislavery movement took place at the Presbyterian Lane Theological Seminary in Cincinnati. For eighteen evenings in February of 1834, the students debated two questions: (1) "Ought the people of the slave holding states to abolish slavery immediately?" (2) "Are the doctrines, tendencies and measures of the American Colonization Society, and the influence of its principal supporters, such as to render it worthy of the Christian public?"[22]

The debates, which took place despite disapproval of the faculty, were organized by Theodore Weld, a brilliant and charismatic student from New York. The first session, regarding whether to abolish slavery, was lively. Eighteen students, all of them with strong Southern ties, gave their testimonials. No one spoke in favor of slavery. All of the students, with the exception of four or five who abstained, voted in favor of the immediate abolition of slavery. The second session, which examined support for the American Colonization Society (ACS), was more sedate. After examining the Colonization Society records and listening to one speaker for each side, the students overwhelmingly voted to disassociate themselves from the course of black repatriation to Africa.[23]

On March 10, the students formed an antislavery society whose purpose was to foster the "immediate emancipation of the whole colored race, within the United States."[24] The faculty and the Board of Trustees ordered the students to disband the organization. Seventy-five students left the seminary rather than obey the order of their more conservative elders. These students became known as the "Lane Rebels." They formed the nucleus of the antislavery movement in the West and North.[25]

The divisions in the church over the question of slavery were evident in the General Assembly meeting held in Cincinnati in May of 1845. The committee on slavery entertained a number of proposals ranging from improving the conditions of slaves to outright abolition. The antislavery delegates asked the assembly to denounce slavery as a "moral evil, a heinous sin in the sight of God, calculated to bring upon the church the curse of God." The apologists, on the other hand, trumpeted the Bible's sanction of the institution. They asked how could the assembly denounce slavery as a "heinous crime" without also denouncing Christ. They argued that the best approach would be to improve the lot of the individual slave by treating him with kindness, prohibiting the breakup of families, and repealing harsh laws. Ultimately, the assembly, more interested in preserving harmony within the church, rejected the antislavery proposals. After all, holding slaves should not be a "bar to Christian communion."[26] The Presbyterians finally split over the issue in 1857, the last major Protestant denomination to do so.[27]

The "mother" Presbyterian Church of Clermont County was organized on June 15, 1821, in New Richmond. The church, known formally as the First Presbyterian Church of New Richmond, was an early advocate of the abolitionist cause.[28] Among the abolitionist Presbyterians known to have spoken at the New Richmond church were George Beecher, John Rankin, Calvin Stowe, Amos Dresser, Alexander T. Rankin, and probably John Gregg Fee.[29]

Rev. George Beecher moderated a session of the church on July 13, 1836. A strongly worded statement condemning slavery was drafted at the session.

And having come to the conclusion from the Word of God and the Universal Consciousness of all of humankind that selling and buying and owning men, women and children as property is unjust and unchristian and a horrid violation of the Community of the Lord our God . . .

Therefore, we do solemnly entreat our sister churches in the United States who may be living in the sin of slaveholding to put the evil away from among them without delay.

Therefore, *Resolved*, That the church hereafter debar all persons from her communion who are guilty of holding men women or children as property or who advocate the system.[30]

This statement was significant not only because of its early date, but also for its tone. This was strong stuff. It was more of a demand than a mere statement of sentiment. It condemned the institution, the slaveholders, and their apologists. And most significantly it called upon the church to withhold communion, the church's most important sacrament, from the malefactors. The statement was sent to the Cincinnati Presbytery. Although it was approved, it was then mysteriously expunged.[31]

The church issued a second antislavery statement drafted by Dr. John Rogers and Rev. Amos Dresser on March 23, 1843.

Whereas we believe American slavery to be a flagrant sin against God and

Fig. 2.3. *The Cranston Memorial Presbyterian Church, founded in 1821, was an integrated, abolitionist church. It is located at Union and Washington streets in New Richmond, Ohio.*

man, and in every form it assumes diametrically opposes to every principle of the Gospel of Christ.

Whereas the Bible denounces the sin of oppression in the strongest terms; a) classes men stealing among such as should be excluded from the Church of Christ b) declaring the man stealer to be guilty of a capital offense & worthy of death &

Whereas the General Assembly of the Presbyterian Church previously to

1818 A.D. declared man stealing and slaveholding to be synonymous terms
&

Whereas making "merchandise of slaves and souls of men" was one of the main charges brought against mystical Babylon an account of which was heard a voice from heaven saying Come out from . . . [illegible] my people, that you be not partaken of her sins and that you not receive of her plagues.[32]

The statement went on to say that the church could not countenance any "who support this sin of sins, this mother of abomination." They asked the Cincinnati Presbytery to dissolve all connections with those churches supporting slavery and warned "that unless such a divorce is effected we shall feel bound to dissolve our present connection with the Presbytery."[33] This statement was issued eleven years before the breakup of the national church over the issue of slavery.

The Rev. Thomas Cole of the New Richmond Presbyterian Church and Rev. Alexander Rankin, John's brother, met with twenty people in Monroe Township, then known as "The Scotch Settlement" (now known as Nicholsville), to form the Monroe Presbyterian Church on November 19, 1831. The church prospered among the Scots until January 1839, when it split into New School and Old School factions.[34]

Amos Dresser, one of the Lane Rebels, made an appearance at the Nicholsville New School church in the winter and early spring of 1842 and 1843. He gathered his congregants together on March 29, 1843, less than one week after the New Richmond church met, to debate the

Fig. 2.4. *The Nicholsville Presbyterian Church issued a strongly worded antislavery statement in 1843. The building, now the Pentecostal Church of God, is located on State Route 222 in Nicholsville.*

Fig. 2.5. *The First Batavia Presbyterian Church was once pastored by George Beecher, the brother of Harriet Beecher Stowe. The church is now located at 277 North Street in Batavia, Ohio.*

issue of slavery. The church drafted a memorial stating that the exercise of slavery "directly or indirectly legalizes" the sins of "adultery, fornication, theft, robbery, extortion, and covetousness." This statement, of all other church statements made in Clermont County, is unique because it links the sin of slavery to secular criminal offenses. It continues,

We shudder at the thought of recognizing as the church of Christ any organization which sanctions this system of inequity. We therefore pray the Cincinnati Presbytery to dissolve all ecclesiastical connections with any such organization & unless such a course is taken we shall . . . dissolve our present connection with the Presbytery.[35]

The Batavia Presbyterian Church was formally organized on December 19, 1829, with eight members. The church was decidedly abolitionist. It hosted a number of antislavery meetings and counted among those who presided at the church such luminaries of the movement as Lyman, George, and Henry Beecher; Lyman and Calvin Stowe; and John Rankin. Brice Blair, an elder of the church, served as the president of the Clermont County Antislavery Society and provided housing to Harriet Beecher when she visited her brother in Batavia.[36]

Rev. Moses H. Wilder presided at the church in 1839. The congregation drafted a statement condemning both "intoxicating drinks" and slavery. With respect to slavery, the statement read,

Resolved, That we will not permit any minister who is guilty of the sin of slavery to occupy our pulpit.

Resolved, That we shall not receive members from slave holding churches into our fellowship, without examination.[37]

The Baptists

The Baptists were the third-largest Protestant denomination in Ohio in 1851, with 551 churches.[38] Like the Methodists and Presbyterians, the Baptists were early critics of slavery. In 1785 Virginia Baptists condemned slavery as "breach of divine law" and in 1790 they denounced it as "a violent deprivation of the rights of nature, and inconsistent with a Republican government and therefore (we) recommend it to our brethren to make use of every legal measure to extirpate the horrid evil from the land."[39]

After 1800, Southern voices defending slavery grew louder. Economic dependence upon slavery, as well as slave rebellions in the 1820s and 1830s, quelled antislavery movements among Southern Baptists. A new proslavery militancy grew in the South in the 1830s. The Charleston Association ridiculed abolitionists as "mistaken philanthropists and deluded and mischievous fanatics."[40]

The Northern Baptists asked their Southern brethren to "confess before heaven and earth the sinfulness of holding slaves" and to admit that it was a crime. Efforts were made to pull back from the brink of schism in the early 1840s. However, these efforts were unsuccessful.

The Baptists split across the slavery divide in 1845.[41]

There were several Baptist churches in Clermont County which took an early and strong opposition to slavery. Among them was the Regular Bethel Baptist Church. The church issued an antislavery statement on September 1, 1860. It read,

The Regular Baptist Church at Bethel, Ohio believing that American Slavery as it now exists is a violation of the laws of God, contrary to the true spirit and progress of the Gospel, and an outrage in the God given rights of man producing injury to the enslaver and the enslaved,

Fig. 2.6. *The Bethel Baptist Church was founded as an antislavery church in 1798. It is located at 211 East Plane Street, Bethel, Ohio.*

Therefore Resolve that it is the duty of our preachers to Preach against slavery and that it is not only the privilege but the Duty of our members to speak against slavery and pray for its Downfall. Believing that in so doing we obey the command of God, who says, open thy mouth for the dumb.[42]

This statement was consistent with the congregation's sixty-two-year abolitionist stand. The church was organized in 1798 with six members: Jeremiah Beck Jr. and Sr.; Obed and Mary Denham; Charity and Kelley Burke.[43]

On December 22, 1805, Jeremiah Beck was appointed to write a letter to the Licking Locust Baptist Church in northern Kentucky to inquire about associating with the church. The Licking Locust church is considered by most scholars to be the "mother church" of the Kentucky emancipation movement.[44] This entry represents the earliest indication that Bethel's Baptists wanted to associate with like-minded abolitionists.

An association of abolitionist churches was formed officially in September 1807. Twenty-six "messengers," or delegates, met at the Ebenezer Baptist Church in Mason County, Kentucky. This association distinguished itself from other Baptist associations by its uncompromising stand against slavery. These churches

professed abhorrence to unmerited, hereditary, perpetual, absolute, unconditional slavery—a system of oppression, by which one part of mankind assumes a right of domineering over another part . . . by whom they are bought and sold, denied the rights of humanity and the comforts of life—tormented, afflicted and abused at the discretion of wicked men.[45]

Jeremiah Beck and Sears Crain were selected to be the messengers from Bethel. Historians have for many years erroneously written that the Bethel Baptist Church mentioned in the association records was located in Kentucky. However, Jeremiah Beck and Sears Crain were clearly members of the Bethel, Ohio, church.[46]

Bethel continued to send messengers to the association, more commonly referred to as "Friends of Humanity." The last meeting of the Friends of Humanity, for which records are known to exist, was held in 1816. Moses Edwards and Jeremiah Beck of Bethel were in attendance. The association was dissolved in 1820 following the death of its leader, David Brown.[47]

A cryptic entry was recorded in the Bethel minute book for August 1, 1829: "The church proceeded to appoint 4 messengers to the secret association."[48] There is no explanation of what was meant by the secret association nor any other references to it in the minutes.

Could it have been a reference to a network of abolitionist churches engaged in the Underground Railroad? It is possible. Underground Railroad activity was recorded in Clermont County as early as the 1820s.[49] A secret association of abolitionist churches with "feeder" churches in Kentucky and an "outlet" church in a river county in Ohio would have formed a perfect network staffed with trusted people. Further, the Baptists were quite successful in gaining converts in the slave community. Therefore, this network would have all the necessary ingredients for a successful slave-running enterprise. Unfortunately, no documentary evidence has been found to support this theory.[50]

The Second Ten Mile Baptist Church, now known as the Lindale

Fig. 2.7. *The Second Ten Mile Baptist Church building was constructed in 1833. It was the home church of Andrew Coombs, an Underground Railroad conductor with ties to John Rankin and Levi Coffin.*

Baptist Church, was organized on August 14, 1819. The church moved to its current site in 1833.[51] Andrew Coombs Jr.—storekeeper, Baptist minister, and Underground Railroad conductor—drafted the church's antislavery statement on August 19, 1844.

Resolved, That we regard slave holding contrary to the principles of the gospel and inconsistent with a profession of Christianity.

Resolved, That it is the duty of Christian Churches and other religious bodies to express their disapprobation of the same and to use their influence for the removal of this great evil.[52]

The slavery issue was thrust upon the Bethel Christian Church in 1852 when Davis Crane and his wife Sarah Denham Crane, the daughter of the town's founder, requested that the church take an official stand opposing slavery. In addition to condemning slavery they wanted the church to bar communion and fellowship with all slaveowners. Sarah Crane expressed their views in the following way:

I do think that all that love the Lord ought to show their disapprobation of the sin of American slavery by withholding from such all communion as hold their fellow beings in bondage.[53]

The request put the church into a quandary. Most of the congregants were antislavery. However, church doctrine prohibited barring anyone from enjoying the sacrament of communion. The church struggled with the issue for nearly one year. Neither the Cranes nor the church budged. An obvious compromise of condemning slavery and permitting communion and fellowship with the slaveholder—hating the sin and loving the sinner—was not reached. The Cranes left the church.[54]

The struggles within Clermont County's religious community were representative of hundreds of others across the country. As Southern members of the three great Protestant denominations began to back away from their earlier disapproval of slavery, those in the North became louder in their condemnation. Each side found support for their position in the Bible. Efforts were made to preserve the unity of the denomination. Neither side retreated, eventually forcing the sects to split.

NOTES

1.   James Finley as quoted by Joyce Oldham Appleby, *Inheriting the Revolution: The First Generation of Americans* (Cambridge, Mass.: Belknap Press, 2000), 186–87.

2.   Winthrop S. Hudson, *Religion in America* (New York: Scribner, 1965) 138.

3.   Hudson, *Religion in America*, 134. Francis Asbury, a Methodist bishop, estimated that more than three million Americans attended camp meetings within ten years; Appleby, *Inheriting the Revolution*, 200.

4.   *Castigator*, August 17, 1824.

5.   Larry Gene Willey, "The Reverend John Rankin: Early Ohio Anti-slavery Leader" (PhD diss., University of Iowa, 1976) 69.

6.   Gen. 14 & 23.

7.   Willey, *The Reverend John Rankin*, 70.

8.   Ibid.

9.   Gen. 15:14.

10.   Isaiah 58:6; Ibid.

11.   Willey, *The Reverend John Rankin*, 70.

12.   Ibid., 75.

13.   Anonymous, "A Friend to Man," *Philanthropist*, February 27, 1838.

14.   Ibid.

15.   Ibid.

16.   Hudson, *Religion in America*, 202.

17.   Peter Cartwright, quoted in Edwin S. Gaustad, *A Religious History of America* (New York: Harper & Row, 1966) 168.

18.   William W. Sweet, *Religion on the American Frontier; The Baptists 1783–1830, a Collection of Source Material* (New York: Cooper Square Publishing Co., 1964) 1:78.

19.   Hudson, *Religion in America*, 203–04.

20.   Ibid., 204.

21. *Cincinnati Journal and Luminary,* January 5, 1837.

22. Lawrence Thomas Lesick, *The Lane Rebels: Evangelicalism and Antislavery in Antebellum America* (Metuchen, N.J.: Scarecrow Press, 1980) 79.

23. Ibid., 79–82.

24. Ibid., 88.

25. Ibid., 131–32.

26. *Clermont Courier,* May 30, 1845.

27. Hudson, *Religion in America,* 204; Gaustad, *Religious History,* 173.

28. Rockey and Bancroft, *Clermont County, Ohio,* 420; Aileen M. Whitt, *Cranston Memorial Presbyterian Church, 1821–1993, New Richmond, Ohio* (New Richmond, Ohio: J. B. Whitt, c1993) 13.

29. Whitt, *Cranston Memorial Presbyterian Church,* 16–19. John Gregg Fee, the second cousin of the Clermont Fees, was a firebrand abolitionist who was exiled from Kentucky during the Civil War. Fee most likely spoke at New Richmond. Unfortunately, records from this period are lost.

30. Ibid., 151–52.

31. Ibid., 150.

32. Ibid., 153.

33. Ibid.

34. Rockey & Bancroft, *Clermont County, Ohio,* 392–93.

35. Aileen M. Whitt, *Monroe Presbyterian Church, Nicholsville, Clermont County, Ohio 1831–1950* (New Richmond, Ohio: A. M. Whitt, c1996) 47.

36. Rockey & Bancroft, *Clermont County, Ohio,* 267–68; Harrison Wright, *History of the Batavia Presbyterian Church* (Batavia, Ohio: 1991) 2.

37. Ibid.

38. C. C. Goen, *Broken Churches, Broken Nation: Denominational Schisms and the Coming of the American Civil War* (Macon, Ga.: Mercer University Press, c1985) 52.

39. H. Leon McBeth, *The Baptist Heritage* (Nashville, Tenn.: Broadman Press, 1987) 383.

40. Ibid., 389.

41. Ibid., 389–90.

42. Bethel Baptist Church (Bethel, Ohio), Minute Book, September 1, 1860. The statement was introduced by N. B. Norris.

43. Rockey & Bancroft, *Clermont County, Ohio,* 330.

44. Bethel Baptist Church, Minute Book, December 22, 1805; Linda M. White, "A History of the Baptized Licking-Locust Association, Friends of Humanity," *The Filson Club History Quarterly,* October 1989, 453.

45. Carter Torrant, moderator, Minutes of the Baptized Licking-Locust Association, Friends of Humanity, September 26–28, 1807, reprinted in William W. Sweet, *Religion on the American Frontier,* 564–67.

46. White, *Filson Club,* 455.

47. Bethel Baptist Church, Minute Book, August 25, 1816; White, *Filson Club,* 465.

48. Bethel Baptist Church, Minute Book, August 1, 1829.

49. Rockey & Bancroft, *Clermont County, Ohio,* 134.

50. Sweet, *Religion on the American Frontier*, 78. An oral tradition exists that the church was involved in the Underground Railroad. It suggests that a small room under the church, now used as the "boiler" room, was used to harbor fugitives. No specifics are available. The tradition has been traced to Hilda Musgrove, a church member, who is now deceased. Walter Carter interview, March 29, 2002.

51. Rockey and Bancroft, *Clermont County, Ohio*, 472; Clifford Hughes, et. al., "The 181 Year History of the Lindale Baptist Church," *Clermont County Bi-centennial* 1800–2000 (Batavia, Ohio: Clermont County Historical Society, 2001) 12.

52. Lindale Baptist Church (Lindale, Ohio) Minute Book, August 19, 1844.

53. Bethel Historical Society, *Bethel 1798–1998* (Bethel, Ohio: Bethel Historical Society, 1998)

54. Ibid., 56–57.

CHAPTER 3

The American Colonization Society

ON DECEMBER 21, 1816, Presbyterian minister Robert Finley convened a meeting of prominent men, including Andrew Jackson, Francis Scott Key, Daniel Webster, and Henry Clay, at the Davis Hotel in Washington, D.C. They met to discuss the issue of the growing population of free blacks. Most of the men at the meeting were slaveowners. They were interested in removing the free blacks, whom they saw as troublesome and a potentially seditious group of people, from the country. A smaller group at the meeting were the "philanthropists." Steeped in Christian benevolence, they were genuinely interested in improving the lives of American blacks. These philanthropists thought whites were so prejudiced against blacks that the two races could never live in harmony. Both groups believed that the answer to the issue was in Africa. The American Colonization Society was formed on January 1, 1817, for the purpose of voluntarily transporting free American blacks to West Africa.[1]

President James Monroe strongly believed in the society and its goals. With his support, Congress appropriated one hundred thousand dollars to recruit and transport colonists and to purchase property in Africa. In January 1820, 88 American colonists set sail on the *Elizabeth* from New York to Africa. Despite early losses to yellow fever, the colony became firmly established. Within ten years, 2,683 American blacks had settled in the new country of Liberia. The colonists, in a show of gratitude to their greatest benefactor, named their capital Monrovia.[2]

The society was strongly supported by the press, both political parties, the business community, and the clergy. Many in Ohio agreed with this editorial in the *Ohio State Journal*:

We are suffering under many of the pernicious effects incident to a slave population, without any of the few benefits which are derived from holding slaves. Immense numbers of mulattoes are continually flocking by tens, and by hundreds, into Ohio. Their fecundity is proverbial. They are worse than drones to society, and they already swarm in our land like locusts.[3]

William Morrow, governor of Ohio, echoed similar thoughts in a message to the Ohio General Assembly.

[H]ow long Ohio will continue to tolerate the emigration [*sic*] to her territory, of this unfortunate and degraded race. Their rapid increase has already given serious alarm to many of our citizens.[4]

He urged the legislature to appropriate public funds to donate to the American Colonization Society for its repatriation efforts.

The efforts of the new organization found favor in the religious community. The Baptists, Methodists, and Lutherans all passed resolutions of support for the society. The Methodists, in particular, urged their clergy to make public speeches of support and to take up collections every Independence Day for the society.[5]

The society hired local agents to represent it in more or less defined territories. Agents spoke at churches and public houses, organized local chapters, raised funds, recruited colonists and arranged transportation to Africa. Local agent Rev. George Gatch, Philip's son, spoke on behalf of the society in Perin's Town (Perintown, Miami Township) on July 7, 1833. The event was given favorable notice in the *Chronicle of the Times*, a county newspaper.

The *Times* reflected the viewpoint of the philanthropist branch of the colonization movement in the following editorial:

Among the numerous objects of benevolence that are almost daily knocking at our doors, there are none of greater magnitude, or that more feeling appeals to the heart of the philanthropist, than the amelioration of the physical and moral condition of the colored population of the United States and among the various schemes devised for this laudable purpose, by the wisest heads and best hearts in the country, none have met with such general favor, or been attended with such general favor . . . as the plan of colonizing them in Africa. On his arrival at this home of the *oppressed*, the colored man no longer feels his degraded condition; and the slave, whose shackles have been knocked off and sent thither, is enabled at once to assert his long defrauded rights and enjoy the independence to which by the laws of God he is entitled.[6]

Robert Hall of Georgetown, Ohio, epitomized those who looked upon the colonization movement as an opportunity to rid themselves of an irritant. He wrote to the national headquarters suggesting a special project: removal of several hundred free blacks from the settlements on White Oak and Brush creeks in Brown County.[7] He mentioned that there were others in the community who also would be willing to contribute money to the project. Hall admitted that these citizens were motivated by self interest. These people were growing increasingly wary of the blacks. Because most of the blacks lived on swampy lands, their farms were only marginally productive, leading many to live in a condition "much more wretched" than slaves of the South. This, he claimed, led them to steal from whites.

Hall, echoing the fears engendered by the Nat Turner slave rebellion of the previous year, wrote that his fellow residents suspected that the blacks "have entertained hostile intentions against the whites."[8] These "hostile intentions" were inspired by black "insurgents from the south" who allegedly had been visiting the black settlements. Because these blacks had been subjected "to many inconveniences" while living among the whites "they have a brotherly feeling for the insurgents" and "look upon the white man as a common enemy in war."[9]

Hall may have had some success in attracting the attention of the American Colonization Society. The *Chronicle of the Times* reported that a scout for three hundred potential colonists from Brown County left Louisville, Kentucky, in April of 1833 bound for Liberia. The scout's mission was to visit the colony and to determine if the conditions were favorable for immigration.[10]

Local chapters of the society were organized throughout Clermont County with the most active at Bethel, New Richmond, and Gilead (Lindale). The Bethel chapter had ninety-eight members who contributed fifty dollars to the cause in 1832. An additional fifteen dollars was raised by Methodist minister John M. Goshorn at two separate meetings in July of the same year.[11]

Rev. George C. Light

Rev. George C. Light, grandson of the founder of New Richmond, accepted a commission as an agent for the society for parts of Kentucky in 1832. Light, a Methodist minister, was described as "a person of more than ordinary note" who was known "for his fervid eloquence and devotion to the interests of the church whose cause he had

Fig. 3.1. *The former home of Rev. George Light, agent of the American Colonization Society, currently The Landing Restaurant located at 401 Front Street, New Richmond, Ohio.*

espoused." Light also served as the county surveyor and state legislator before accepting his commission as an agent.[12]

Evidently, Light was a better recruiter than fundraiser. Robert Finley informed the parent organization in Washington that Light had arranged for the transportation of sixty emigrants, but had not found enough money to pay for the trip. John Edgar expressed similar thoughts four months later. Edgar wrote that between eighty and ninety emigrants had committed to go to Liberia. The Kentucky Board of Managers was "seriously apprehensive that the funds will not be adequate to meet the expenses" of the venture. He asked the national organization for help.[13]

Light wrote a lengthy letter to his boss on April 1, 1833. He reported that seventy-two colonists left Louisville for New Orleans on March 23. Thirty-three others joined the party downstream. "These emigrants," he wrote, "are in the general young and healthy. Some of them are mechanics. Others can read and write." Among the party was Samuel Jones of Brown County, who was expected to return to Ohio to report on the conditions found at the colony. His way was paid by the Brown County Colonization Society. Light also advised that he had indeed raised all the money necessary to pay for the trip.[14]

The *Louisville Herald* criticized Light for taking what appeared to be an exorbitant salary as agent. The paper reported that he had raised $1,113.67 for the society, but had deducted $725.00 as salary and another $15.00 in expenses. The paper opined, "If so small a part of the amount collected for the benevolent purposes of colonization, finds its way into the Treasury of the society, we apprehend that many who are favorably disposed to it will withhold their aid."[15] Despite the criticism, Light continued to work on behalf of the organization. Light sided with the proslavery Southern branch of the Methodist Church and later became a bishop. He died in Vicksburg, Mississippi, in 1860 at the age of seventy-five.[16]

Fissures began to undermine the society. Free blacks began to increasingly see themselves as Americans rather than Africans. They wanted to remain in America and work to abolish slavery. In 1828 Massachusetts blacks formally denounced the society and demanded an end to slavery. White philanthropists also began to leave the organization in the 1830s as they came within the orbit of British activists who demanded an immediate end to slavery. Poor fundraising also took a toll on the colonization movement. A large debt of forty-five thousand dollars led to a temporary suspension of trips to Africa. Though the society survived until the twentieth century, it inexorably lost influence as events passed it by.[17]

NOTES

1.   Appleby, *Inheriting the Revolution*, 228; Greg [—?—], "The American Colonization Society: The Movement Begins," *Back to Africa: The Colonization Movement*, http://beatl.barnard.columbia.edu/students/his3487/lembrich/seminar 62.html (hereinafter Barnard); *The American Colonization Society*, http://nebby.ccdennison.edu/waite/liberia/history/acs.html (hereinafter Webby).

2.   Webby, 1; Barnard, 1.

3.   *State Journal*, July 12, 1827, reprinted in *African Repository*, July 1827, 157.

4.   *African Repository*, December 1827, 316.

5.   Ibid., 315–316.

6.   *Chronicle of the Times*, June 29, 1833.

7.   Hall was referring to blacks living in those Brown County communities more commonly known as the Gist Settlements. Samuel Gist was a Virginia slaveholder who died in 1815 and manumitted three hundred slaves by will. Much of his estate was to have established a trust fund for his former slaves. His family contested the will and received most of the estate's assets. A smaller portion was used to purchase property in Brown County. The "Gist Settlers" came to the land in June of 1818.

8.   Keith P. Griffler, *Frontier Line of Freedom, African Americans and the Forging of the Underground Railroad in the Ohio Valley* (Lexington, Ky.: University Press of Kentucky, 2004) 12–14. Nat Turner was a charismatic mystic who led dozens of slaves in a rebellion in South Hampton County, Virginia, on August 22, 1831. He and his insurrectionists killed sixty whites and destroyed thousands of dollars in property. Nearly two hundred blacks, a number of whom were innocent, were executed afterwards.

Elliot Gorn, et al., eds., *Constructing the American Past* (New York: Longman, 2002) 1:150.

9. Robert Hall to Robert Finley, January 31, 1832, American Colonization Records, vol. 37, Library of Congress, Washington D.C.

10. *Chronicle of the Times*, April 27, 1833.

11. Robert Porter to the American Colonization Society (ACS), August 11, 1835, ACS Records, Library of Congress, vol. 61. Robert Porter was the secretary of the New Richmond chapter. He was a merchant who served several terms as treasurer of the Village of New Richmond.

12. P. J. Staudenraus, *The African Colonization Movement, 1816–1865* (New York: Columbia Univ. Press, 1961) 14; *Chronicle of the Times*, March 16, 1833; Rockey & Bancroft, *Clermont County, Ohio*, 73, 129, 287.

13. Robert Finley to Ralph Gurley, October 30, 1831, ACS Records, 45:5; John Edgers to Ralph Gurley, February 28, 1833, ACS Records, vol. 47.

14. George C. Light to Ralph Gurley, April 1, 1833, ACS Records, vol. 47. The fate of Samuel Jones is unknown.

15. *Louisville Herald* as reprinted in the *Chronicle of the Times*, March 16, 1833.

16. Rockey & Bancroft, *Clermont County, Ohio*, 287.

17. Appleby, *Inheriting the Revolution*, 228; Staudenraus, *The African Colonization Movement*, 224–285. The descendants of the former American slaves, known as Americos, have held power in Liberia ever since the founding of the country. The native-born Africans have resented the Americo's for many years. This resentment spawned the most recent eruption of civil war in Liberia. The "special relationship" that America has with Liberia was the reason the congressional black caucus called for the U.S. to intervene in Liberia. Kenneth Timmerman, *Shakedown: Exposing the Real Jesse Jackson* (Washington, D.C.: Regnery Pub., 2002) 298.

CHAPTER 4

The American Antislavery Society

WILLIAM LLOYD GARRISON, the balding, bespectacled editor of the *Liberator* newspaper, called upon abolitionists, both black and white, to meet in Philadelphia in December 1833 to form a national abolitionist society. Sixty men from eleven states responded to the call. Characteristically, the meeting opened with a Scripture reading: "Cry aloud, spare not, lift up thy voice like a trumpet, and show my people their transgressions; and the house of Jacob their sins."[1]

A ten-member committee was chosen to draft a constitution for the new organization. Garrison wrote a "declaration of sentiments" for the society. He harkened back to the American Revolution, just fifty-seven years before, when "a band of patriots convened in this place to devise measures for the deliverance of this country from the foreign yoke." However, since nearly two million people "are recognized by law and treated by their fellow beings, as brute beasts" and "are plundered daily of the fruits of their toil without redress,"[2] the revolution is incomplete.

Garrison noted that the United States Constitution recognized the legality of slavery, but he declared it and all other laws supporting slavery immoral and, therefore, "utterly null and void," and consequently, they "ought to be instantly abrogated." The new organization vowed "to remove slavery by moral and political actions." The declaration concluded,

These are our views and principles—these are our designs and measures. With entire confidence in the overruling justice of God, we plant ourselves upon the Declaration of our Independence and the truths of Divine Revelation, as upon the Everlasting Rock.[3]

The convention created a new organization, known as the Ameri-

Fig. 4.1. *James G. Birney, a former slaveowner, became editor of the antislavery newspaper—the* Philanthropist—*first printed in New Richmond, Ohio. He later ran for president as the Liberty Party candidate in 1840 and 1844.*

can Antislavery Society. It promised to dedicate itself "to bring about the extinction of slavery" by appealing to the "consciences, hearts, and interests of the people" through reasoned argument and not by "resorting to physical force."[4]

The society was immediately successful. Within five years, 1,350 local chapters had been formed with a total membership of 250,000.[5] Some of the members were new to the movement. Others were defectors from the American Colonization Society, the most prominent of whom was James G. Birney.

Birney was a Kentucky-born lawyer and legislator who immigrated to Alabama. He became an agent for the American Colonization Society for the Southwest. Over time he began to have doubts about the morality of slavery and the efficacy of the colonization movement. He freed his own slaves. In 1834 he renewed a friendship with Theodore Weld, the charismatic organizer of the Lane Seminary debates, who had recently accepted a position with the Antislavery Society. Weld urged Birney to publicly renounce his allegiance to the Colonization Society, arguing that a public renouncement statement from Birney would bring many others to the cause. Birney agreed, but stated that he needed a job to support his growing family. A deal was struck: Birney would come aboard in exchange for a one-year appointment as an agent for the Antislavery Society at a salary of fifteen hundred dollars.

Birney published his renouncement in the *Lexington Intelligencer.* He called colonization "an opiate of the consciences" of Americans. The organization served to divert the American people from seeing "the injustice and the sin of slavery." The statement was sensational. It, and subsequent conversations, convinced Gerrit Smith, the Colonization Society's largest contributor, to defect.[6]

Organizationally, the society was similar to the Colonization Society. There was a national board of managers with paid officers. State and local chapters were formed. But at the heart of the organization was the local agent.

Agents were assigned to a more or less defined geographical territory. They spoke to local groups, usually at churches. They formed auxiliary chapters, raised funds, organized petition drives, and circulated the society's antislavery publications.

These agents were no shrinking violets. They were muscular, evangelical Christians who were totally committed to the cause; they knew they were doing God's work. They possessed a remarkable physical fortitude. They were often on the road for weeks, frequently braving foul weather and hostile crowds. Often, they would speak two or three times a day, frequently for hours at each session.

Rev. John Rankin, of Ripley, Ohio, was the agent for Clermont County. Rankin was generally, though not always, well received in the county. In Williamsburg he was hit in the neck with a stick following a speech at the schoolhouse. His speech in Withamsville was interrupted by rowdy boys. At other times he was pelted by eggs.[7]

During the month of September 1836, Rankin went on an extensive speaking tour in Clermont County. At the Batavia Presbyterian Church, he delivered a two-hour oration which was well received despite the "missile" that was thrown through the window of the church by a "badly trained boy." The meeting concluded with the formation of a new twenty-member chapter led by President Brice Blair, Secretary John Jolliffe and Corresponding Secretary Rev. George Beecher. Batavia's pastor George Beecher, the son of Lyman Beecher, particularly impressed Rankin. "He is a young man of talents and zeal," repeated Rankin, "and has already extensive influence in Clermont County, and is still gaining more." Rankin also gave special notice to John Jolliffe, Clermont County's prosecuting attorney. He predicted Jolliffe's membership would spur his fellow Methodists to join the cause.[8]

Six new chapters were formed in Clermont County in September of 1836—three of them in just three days. Rankin was very pleased with his work in the county writing, "Such is the state of society in this county, that the mobocrats have as yet been unable to get up a mob." The developments in Clermont County were significant because "Clermont is a populous and highly important county, as it borders on a slave state, and is near to Cincinnati. It will throw its moral influence upon that city, and across the river in Kentucky."[9]

Rankin's brother, Alexander, also a Presbyterian minister, worked in Clermont County as well. He spoke at the Judge Embry schoolhouse in Miami Township, lectured with his brother at the Bethel Presbyterian Church, and organized a new twenty-two member chapter at Goshen.[10]

By September of 1837 there were ten chapters in the county: New Richmond, Felicity, Neville, Bethel, Batavia, Goshen, Milton, Grassy Run, Monroe Township, and Gilead (Lindale). Andrew Coombs Jr., president of the Gilead chapter, reported that there were few abolitionists in his community just one year before. Now, there were sixty members in his chapter. The society maintained a circulating library of antislavery newspapers and tracts.[11]

The Clermont County Antislavery Society was organized on November 23, 1836, in Batavia. Present at the meeting were Thomas Morris, U.S. senator; Reverend Rankin; and James Birney. A six-article Constitution was drafted and officers elected. The officers were Dr. John Rogers, president; Ezekiel Dimmitt, John Shannon, Andrew Coombs, Dr. Samuel Meek, Dr. Andrew Hopkins, John O. Butler, William S. Patterson, Jesse Ellis, and Lemuel Slade, managers; Brice Blair treasurer; Rev. George Beecher, corresponding secretary; and John Jolliffe, recording secretary.

The society's purpose, in accordance with the Declaration of Independence and the Constitution of Ohio, was to abolish slavery in America. It would accomplish this goal "by the diffusion of Knowledge calculated to convince their fellow citizens that slaveholding is a heinous sin against God." The organization would also work "to elevate the character and condition of the colored people by encouraging their intellectual, moral, and religious improvement."[12]

The tone of the local meetings took on the look and feel of the camp revival. This was no accident. Theodore Weld, the de facto chief of local operations for the national organization, was a camp revival veteran. He knew very well the powerful hold that the personal "conversion" phenomena had with nineteenth century Americans. As a result, the Antislavery Society meetings opened with prayer and scriptural readings. Gospel hymns were sung. Testimonials from former slaveowners were solicited. Former slaves were invited to give their stories. Invitations for altar calls were made. New converts to the cause tearfully confessed their previous errors and were enthusiastically welcomed into the community of believers. Featured speakers delivered their "homilies" about slavery as a sin. Business sessions generally followed. The society issued resolutions on slavery-related issues of the day. Meetings usually concluded with a benediction.

What did Clermont County abolitionists really think or feel about slavery in their private, unguarded moments? What motivated them to become a part of the movement to free the slave? Unfortunately, with the exception of Philip Gatch, journals and letters of Clermont County's abolitionists have rarely been found. So we must search for these answers in the public pronouncements of the groups of which they were members.

Clermont County's abolitionists were, as has been described, evangelical Christians who believed that slavery was a sin. The Antislavery Society condemned slavery as such and believed that all who "uphold this iniquitous system are unworthy of admission with the churches of Christ."[13]

They thought that slavery should be abolished immediately through peaceful means,[14] and that they could accomplish this goal by exerting their "moral influence" and persuasion.[15] These were important points.

A more moderate strain of antislavery sentiment known as *emancipationism* surfaced at this time. The emancipationists agreed that slavery was evil, but felt that it should be ended gradually within several decades in order to give the South an opportunity to evolve into a free labor economy.

Slaveholders and conservative Northerners frequently charged that abolitionists incited slaves to violent rebellion. In response, abolitionists reiterated again and again that they did not advocate violence. Clermonters derided this accusation with sarcasm. They wrote that Southerners, themselves, often resorted to violence by "hanging up" a man like a dog, "because they thought him an abolitionist." Southerners also charged that abolitionist tracts sent to the South through the mail would incite violence. To this, the abolitionists replied, "Well, suppose some of the Southern men, in revenge, should write letters to our horses and cows, exhorting them to insurrection, they would be amply revenged, for who among the slaves knows how to read? Not one in twenty."[16]

What did these white abolitionists think about blacks? Were they equal to whites? At that time, opposition to slavery did not necessarily mean that one believed in equality. The public pronouncements of the Clermont County Antislavery Society seemed to indicate its members sought not only freedom for blacks but equality as well.

Clermont County's abolitionists invoked the Declaration of Independence by proclaiming that all men are born free and equal.[17] They condemned Ohio's Black Codes that excluded "Negroes and mulattoes from courts of justice in civil and criminal cases,"[18] prohibited black and biracial people from settling in Ohio without a bond for good behavior, excluded black children from attending public schools, and penalized employers for hiring free people of color.[19] Not only did they condemn the Code, but they also pledged to "Petition the legislature of Ohio . . . until our petitions result in their abrogation."[20]

They also endeavored to "elevate the character and condition of coloured people."[21] To twenty-first-century eyes this may seem to be patronizing, but, within the context of the times, it was a most benevolent and progressive sentiment.

The Petition Drive

The First Amendment to the United States Constitution guarantees, among other things, the right of the people to "petition the Government for a redress of grievances."[22] This right is an ancient one whose origins can be traced to the Magna Carta of 1215. The act of petitioning the government was popular in both England and the colonies. It was spectacularly successful in abolishing slavery in England. It was natural, considering the English influence among American abolitionists, that the American Antislavery Society would adopt the practice.[23] Antislavery activists utilized the petition in an unsuccessful attempt to outlaw slavery in the District of Columbia as early as 1828. They agreed with the proslavery forces that the Constitution granted the right to decide the slavery question to the individual states. But they believed that, since the District of Columbia was a creature of Congress, Congress had the legal authority to abolish slavery within the District. They also held that the same applied to the territories and pointed to Article VI of the Northwest Ordinance as support.[24]

Congress, dominated by slaveholders and their apologists, responded to the antislavery petitions by creating a select committee to decide the issue. A report was issued by the committee explaining that it was inappropriate to abolish the institution of slavery. An acrimonious debate broke out when a small antislavery minority disputed the committee's finding. Congress avoided the issue by deciding not to hear it.[25]

In December of 1834 the American Antislavery Society undertook a national petition drive to abolish slavery in the District of Colombia. Theodore Weld drafted a number of forms opposing slavery and requesting Congress to abolish it in the District of Colombia. Aided by the newly invented steam-driven presses, the society printed tens of thousands of typed petitions. These were distributed to state and local chapters, whose agents organized the grassroots to obtain signatures[26]

Southerners, and their Northern allies, feared that the mere acknowledgment of the petitions would recognize the right to petition on this issue, which could lead to the abolition of slavery in the District of Columbia and, possibly, throughout the country. They resolved to end the matter before it could gain any momentum. Therefore, the House of Representatives enacted House Rule 25, known as the Gag Rule, prohibiting even the acceptance of the petitions.

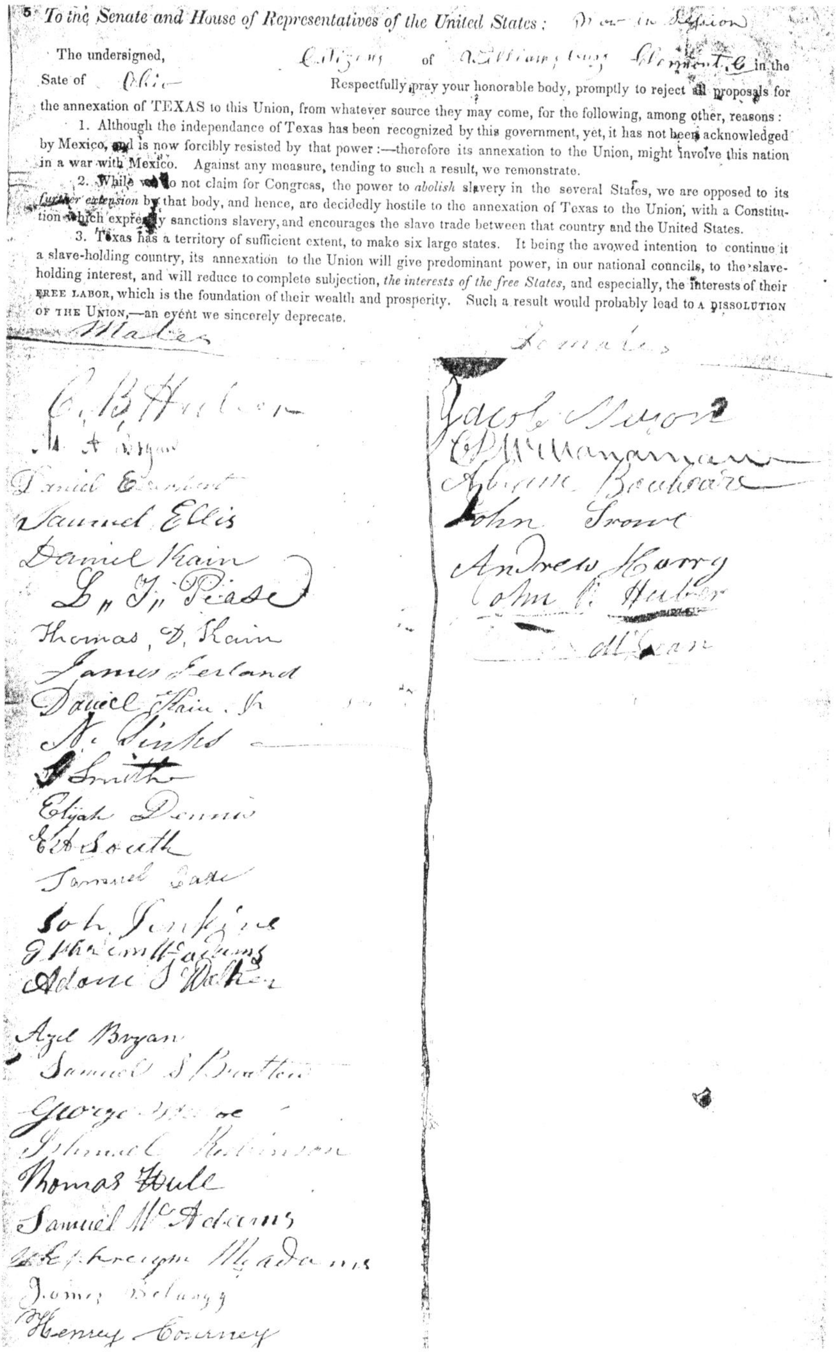

5 To the Senate and House of Representatives of the United States:

The undersigned, Citizens of Williamsburg Clermont C. in the Sate of Ohio— Respectfully pray your honorable body, promptly to reject all proposals for the annexation of TEXAS to this Union, from whatever source they may come, for the following, among other, reasons :

1. Although the independance of Texas has been recognized by this government, yet, it has not been acknowledged by Mexico, and is now forcibly resisted by that power :—therefore its annexation to the Union, might involve this nation in a war with Mexico. Against any measure, tending to such a result, we remonstrate.

2. While we do not claim for Congress, the power to *abolish* slavery in the several States, we are opposed to its *further extension* by that body, and hence, are decidedly hostile to the annexation of Texas to the Union, with a Constitution which expressly sanctions slavery, and encourages the slave trade between that country and the United States.

3. Texas has a territory of sufficient extent, to make six large states. It being the avowed intention to continue it a slave-holding country, its annexation to the Union will give predominant power, in our national councils, to the slave-holding interest, and will reduce to complete subjection, *the interests of the free States*, and especially, the interests of their FREE LABOR, which is the foundation of their wealth and prosperity. Such a result would probably lead to A DISSOLUTION OF THE UNION,—an event we sincerely deprecate.

Fig. 4.2. The *American Antislavery Society*, evoking the *First Amendment right to petition the government*, initiated a petition drive in 1837 opposing the annexation of Texas. This petition was signed by citizens of Williamsburg, Ohio.

Clermont County's abolitionists favored the petition drive. They divided the county into districts and circulated the antislavery petitions throughout.[27] They pledged to continue exercising their constitutional right to petition for the abolition of slavery in the District of Columbia and praised the members of Congress who "defended with manly boldness the right to petition that body."[28]

The abolitionist movement began to take guarded steps toward becoming a political movement as a result of their utter failure to force the Congress to recognize their right to petition. The purists, led by William Lloyd Garrison, wanted to avoid Congress and depend solely upon the force of "moral suasion" to obtain their goals. Pragmatists such as James Birney, Henry Stanton, and Louis Tappan, recognized that short of war, politics was the surest means to abolishing slavery. Tappan specifically pointed to the Congressional action as evidence. By simply ignoring the petitions, Congress relegated them "to the dust and cobwebs of oblivion."[29] This disagreement eventually led to the disintegration of the National Antislavery Society.

Abolitionists in Clermont County sided with the pragmatists, though they moved guardedly in that direction. New Richmond, the hot seat of abolitionism in the county, held a unique antislavery Fourth of July celebration in 1838. The celebrants assembled at 11:00 a.m. at the Presbyterian Church. Following an opening of instrumental and vocal music, seven young men delivered speeches of famous abolitionists. The scene, according to the reporter, was "too sublime," for the "stomping of feet, clapping of hands, firing of guns . . . drinking of toasts with intoxicating liquors" that typically accompanied the day. The editor was then asked, "do you not think such a celebration preferable to those distinguished by pseudo-republican boasting, and stimulated with whiskey and gun powder?"[30]

Despite their best efforts, abolitionists made little headway in Congress. Many abolitionists began to believe that Garrison's moral suasion was not enough. They came to the conclusion that they had to enter the political arena if they were to influence the system.

NOTES

1.   *Abolitionists* were people who wanted to end or abolish slavery immediately as opposed to *emancipationists* who wanted to end the institution gradually. Henry Mayer, *All on Fire: William Lloyd Garrison and the Abolition of Slavery* (New York: St. Martins Press, 1948) 173–175; Isaiah 58:1.

2.   William Lloyd Garrison, *The Declaration of Sentiments*; Mayer, *All on Fire*, 175.

3.   Ibid., 175, 176.

4.   Multi Educator, Inc., "Constitution of the American Anti-slavery League— 1833," *History Central*, www.historycentral.com/documents/antislaveryleague.html. 2000.

5.   U.S. Department of State, "The American Antislavery Society," *International Information Programs: USINFO.State.Gov*, wtp://usinfo.state.gov/usa/infousa/facts/ democrac/18.htm.

6.   Staudenraus, *The African Colonization Movement*, 229–232.

7.   Ann Hagedorn, *Beyond the River: The Untold Story of the Heroes of the Underground Railroad* (New York: Simon & Schuster, 2002) 115–116.

8.   *Emancipator*, October 29, 1836.

9.   Ibid.

10. *Philanthropist*, December 23, 1836; February 3, 1837.

11. Ibid., September 9, 1837.

12. "Constitution of the Clermont County Antislavery Society (CCAS)," *Clermont Courier*, December 31, 1836.

13. "CCAS Resolution, April 13, 1838," *Philanthropist*, May 8, 1838; "CCAS Resolution, March 22, 1837," *Clermont Courier*, March 3, 1837.

14. "CCAS Resolution, March 3, 1837," *Clermont Courier*, March 22, 1837; "CCAS Resolution, April 18, 1838," *Philanthropist*, May 8, 1838.

15. "CCAS Resolution, February 22, 1837," *Clermont Courier*, March 3, 1837.

16. Rev. George Beecher, John Jolliffe, Daniel Fee, Rev. Daniel Parker, and Dr. John Rogers, Letter to the Editor, *Clermont Courier*, April 22, 1837.

17. "Constitution of the CCAS," *Clermont Courier*, December 31, 1836, art. 2.

18. "CCAS Resolution, February 22, 1837," *Clermont Courier*, March 11, 1837.

19. "CCAS Resolution, January 1, 1838," *Philanthropist*, January 30, 1838.

20. "CCAS Resolution, February 22, 1837," *Clermont Courier*, March 3, 1837.

21. "CCAS Resolution, November 23, 1836,"*Clermont Courier*, December 31, 1836, art. 3.

22. U.S. Constitution, amend. 1.

23. William L. Miller, *Arguing About Slavery: The Great Battle in the United States Congress* (New York: Vintage Books, 1998) 106–07.

24. Northwest Ordinance, art. 6, passed by the Confederation Congress in 1787, reads in part: "There shall be neither slavery nor involuntary servitude in said territory."

25. Miller, *Arguing About Slavery*, 107.

26. Mayer, *All on Fire*, 94 & 108; Miller, *Arguing About Slavery*, 107.

27. "CCAS Resolution, November 23, 1836," *Clermont Courier*, December 31, 1836.

28. "CCAS Resolution, February 22, 1832," *Clermont Courier*, March 3, 1837.

29. Mayer, *All on Fire*, 263.

30. Rev. Daniel Parker, Letter to the Editor, *Philanthropist*, July 24, 1838.

CHAPTER 5

Slavery and Politics

GATHERING IN ALBANY, NEW YORK, in April of 1840, one hundred radical abolitionists considered their options. They were frustrated. Their petition drive protesting slavery was wildly successful in generating the signatures of thousands of Americans, yet Congress, through parliamentary guile, had refused even to recognize their existence. The abolitionists had turned to screening candidates for state and federal offices to ascertain their position on slavery, but the questionnaires were routinely ignored.[1] It was clear that the current political power structure would not take them seriously until they, too, acquired political power. The only option left was to form a political party opposed to slavery.

Conservative abolitionists urged caution. They believed their campaign of moral suasion would, if given more time, carry the day. Further, politics was an unsavory business. The mere act of engaging in politics, they argued, would taint the antislavery movement.[2] Despite these objections, the radicals pushed forward. They formed the Liberty Party, with abolition of slavery as its single-plank platform. They chose former slaveowner and newspaper publisher James Birney as its presidential candidate and James Earle of Ohio as his running mate.[3]

The new party faced nearly insurmountable odds. America's political tradition discouraged third parties. The new party's appeal, based solely upon opposition to slavery, was limited. Slavery, at that time, barely registered as a public issue. Most Americans were still concerned about financial woes stemming from the panic of 1837. And ferocious competition was sure to come from the two established parties of the day: the Democrats and the Whigs. The Democratic Party was the party of the slaveholding interest. Time and again the party stated and voted its support of the institution. There were antislavery Democrats, but their influence was limited. The Whig Party rose as a party of opposition to "King" Andrew Jackson. A Virginia newspaper captured the essence of the party when it declared that a Whig was "one who prefers liberty to tyranny . . . the constitution and the laws of the country against the predominance of the Crown or Executive Power."[4] The Whigs were divided on the subject of slavery.

The developments in Albany were met with great enthusiasm by a small cadre of men living in New Richmond, Ohio. The men, led by the venerable Dr. John Rogers, were all committed antislavery Democrats. This same group fomented an insurgency against the party regulars three years earlier when they fielded a slate of candidates known as the "People's Ticket." They were able to elect four of their own to local offices. Now they were ready to bolt from the party altogether.[5]

As in many places in the Old Northwest, the Liberty Party faced formidable opposition. Clermont County was a rock-ribbed Democratic stronghold. Presidents Jefferson, Madison, and Monroe easily carried the county. But it was not until the rise of Andrew Jackson that the Democrats gained a strong, unyielding, grip on the county's voters. In 1840 they were still in his thrall.[6]

The Clermont County Democrats were divided on the issue of slavery. The champion proslavery Democrat was Thomas J. Buchanan. The prominent Washington Township attorney was first elected to the Ohio General Assembly in 1837. He earned the everlasting ire of abolitionists in 1839 when, in response to antislavery petitions sent to the Ohio legislature by black citizens, he stated, "Negroes have no more right to petition than dogs." He also wrongfully accused prominent New Richmond businessman and abolitionist Thomas Donaldson of promoting the "amalgamation of the races."[7]

There were prominent antislavery Democrats as well. Senator Thomas Morris of Bethel had well-known antislavery sentiments. Dr. William Doan of Withamsville was president of the Mt. Gilead Antislavery Society before being elected to two terms in the United States Congress. Dowty Utter, of Washington Township, was a long-time Democratic state legislator and an Underground Railroad operative. Oliver Perry Spencer Fee was a Stephen Douglas delegate to the 1860 Democratic Convention and was known as the "High Priest" of the Felicity Underground Railroad network.[8]

The Whigs were also active in Clermont County by 1840. Their success, however, was limited. The *Clermont Courier*, the party's mouthpiece, generally issued a post-election concession statement that gauged the measure of the party's defeat. For example, the *Courier* wrote the following in 1842: "This county as usual, has gone for the Locofocos. We acknowledge ourselves beaten worse than we anticipated."[9]

Dr. Rogers and his group must have entered the 1840 presidential campaign with optimism. They had shown in the 1837 election that Clermont County Democrats were willing to buck the party hierarchy. And John Jolliffe, an avowed abolitionist, had defeated John Lowe for the position of prosecuting attorney.[10] Would they be able to shear off enough antislavery Democrats to vote for the new party?

The Democrats ran incumbent Martin Van Buren, "The Magician." The Whigs countered with war hero "Tippecanoe" William Henry Harrison. The country had recently loosened voter qualification, bringing thousands of new voters into the process. The Whigs realized that they had to pull out all the stops to bring the masses to the polls. Large rallies with log cabin raisings were held to show that Harrison was a man of the people. Barbecues with barrels of free cider and long-winded oratories were staged. Huge balls of twine with anti–Van Buren signs attached were pushed through communities to indicate that Harrison would "roll over" Van Buren. Quite simply, the campaign was the most raucous, boisterous, silliest in American history. The Liberty Party was lost in all of the hoopla.[11]

Not to be outdone in showing their support for Harrison, ten thousand people poured into Batavia on August 8, 1840, to demonstrate their affection for "Ole Tippecanoe." Flags and banners festooned the county seat. A log cabin was raised by four veterans of the War of 1812. A monster parade wound through the village. A large canoe, filled with fifty people, was pulled by a team of six horses. A band from Georgetown, Ohio, provided the musical entertainment. A thousand "farmers and mechanics" from Miami and Goshen townships approached Batavia along the East Fork River pulling a log cabin on wheels; the cabin draped with banners "fluttering in the wind."[12]

As expected, Van Buren carried Clermont County. Statewide, however, Harrison prevailed with a comfortable 23,271 vote majority. The Birney ticket mustered just 903 votes in the entire state of Ohio.[13] Just thirty-nine votes were cast in Clermont County for Birney, twenty-three of which were cast in Ohio Township.[14] Birney's supporters expected better results, considering there were more than one hundred members in the county's various antislavery societies. What happened?

Upon reflection, the results are not all that surprising. The party had been formed just a few months before the election. Further, it was a single issue that was of marginal interest to the larger public. Therefore, its appeal was limited. The tug of that one issue was not enough to pull antislavery Democrats and Whigs from their traditional party allegiances.

The party was also the victim of a dirty trick. The Whigs, fearful of losing its antislavery constituents, circulated a baseless rumor, widely repeated in Ohio newspapers, that Democrats were passing out Birney campaign literature. The implication was that Birney was merely a stalking horse for the Democrats to pull away Whig votes.[15]

But much of the fault for the poor showing must lie with the Liberty Party itself. They looked upon the mechanics of running a party with disdain, believing that such activity was corrupting. They had virtually no local organization and were grossly underfunded. Consequently many counties did not have literature or sample ballots for voters.[16] And Birney himself left the country to attend an antislavery convention in England. Birney's son, William, summed up the defeat nicely in a letter to his father: "Your third party politicians are better

Fig. 5.1. *An 1888 drawing by Rem Lane of Batavia from an earlier sketch depicting the raising of a cabin in Batavia, Ohio, for a William Henry Harrison campaign rally.*

men than they are tacticians. The state [Ohio] was poorly supplied with tickets and half of the people supposed that you had withdrawn from the canvas."[17]

Undeterred, the Liberty men began preparing for the next presidential campaign from the bottom up. They staged events, scheduled speeches, and, in Clermont County, ran full slates of candidates for local offices. Despite their efforts, the third party barely dented the ballot box. In the race for state senate, former county prosecutor John Jolliffe received but 21 votes out of 4,077 votes cast, or barely one-half of 1 percent of the total.[18]

In 1842 the Liberty Party ran Leicester King for Ohio governor. He crashed in Clermont County, receiving only fifty-five votes. Statewide, however, he did surprisingly well, garnering four thousand votes. The Whigs were worried because much of that support came from their traditional power center in the Western Reserve area of northeast Ohio. The *Ohio State Journal* blamed the Liberty Party for throwing the state into political chaos: "The abolitionists have thrown the entire legislature into the hands of men who will gerrymander the state and fill Congress with the allies of the slave power."[19]

Slavery, or rather its westward expansion, appeared for the first time in a presidential campaign in 1844 when the Republic of Texas, in which slavery was legal, asked to be admitted to the United States. President John Tyler submitted the treaty to the U.S. Senate for ratification. He sent his secretary of state, John C. Calhoun, to the U.S. Senate to speak on behalf of the treaty. He not only spoke on behalf of the treaty, but offered an impassioned defense of slavery. Calhoun played directly into the hands of the opponents of slavery, such as Thomas Morris, who had been decrying the "slave power conspiracy." The speech ignited a firestorm of criticism in the North. The annexation treaty was defeated, guaranteeing that it would become a major issue in the 1844 presidential election.[20]

The Democrats nominated James K. Polk, a forty-eight-year-old Tennessee slaveholder. Polk, the former Speaker of the United States House of Representatives, was a strong advocate of "manifest destiny." He naturally supported annexation. Henry Clay was chosen by the Whigs by acclamation. The two-time presidential candidate and former secretary of state originally seemed to favor annexation. But once the campaign started, he began waffling on the issue, arguing that annexation may be dangerous at the present.[21] The Liberty Party offered

James Birney again. Thomas Morris, of Clermont County, the sixty-eight-year-old former U.S. senator, was chosen as Birney's running mate. Morris, who had been excommunicated by the Democrats because of his antislavery views, brought a certain *gravitas* to the fledgling party.

Ohio's state races were held in October. Clermont County's Liberty Party kicked off the campaign season by holding its convention in New Richmond in September. They again fielded a full ticket. This time, they "aggressively" campaigned by placing advertisements in two consecutive issues of the Whig paper, the *Clermont Courier*. Leicester King ran again as the party's candidate for governor. This time, he doubled his vote total from two years earlier.[22]

It was a Whig year. The party captured the Ohio Governor's Office and a controlling majority in both branches of the General Assembly. The Whigs in Clermont County, despite local losses, were ecstatic. A torch-lit parade marched to the Batavia Hotel; Whig homes "were generally illuminated and the whole presented a cheerful spectacle." The *Courier* exhorted its readers, "You have done nobly; but you can and will do better on the first of November, when the great contest is decided. . . . Organize—Organize effectually ORGANIZE THOROUGHLY! . . . Are you ready? Charge!"[23]

Abolitionists were unsure of Clay. At one time, he stated he was against slavery, yet he owned slaves. They saw his waffling about Texas as a disingenuous political ploy. He was denounced by some as a cruel master.[24]

Antislavery Whigs, known as Conscience Whigs, faced a difficult choice: either stay with Clay, whose position on slavery was muddled; or, bolt from their party, and register their protest, thereby electing the proslavery Polk? James Sullivant of Columbus, Ohio, was characteristic of these troubled Whigs. Sullivant, an abolitionist and a distant relative of Birney, recognized that Polk was "the candidate of the Slave Power." He held Birney in high esteem and would happily vote for him if he knew that to do so would "advance the grand principles of human liberty." Ultimately, he voted for Clay because he thought that Clay had a better chance of winning.[25]

The Whig Party was worried about its abolitionist voters. The party machinery emphasized that since Birney was unelectable, a vote for him was really a vote for the Democrat, Polk. On election eve, a letter, now known as the "Garland Forgery," surfaced in Northern newspapers, charging that Birney had admitted that he actually supported slavery. Birney issued an immediate denial, but the damage was done.[26]

A similar tactic was used against Birney's running mate in Clermont County. The Democratic *Ohio Sun* accused Morris of going "the whole hog for Clay and slavery." Morris denied the allegation, declaring that he had voted "a Liberty ticket" and suggested that anyone who cared could look at it. He also promised to burn "the brand of falsehood" into the "foreheads" of his accusers. Then he called them out: "They know where I live and they know their remedy." It appears that the old warhorse was actually challenging his accusers to a duel.[27]

James K. Polk, the champion of slavery, won the election, but it was very close, a mere 38,181 votes separated Polk from Clay. The number of votes received by the Liberty Party Nationals increased ninefold from 1840. Its 62,300 votes were clearly more than Polk's margin of victory. The four-year-old, single-issue Liberty Party had played the role of spoiler. This was no more apparent than in New York, where it polled 5,812 votes. Clay lost the state to Polk by 5,106 votes. Had Clay carried New York, he would have been elected president.[28] The prospects for the Liberty Party looked bright. It had succeeded in putting slavery into the mainstream of public debate. It had substantially increased its national vote totals. And it had played the role of spoiler.

But there were disquieting signs as well in the electoral tea leaves. The actual vote totals were far below the 160,000 predicted by party insiders. Further, the party had failed to carry even one of the five hundred counties in the North.[29]

The results in Clermont County can only be called humiliating for Thomas Morris. Morris had lived in the county most of his adult life, was a prominent attorney, and had served in the Ohio General Assembly for years. And yet he could secure only 105 votes for the party, 9 votes fewer than King received in the state election one month earlier.

Party pragmatists argued that they had to expand the party's appeal beyond the abolition of slavery. Ohio leaders, meeting in 1846, called for educational reform, modification of tariff policies, and federal action to secure overseas markets for agricultural products. The Liberty Party in Clermont County ran another ticket in 1846 with the expanded platform. The results were the same—utter defeat. Nationally, the story was the same. The end appeared near.[30]

The Liberty Party failed, as do most third parties in America. Most Americans at this time did not consider slavery to be a burning political issue. Those who did were simply not ready to abandon their traditional political home for the fledgling single-issue party. It did succeed, however, in pushing the topic onto the national public arena.

The acquisition of new territories resulting from the successful War with Mexico focused attention on slavery. Were the new territories to be slave or free? Both sides of the debate were poised for the dispute. David Wilmot, a congressman from Pennsylvania, struck first. He introduced a bill in Congress prohibiting the expansion of slavery into those new territories. Wilmot explained his position: "Slavery has within itself the seed of its own destruction. Keep it within limits, let it remain where it is now, and in time it will wear itself out."[31] The Wilmot Proviso, as the legislation came to be known, was passed in the House, but failed in the Senate. Northerners generally agreed that slavery was legal where it then existed. They felt, however, that Congress had the constitutional authority to prohibit its extension. Many Southerners, however, agreed with the position of former vice president John C. Calhoun who argued that slaves were property no matter where they went.[32]

Ohio Whig John Sherman clearly saw the future impact that the debate over the expansion of slavery would have upon the nation's politics. He asserted, "The question of slavery in the newly conquered territory, the relative influences of the north and south . . . will in my opinion breakdown the old parties and build up new ones, divided by different principles and led by different men."[33] Sherman could very well have been talking about his own party. Tensions within the Whigs over slavery roiled beneath the surface, but were tamped down in the name of party unity. Cleavage between the factions appeared in 1844 over the admission of Texas. Just four years later, the dispute threatened the party's very existence.[34]

The Free-Soil Party

Conscience Whigs called for a convention of the like-minded to form a new political party. Twenty thousand people responded to the call and converged upon Buffalo, New York, during the first week of August 1848. Old Liberty men, advocates of free labor, and antislavery Democrats from New York, known as Barnburners, came to Buffalo as well.[35] Clermont County sent a three-man delegation to the convention. Dr. John Rogers, his son-in-law Jacob Ebersole, and Thomas Glisson were chosen at a "large enthusiastic meeting" held at the New Richmond Market House. They came armed with a resolution supporting former president Martin Van Buren for president and Cincinnatian John McClean for vice president.[36]

Fig. 5.2. *Salmon P. Chase*

The convention's first order of business was to draft a party platform. Ohioan Salmon P. Chase was chosen for this task. He crafted an inclusive, multiplank platform that opposed the expansion of slavery into the new territories and supported cheap postal rates, free land to settlers in the West, harbor and river improvements, and tariff reforms.

Van Buren was chosen as their candidate for president. Intellectual Charles Francis Adams, the son of John Quincy Adams, was selected as Van Buren's running mate. With the slogan "Free Soil, Free Speech, Free Labor, and Free Men" still ringing in their ears, the delegates adjourned and returned home to prepare for the 1848 campaign.[37]

Supporters of the Free-Soil Party were a diverse group. In addition to core abolitionists, Free-Soilers included many who were largely ambivalent about slavery. These members were Northern industrial workers who were fearful of cheap labor represented by slavery. A statement appearing in Cincinnati's *Daily Unionist* newspaper is characteristic of this viewpoint: "We are no abolitionists in the popular sense of the term, but we would belie our convictions of democracy if we did not oppose slavery's expansion over new lands."[38]

Lewis Cass of Michigan was chosen by the Democrats as their 1848 candidate for president. He endorsed popular sovereignty, allowing the voters of the territories to decide the issue of slavery. His Whig opponent was the popular Mexican War hero Zachary Taylor, a slaveholding Southerner. Taylor tried to sidestep the slavery issue altogether by not addressing it in his party's platform.[39]

Ohio's Whigs were worried about Van Buren and the third-party challenge. They were uncomfortable with what they saw as Van Buren's "previous subservience to the claims of the South." They conceded that most of the Free-Soilers were "honest and conscientious," but decided to stay with their party. They tried to outflank the Free-Soilers by introducing a resolution in the Ohio House of Representatives opposing slavery's expansion. They cited the prohibition of slavery in the Northwest Ordinance as precedent. The resolution passed 44–8. Among the nays was Democrat Shepherd Norris of Clermont County. The *Clermont Courier* condemned Norris's vote as a "signal exhibition of dough-faceism" and called upon the county's voters to remember it in the upcoming election.[40]

The local Free-Soilers, also called Free Democrats, held a convention at the Clermont County Courthouse to choose candidates for the upcoming state and local offices. Former prosecuting attorney John Jolliffe delivered "a highly inflammatory" address to the gathering. Daniel Fee of Monroe Township was chosen to run against the nefarious Shepherd Norris.[41] Not surprisingly, Norris and every other Democrat were returned to office. There were signs, however, that the Democrats were losing their stranglehold on county politics. Their margins of victory were smaller. For the first time, openly antislavery candidates Daniel Fee and James Robb actually carried four townships in their respective races. Perhaps the tide of antislavery politics was rising in Clermont County.[42]

John Lyons of Felicity, Ohio, was typical of many antislavery voters that year. Would he vote his conscience or hold onto his traditional party allegiance? He said that he was a Free-Soiler at heart, but was disappointed with their poor showing at the recent state election. He predicted a similar result in the upcoming presidential election. He rejected Democrat Lewis Cass "because he has said that Congress has no power to enact laws having reference to slavery in the new territories." In the end, he voted for Zachary Taylor because Taylor promised not to veto any act, presumably relating to prohibiting slavery's extension. He concluded that Taylor was an "honest soldier and patriot" who could be trusted.[43]

In the November national election, Van Buren received a respectable 291,763 votes, representing 10 percent of the total. His strong showing in his home state swung New York to Taylor, and thereby the election to the Whigs.[44] The Free-Soilers showed a similar strength in Ohio, receiving 35,523 votes—nearly 10 percent of the total. Van Buren actually outpolled Taylor in the Whig stronghold of northeast Ohio. Voters in Clermont County did their part for Van Buren as well, casting 417 votes for the former president. This total represented a 400 percent increase in antislavery votes from Birney's 1844 total. Van Buren received votes in every township in the county, a first for an antislavery candidate.[45]

The 1848 state elections dramatically altered Ohio's political landscape. The Whigs had been losing antislavery voters for some time. Their previous ploys had failed to stanch the hemorrhaging. The Whigs gerrymandered their traditional strong voting districts in the Western Reserve and in Hamilton County in order to boost their number of safe seats. The tactic failed miserably. Free-Soilers were elected instead, giving the new party the balance of power in the General Assembly. After months of struggle, a coalition of Free-Soilers and anti-South Democrats was formed.[46] The Democrats were given the opportunity of organizing the state's House of Representatives. In exchange, Free-Soil leader Salmon P. Chase of Cincinnati was selected as Ohio's new U.S. senator. Additionally, Ohio's notorious Black Codes, which, among other things, prevented blacks from providing evidence in a legal case against a white, were repealed.[47]

To Chase, the repeal of the Black Codes was "an object dearer . . . than political elevation." Their repeal was "a great victory of humanity and justice." Considering Chase's well-known interest in political elevation, this must be seen as quite an accomplishment.[48]

The repeal of the Black Codes was not without some controversy in Clermont County. State representative Shepherd Norris refused to vote on the bill. "He skulked the Question," opined the *Clermont Courier*, and "dared not take the responsibility of recording his vote upon it. The bill was brought to the floor again the next day. And again Norris abstained. He acted "the sneak, a character for which nature has so admirable [*sic*] qualified him," chastised the paper.[49]

Party allegiance for antislavery voters was still volatile. They tried to find a party home in which their votes would count toward the elimination of slavery. James Robb of Ohio Township was one such voter. He was originally a Democrat, but concluded that his party was "merely hewers of timber and drawers of water for the Southern slaveholder. . . . Slavery and democracy are inseparably connected," he concluded. After a brief flirtation with the Free-Soilers, whom he saw as "unsolid," he migrated to the Whigs because he felt they were a stronger force against slavery. Hereafter, he called himself a Free-Soil Whig.[50]

The Clermont County Free Democrats met at Slade's Tavern in Pierce Township on August 31, 1852, to ratify the national party's selection of John P. Hale for president and George W. Julian for vice president. The local delegates supported their party's platform calling for cheap postage and river and harbor improvements. Sensing the growing national outrage over the newly enacted Fugitive Slave Act, the party called for "the final repeal" of the law.[51]

Julian paid a campaign visit to Felicity after stops in northern Kentucky. While there, a speech was delayed one day following the escape of forty slaves from Mason County, Kentucky. In Bracken County, Kentucky, Julian gazed upon "a large crowd of that brutalized rabble element which formed the background of slavery everywhere." The aboriginal creatures, though menacing, did not interrupt the meeting.

Congressman Julian was expected in Chilo, just across the river from Bracken County. Party activist Rev. Silas Chase sent a young man to escort Julian from Chilo to Felicity, four miles away. While waiting for the candidate to arrive, the young man was accosted by several drunken proslavery Kentuckians. They seized the young man and threw him into their skiff, whereupon they threatened to "give him the best lynching he had ever known." The lynching was foiled by an unknown former resident of Felicity who persuaded the rowdies to release their victim. Julian arrived a little later and was safely escorted to his engagement.[52]

The Free Democrats had entered the race with high hopes, expecting to build upon the 10 percent vote total Van Buren received four years before. However, many of the Van Buren Barnburners returned to their Democratic roots. As a result, they managed to poll only 5 percent of the presidential vote. The Democrats, running on the slogan "We Polked 'em in 44; we'll Pierce 'em in 52," elected their candidate, Franklin Pierce. The Whigs lost with General Winfield Scott.[53]

The Republican Party

Stephen Douglas, the Little Giant, of Illinois, introduced his Kansas-Nebraska bill in January of 1854. The bill enshrined his concept of popular sovereignty, allowing the people of those two territories to decide by referendum whether to permit slavery or not. During the debate on the bill, Salmon Chase predicted that its passage "will hasten the inevitable reorganization of parties" and warned, "It will light up a fire in the country which may, perhaps, consume those who kindled it."[54] Six months later, the accuracy of Chase's prediction was borne out. Albert Bovay, an antislavery Democrat, convened a meeting on July 28, 1854, in Rippon, Wisconsin, to organize opposition to the Douglas bill. A similar meeting was held in Jackson, Michigan. Opposition to the Kansas-Nebraska Act was widespread. Chase called for a meeting on the subject for March of 1854. Between twelve hundred and fifteen hundred people attended the meeting at the Columbus, Ohio, Town Street Methodist Church. John Bond and Daniel Fee represented Clermont County at the meeting. A new party, variously known as the Anti-Nebraska Party, the People's Party, and the Fusion Party, was formed. Whatever the name, the theme was the same, opposition to the Kansas-Nebraska Act and the concept of popular sovereignty. Several newspapers began referring to it as the Republican Party. The name stuck.[55]

The 1854 Congressional elections were a spectacular success for the new party. All twenty-one of Ohio's districts sent Republicans to Congress. James Ernie was chosen as representative of the Sixth Congressional District, comprising Clermont, Adams, Brown, and Highland counties.[56] Momentum was building for the crucial governor's race of 1855.

Salmon Chase was chosen by the Republicans to run for governor. A controversial figure, Chase was seen as a clever manipulator with unbounded personal ambition.

The *Clermont Sun* denounced Chase's candidacy.

The name of Salmon P. Chase is connected closely with every bargain and sales transaction that has ever occupied in Ohio—he has been repudiated by every party to which he has ever belonged. . . . Further Chase is an abolitionist of the first water: he stands at the very head of the heap of Ohio Know Nothingism which is claimed to be the fossil remains of the Whig Party.[57]

The *Sun* dismissed the Republican candidates for state representative as "clever men," but abolitionists. Thomas Glen, the Republican candidate for county treasurer, was cast as a "very clever man," but an "ultra abolitionist of the first water." Incredibly, slavery had become, by 1855, the litmus test for Clermont County's treasurer! The very clever young men were elected.[58]

The statewide campaign was hard fought. Chase eked out a slim victory in a three-way contest with Democratic incumbent William Medill and former governor Allen Trimble of the American Party. Chase's victory gave the Republicans access to the levers of statewide power in the upcoming 1856 presidential campaign, the first for the Republicans.[59]

The Republicans met in Philadelphia to nominate their candidate. Joseph Parrish of Felicity was there representing Clermont County. The convention chairman set the tone: "You are here today to give direction to a movement which is to decide whether the people of the United States are to be hereafter and forever chained to the present national policy of the extension of slavery." The party expressed its belief that Congress had the authority to prohibit the expansion of those twin relics of barbarism—polygamy and slavery." The Republicans also supported the admission of Kansas as a free state, the construction of a transcontinental railroad, and the improvement of rivers and harbors.[60]

John Charles Fremont, celebrated for his western explorations, exploits in the Mexican War, and his rabid abolitionist sentiments, was chosen as the Republican nominee. With a catchy campaign slogan, "Free Soil, Free Speech, Freemen, Fremont," in the air, the Republicans enthusiastically adjourned the convention. They were poised to face the "dough face" James Buchanan from Pennsylvania in the November election.[61]

The campaign took on the appearance of a revival. To his followers, Fremont's election became a moral crusade to end the sin of slavery. Supporters throughout the small towns of the North flooded the streets speaking the word, poetry was read about Fremont, huge rallies were held, parades were formed, and torch-lit marches were conducted.

Fremont, the Pathfinder, was not shy about stating his views on the campaign's great issue: "I am opposed to slavery in the abstract and upon principle and made habitual by long settled convictions. I am . . . inflexibly opposed to its extension beyond its present limits."[62] He was vilified by the Democrats. Fremont was called a drunk, a slaveowner, a fraud, a deserter, and a man of low morals. It was said that his election would split the country apart. Even his own father-in-law opposed his election for that reason.

Northern big businessmen, fearful of losing Southern trade, contributed enormous sums of money to Buchanan. The Democrats outspent the new party ten to one. This infusion of cash was crucial in the outcome.[63]

Fremont lost the campaign, but actually did quite well with 33 percent of the popular vote and 114 electoral votes. In Ohio the tally was even more impressive, 48.5 percent, enough to put the state into his column. Fremont did surprisingly well in Clermont County as well, with 34 percent, but failed to carry the county.[64]

Post-election analysis revealed that Fremont found strong support in New England and the upper Midwest. Farmers, small businessmen, and skilled artisans voted for him as well. Ethnically, the Scots, Welsh, English, Scandinavians, and Free-thinking Germans tended to cast their ballots for Fremont.[65]

A strong drum beat of events further polarized the country following the 1856 election. The violence between pro- and antislavery advocates in Kansas and Nebraska was followed by the infamous *Dred Scott* Supreme Court decision, which said that blacks had no rights white men were bound to respect. The North was outraged. The Ohio General Assembly passed resolutions against slavery and condemning the kidnapping of free blacks. And then came John Brown's Raid, a vision of the coming apocalypse.[66]

Ohioans went to Chicago in the summer of 1860 committed to vote on the first ballot for their favorite son, candidate Salmon P. Chase. Like many others from the Ohio delegation, Reader W. Clarke, of Batavia, bolted from Chase on the second ballot to vote for Abraham Lincoln. On the third ballot, Lincoln was selected. Following their national convention, Ohio Republicans met in Columbus to map out their campaign strategy. Traveling to Columbus was a seven-man delegation from Clermont County.[67]

In keeping with nineteenth-century tradition, Lincoln remained at home in Springfield, Illinois, and conducted the campaign from his front porch. Thousands of surrogates, however, swarmed throughout the country on his behalf. The Clermont County campaign was hotly contested. Liberty poles were raised throughout the county. Wide Awakes, clothed in oil capes and carrying torches, marched in Neville. A large rally, with "German speakers," was held at the Clermont County Fairgrounds. There, a wagon parade was staged. One wagon carried thirty-three "Lincoln Girls" dressed in white and one girl, representing "Bleeding Kansas," garbed in black mourning clothes. Another wagon featured men splitting "Lincoln rails."[68]

The tone of the campaign was decidedly racist. The *Clermont Sun* claimed that the Republicans were "nigger lovers and Negro Equalitists." The *Courier* countered with its "short Catechism of Negro Equality," claiming that it was the Democrats who gave blacks the right to vote in New York. The *Courier* also claimed that Democrats fostered amalgamation of the races, pointing out former vice president and Democrat Richard Johnson's child of mixed heritage as evidence.[69]

The *Courier* attacked Stephen Douglas, the Democratic contender, for his reputed bouts with the bottle.

Who then is the Little Giant Inn Disposed?
When he was seen Aleing for a few days.[70]

When all was said and done, Lincoln was elected with the help of Ohio's voters. The *Courier* declared that in Batavia, "A shout went up that would have raised even Rip Van Winkle from his slumbers, and all day long the excitement has been intense." This time, though, the Democrats took the county by only 241 votes.[71]

It took twenty years and five presidential elections for slavery to move from the shadows to become the predominant, decisive issue in the country. By then it was too late to resolve the controversy peacefully. All of the diplomacy, compromise, and negotiations were not enough. The final arbiter of the issue would be war.

NOTES

1.   Mayer, *All on Fire*, 277; Richard Sewell, *Ballots for Freedom: Antislavery Politics in the United States, 1837–1860* (New York: Oxford University Press, 1976) 73. The Clermont County Antislavery Society met at the Williamsburg Presbyterian Church to draft their questionnaire. They asked candidates for Congress these three questions: Are you in favor of the immediate and unconditional emancipation of all the slaves in the District of Columbia and the Territory of Florida? Are you in favor of annex-

ing Texas to the Territory of the United States? And are you in favor of the abolition of the interstate trafficking of slaves?

To the candidates of the Ohio General Assembly they asked two questions: Are you in favor of the right to petition for all persons? And, if elected, will you work to repeal Ohio's Black Code?

There is no evidence that the questionnaires were actually circulated in Clermont County. *Clermont Courier*, August 14, 1838.

2.   Sewell, *Ballots for Freedom*, 12.

3.   Ibid., 73.

4.   Michael Holt, *The Rise and Fall of the American Whig Party: Jacksonian Politics and the onset of the Civil War* (New York: Oxford University Press, 1999) ix, 29.

5.   The group was composed of Dr. John Rogers, Eben Ricker, Rev. Caleb Walker, William Carnes of New Richmond, and attorney John Jolliffe of Batavia. The "Renegades" campaign consisted of purchasing poetic advertisements in the *Clermont Courier*. The advertisement for Dr. Rogers, an unsuccessful candidate for state representative, ran like this:

John G. Rogers, a man of sense,

To him this boon we will dispense;

Let us our rights to him intrust,

Believing that he will be just.

Clermont Courier, September 30, 1837. The four elected to office were John Robinson, county treasurer; John Beatty, auditor; William Roudebush, commissioner; and Edward Frazier, sheriff. *Clermont Courier*, October 14, 1837.

6.   Rockey and Bancroft, *Clermont County, Ohio*, 125.

7.   Ibid., 366A, 138; *Philanthropist* as reprinted in the *Clermont Courier*, October 27, 1839; Thomas Donaldson to the *Philanthropist*, February 18, 1840.

8.   Rockey and Bancroft, *Clermont County, Ohio*, 430A, 191–193; *Emancipator*, September 29, 1836; *Felicity Times*, July 6, 1893; Oliver Fee obituary, *Felicity Times*, undated.

9.   *Clermont Courier*, October 15, 1842. *Locofocos* was a derogatory term for radical working-class Democrats used by Whigs. The term was coined in 1836 when conservative New York Democrats walked out of a meeting when radicals upset them. The conservatives turned out the gas lights. The radicals responded by striking the newly invented "locofoco" matches and lit candles. Paul F. Boller, *Presidential Campaigns* (New York: Oxford University Press, 1984) 63.

10.   Lowe, an émigré from New Jersey, who had married well, raised the issue of abolitionism. He told the *Clermont Courier*, "I am no abolitionist, neither do I regard the institution of slavery as right," in a veiled reference to Jolliffe he continued, "but the ultra proceedings of the abolitionist are . . . not only injurious to the cause of the oppressed; but their practical operation will endanger the peace, if not the very existence of the Union." He later boasted that he prevented a mobbing of James Birney when the latter spoke at the Batavia Presbyterian Church. Jolliffe won the election 1,526 to 1,154. Lowe later commanded the Twelfth Ohio Volunteer Infantry in the Civil War and was killed leading his men at the Battle of Carnifex Ferry, the first

Ohioan with a field grade commission. See, Clermont County election results, 1839, MS 4283, Cincinnati Historical Society, Cincinnati, Ohio; Rockey & Bancroft, *Clermont County, Ohio*, 199–200; to be killed in the war, see Whitelaw Reid, *Ohio in the War* (Cincinnati, Ohio: 1895) 1:1010.

11. Richard Shenkman, *Presidential Ambition: How the Presidents Gained Power, Kept Power, and got Things Done* (New York: Harper Perennial, 2000) 65; Boller, *Presidential Campaigns*, 65–66, 77.

12. Rockey & Bancroft, *Clermont County, Ohio*, 126; *Clermont Courier*, August 8, 1840.

13. *Clermont Courier*, November 21, 1840.

14. Ibid.

15. Sewell, *Ballots for Freedom*, 77.

16. Ibid., 75–76.

17. Quoting William Birney, Ibid., 78.

18. Clermont's papers often referred to the party as "The Liberty Vote," "The Abolition Vote." The party's local candidates were usually the same each time—Dr. John Rogers, John Jolliffe, Absalom Douglas, William Keyes, Eben Ricker, Benjamin Morris, and Charles Huber. Most of the vote they did receive was from Ohio, Franklin, and Williamsburg townships, all future centers of Underground Railroad activity. *Clermont Courier*, October 21, 1843, October 22, 1842; *Ohio Sun*, October 8, 1842.

19. The *Ohio State Journal* as reprinted in the *Clermont Courier*, October 22, 1842. Gerrymander is the term describing the extreme redrawing of the boundaries of congressional districts following the census to favor the dominant political party. The first such redrawing was by Elbridge Gerry of Massachusetts. The district appeared to be like a salamander, thus the name.

20. Boller, *Presidential Campaigns*, 79.

21. Ibid.; Irving Stone, *They also Ran* (New York: Signet, 1968) 72–73.

22. The Liberty candidates for local office were William Keyes, Congress; Caleb Walker, state representative; Eben Ricker, county commissioner; Thomas J. Morris, recorder. All were defeated. King registered 113 votes of 4,888 cast. Ohio Township provided 57. *Clermont Courier*, October 19, 1844.

23. *Clermont Courier*, October 19, 1844.

24. Robert V. Remini, *Henry Clay: Statesman for the Union* (New York: W. W. Norton, 1991) 652.

25. The *Ohio State Journal* as reprinted in the *Clermont Courier*, October 26, 1844.

26. Edgar A. Holt, *Party Politics in Ohio* (Columbus, Ohio: The F. J. Heer Printing Co., 1931) 206.

27. *Clermont Courier*, November 30, 1844.

28. The popular vote total for the election was Polk, 1,337,243; Clay, 1,299,062; Birney, 62,300. Polk's electoral votes were 170 to Clay's 105. Clay carried Tennessee, Polk's home state. Remini, *Henry Clay*, 663.

29. Sewell, *Ballots for Freedom*, 110, 113.

30. *Clermont Courier*, October 16, 1846; Sewell, *Ballots for Freedom*, 111; Stephen E. Maizlish, "Ohio and the Rise of Sectional Politics," *The Pursuit of Public Power: Political Culture in Ohio, 1787-1861*, eds. Jeffery P. Brown and Andrew R. L. Clayton (Kent, Ohio: Kent State Univ. Press, 1994) 127.

31. David Wilmot as quoted in Bruce Levine, *Half Slave and Half Free: The Roots of Civil War*, rev. ed. (New York: Hill and Wang, 2005) 181.

32. Ibid.

33. John Sherman as quoted in Maizlish, "Sectional Politics," *Public Power*, 127.

34. Michael F. Holt, *American Whig Party*, 226–27.

35. The "Barnburners" were so named because they were "willing to burn down the barn in order to get rid of the rats," a reference to their apparent willingness to destroy the Union in order to destroy slavery. Boller, *Presidential Campaigns*, 84.

36. Other activists chosen for leadership roles in the new local party were William Hobson, Samuel Siler, Col. A. G. Monroe, Thomas Gowdy, and E. G. Beck. John McLean was well known to Clermonters. He lived in nearby Warren County and was among the first men admitted to practice law in Clermont County. He later became an associate U.S. Supreme Court Justice and wrote the dissent in the *Dred Scott* case. *Clermont Courier*, August 17, 1848.

37. Sewell, *Ballots for Freedom*, 157; Boller, *Presidential Campaigns*, 84–85.

38. *Cincinnati Daily Unionist* as quoted in Levine, *Half Slave and Half Free*, 177.

39. Maizlish, "Sectional Politics," *Public Power*, 126–27.

40. "Dough faces" were Northerners who supported Southern interests. *Ohio State Journal* as printed in the *Clermont Courier*, August 17, 1848; *Clermont Courier*, September 21, 1848.

41. James Robb, of Ohio Township, was offered as county commissioner; Thomas Jefferson Morris, son of Thomas Morris, the former U.S. senator, announced his candidacy for Congress, a few days later. *Clermont Courier*, September 8, 1848.

42. The four townships were Batavia, Tate, Williamsburg, and Franklin. The vote totals in antislavery-rich Ohio Township were disappointing. *Clermont Courier*, October 19, 1848.

43. John Lyons to the *Clermont Courier*, October 26, 1848.

44. The popular vote total was Taylor, 1,360,099; Cass, 1,220,544; Van Buren, 291,763. See Boller, *Presidential Campaigns*, 86.

45. Maizlish, "Sectional Politics," *Public Power*, 130; *Clermont Courier*, November 9, 1848.

46. Holt, *American Whig Party*, 378–400.

47. The first black laws were enacted in 1804 and supplemented in 1807. Other provisions included a requirement for blacks living in Ohio to prove their freedom, registering a certificate of freedom in the county clerk's office, fining employers who hired blacks without the certificates, and criminalizing helping runaways. Mary Ann Yannessa, *Levi Coffin: Breaking the Bonds of Slavery in Ohio and Indiana* (Richmond, Ind.: Friends United Press, 2001) app. B.

48. Sewell, *Ballots for Freedom*, 181, N 34.

49. *Clermont Courier*, February, 1849.

50. Ibid., September 25, 1851.

51. *Herald of Freedom*, September 17, 1852.

52. George W. Julian, *Political Recollections, 1840–1872* (Chicago: Jansen, McClurg & Company, 1884) 125–127; *Herald of Freedom*, October 22, 1852.

53. Boller, *Presidential Campaigns*, 88–90. Hale did a little better in Ohio with 8.8 percent of the vote. Hale's performance in Clermont County mirrored the state's outcome, pulling 409 votes. Maizlish, "Sectional Politics," *Public Power*, 135; Rockey and Bancroft, *Clermont County, Ohio*, 129.

54. Salmon P. Chase quoted in Levine, *Half Slave and Half Free*, 193.

55. Vernon Volpe, "The Ohio Republican Party," *The Pursuit of Public Power*, 158; Joseph P. Smith, ed., *History of the Republican Party in Ohio* (Chicago: Lewis Publishing Co., 1898) 1:20, 21, 25.

56. Volpe, "The Ohio Republican Party," 158.

57. The Know-Nothing Party was the commonly used name for the American Party. It acquired the moniker because its members responded to questions about the party by saying "I know nothing." The American Party was nativist, standing against immigrants, especially Irish Catholics. They believed that immigrants should have to live in the United States for twenty-one years before gaining citizenship and that all immigrants should be banned from public office. Boller, *Presidential Campaigns*, 93; *Clermont Sun*, October 4, 1856.

58. *Clermont Sun*, October 4, 1856.

59. Chase was elected with a 48.5 percent plurality of the votes. In Clermont County the totals were Medill, 2,423; Chase, 2,336; and Trimble, 436. The Republicans showed strength in the traditional antislavery areas of Williamsburg, Tate, Franklin, and Ohio townships. Chase actually carried Jackson Township 142 to 95 over Medill. *Clermont Sun*, October 18, 1956.

60. Smith, *History of the Republican Party in Ohio*, 1:52, 55. Boller, *Presidential Campaigns*, 92. Polygamy was a major issue of the time because of the difficulties with the Mormons in Utah. The Mormon Church sanctioned polygamy. Its abolition was the price it paid for statehood.

61. Boller, *Presidential Campaigns*, 92.

62. Irving Stone, *They Also Ran*, 172; Volpe, "The Ohio Republican Party," 161.

63. Stone, *They Also Ran*, 173–74.

64. The final total in Clermont County was Buchanan, 2,754; Fremont, 2,188; and Millard Fillmore, American Party, 795. See Boller, *Presidential Campaigns* 94; Volpe, "The Ohio Republican Party," 165; *Clermont Sun*, November 6, 1856.

65. Levine, *Half Slave and Half Free*, 208–209.

66. Stamp, *American in 1857*, 105.

67. The seven men from Clermont County were Andrew Ermie, Thomas Fitch, Louis Logan, Alexander Smith, Charles Burkhardt, William Urley, and Abraham Teeter. See Boller, *Presidential Campaigns*, 101; See also, Smith, *History of the Republican Party in Ohio*, 1:117, 128.

68. *Clermont Courier*, November 7, 1860.

69. Richard M. Jackson was a Kentucky Indian fighter who became Martin Van Buren's vice president. He lived with a black woman and fathered two children with her. Ibid., October 1860; Boller, *Presidential Campaigns*, 60.

70. *Clermont Courier*, October 31, 1860.

71. Ibid., November 7, 1860; Rockey & Bancroft, *Clermont County, Ohio*, 129.

CHAPTER 6

Slavery and the Law

THE LAW WAS HEAVILY WEIGHTED toward slavery. The Constitution protected it. Congress enacted laws in 1793 and 1850 to help slaveholders retrieve their property when they escaped into the free states. The conservative nature of the law itself served to protect the status quo. Nineteenth-century judges were typically constructionists who saw their role as interpreting the law, not making it. Further, the law in the nineteenth century was highly technical. More often than not, the case would turn on some arcanum of procedure rather than the underlying facts at issue. Ohio, despite being a "free state," gave deference to slaveholding interests. Despite the long odds, there were attorneys such as Rutherford B. Hayes, Salmon Chase, and Clermont County's former prosecuting attorney John Jolliffe, who challenged the system.

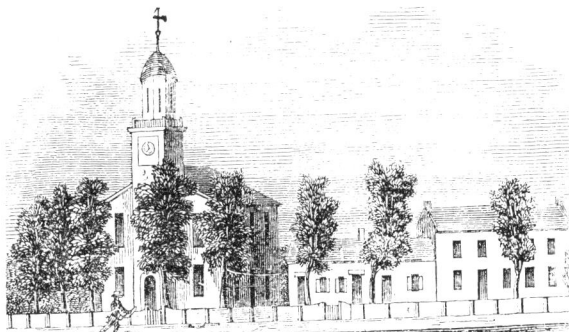

Fig. 6.1. *This Clermont County Courthouse was built in 1829 and was razed in 1935.*

Layered deep within the technicalities and legal abstractions of each case were its facts. The facts were the who, what, and where—the blood, bone, and sinew of the case. The facts put a human face upon the abstractions. Most of the cases were legal losers for the abolitionists. They could, however, have a great impact beyond the courthouse if they were exploited successfully.

The antislavery movement eagerly seized upon the most egregious and sensational cases and parleyed them into political victories. The *Philanthropist*, the official newspaper of the Ohio Antislavery Society, was particularly adroit at capitalizing upon the slaveholders' excesses. The paper appealed to Northerners' basic humanitarian impulse by portraying the slaves and conductors as helpless victims ensnared within the slaveholder's web. The slaveholders were shown as greedy, arrogant sinners. The paper also, especially early on, targeted a larger audience: those who were insulted by the overweening grasp of the "slaveocracy" that assaulted Ohio's sovereignty with their incessant demands.

Over the period there were a number of high-profile slavery-related cases that had a much greater impact upon society and politics than they did upon the law. We will examine three of these high-profile, high-impact cases.

Eliza Jane Johnson

Eliza Jane Johnson was a thirty-two-year-old free woman of color who lived with her husband, Gabriel, and their five children in Murraytown, Brown County, Ohio. On September 23, 1837, a party of four armed men broke into the Johnson home, whipped Eliza into submission and carted her off to Kentucky. The kidnappers claimed that she was a runaway slave.[1]

Chase was given by residents of Sardinia. More recruits joined in from Red Oak. The kidnappers avoided Ripley, the "abolitionist hell hole," and proceeded two miles downstream to Levanna to cross over to Kentucky. William Kephart, one of the posse, reached the bank of the Ohio River. He had the four kidnappers and Eliza in view, and went after them. As he approached, his horse stumbled on a tree root. Kephart's face smashed into the rocky beach, severely injuring him. The kidnappers, seeing the accident, let out a victory shout, pushed Eliza into an awaiting boat, and rowed her to Kentucky.

Two of the kidnappers, Peyton Huff of Brown County and Mr. Cruet of Highland County, were left on the shore when the rest of the posse arrived. Pistols were drawn. The kidnappers threatened to shoot anyone who attempted to arrest them. However, upon calculating their survival odds, they relented and submitted to arrest. They were taken to Georgetown, where a "straw bail" was set. After posting the low bond, the two promptly fled the state.[2] The editors of the *Cincinnati Journal and Luminary* captured the sentiments of the times.

This outrage on humanity has occasioned no little distress in the neighborhood. It produced an intensity of feeling that cannot be described. Will not the humanity of the citizens of our sister state induce them to return this poor woman to her husband? Can friendship between the states be maintained, while such outrages are perpetrated by private citizens, and then sustained by the civil authorities. The woman it is certain never belonged to Kentucky of course, the citizens of that state have no pretext, in her case, for such deeds of horror.[3]

The paper pressed home its argument. Kentuckians should not rely upon kidnapping to retrieve alleged slaves. They must press their case first in Ohio courts before taking the fugitives back to Kentucky for further disposition. Eliza Jane Johnson "must be replaced under the jurisdiction of Ohio," demanded the paper, "before any court can entertain jurisdiction of the question of freedom and slavery. . . . Unless these private outrages stop," the paper warned, "border warfare will erupt."[4] A stronger appeal to the "sovereignty" audience could not have been made.

Arthur Fox, the leader of the kidnappers and son of the Mason County, Kentucky, sheriff, went to Eliza's cell to look at his "property." He was astonished to find that Eliza was not the slave he lost four years ago.[5] This was nothing more than a case of mistaken identity. It should have been over, but Kentucky wasn't through with Eliza Jane Johnson.

John Rankin and others appeared at the Mason County courthouse to demand a habeas corpus hearing, arguing that Eliza was a free woman and, therefore, not subject to the jurisdiction of Kentucky. A hearing was held on October 1, 1837. Eliza testified that she had been born a slave, but had escaped four years prior. After reaching Cincinnati she had been presented with her manumission papers. Rankin argued that whatever her past, the fact that she had lived in the free state of Ohio for the past four years made her free and that she should be released immediately. Judge Walker Reid, a slaveowner and former state legislator, disagreed. He reasoned that Kentucky law required him to think that every "person of color" must be considered a slave until proven otherwise. This was so, despite the fact that Ohio law compelled the putative master of the fugitive slave to prove the person held was indeed a slave. "For the present," he concluded, "Eliza Jane Johnson is remanded to jail as a fugitive slave."[6]

On their way home, James Huggins, a member of Rankin's party, was set upon by several Kentuckians, tied to a tree and severely whipped. Rankin saw clearly from this incident and the opinion of Judge Reid that Eliza Johnson would not see justice in Kentucky. They decided to take the matter out of the courts and insert it into the political realm by petitioning the Ohio General Assembly and the governor for help.

The Clermont County Antislavery Society took up the cause. At its meeting on January 5, 1838, a resolution was passed that condemned the Kentucky court's action for "consigning her [Johnson] to perpetual slavery. . . . The tearing of this woman from her husband, immuring her in prison for months and consigning her to slavery, is a barbarity that should make even the most savage ashamed."[7] According to the society, the kidnapping and subsequent incarceration of Eliza was "an outrage upon the humane feelings of the citizens of Ohio that the execration of all good men, and threatens to destroy every vestige of friendship existing between the States." A committee comprised of John Jolliffe, Dr. John Rogers, Rev. Daniel Parker, and William Gage, was formed to express the sense of the society that the incident was "an indignity upon the laws of Ohio" and to demand the immediate attention of the governor and legislature.[8]

Not everyone in the county was of the same mind. A group of Tate Township citizens met to consider their own resolution. They believed that the Antislavery Society's resolution was "ungenerous, unnatural, and contrary to the true spirit of our political and religious institutions at war with our peace and happiness, as it exists between us and the citizens of the Southern states." They disapproved of the "course pursued by the abolitionists and consider them to be agitators and disturbers of the peace and ought to be looked upon as a lawless gang of mobocrats." Specifically, they condemned the abolitionist's reaction against Judge Reid's decision as an "unwarrantable attack" on the judge's character that is "unbecoming and unworthy of the notice of any man (abolitionists excepted)." Finally, the resolutions adopted at the New Richmond meeting of the Antislavery Society represented a "dark and boisterous appearance, a revengeful spirit, hatred and enimity, claiming unto themselves the charity and benevolence not withstanding."[9]

"Originous" responded to the foregoing. He wrote that the very preamble of the resolution, "Citizens of Tate Township," was misleading. There were forty-two people at the meeting, twelve of whom were from different townships. Only about eight of the attendees actually participated in drafting and voting upon the resolution. Most remained "silent . . . out of disgust at the proceedings," or were merely entertained by the proceedings. Nevertheless, there was certainly no unanimity of opinion. Originous wanted the rest of the county to know

they were not concerned in the slander so unjustly heaped upon a portion of their fellow citizens (abolitionists) for it is believed that no unprejudiced reader of the resolutions passed at New Richmond, can correctly draw the conclusion that the abolitionists have the remote idea of disbanding the Union, or taking up arms, as represented by one of the eight patriots at the aforesaid meeting, unless in self-defense, if attacked by some "lawless band of mobocrats."[10]

Senator Thomas Morris became embroiled in the affair. When returning to his home from Washington City by boat, he decided to have dinner with his friend Alexander Campbell at a Ripley hotel. A man who described himself as "a citizen of Kentucky" and a friend of the senator's overheard a portion of the dinner conversation between Morris and Campbell. In a letter to the *Maysville Eagle*, "Citizen" castigated Morris's heated denunciation of Judge Reid's decision in the Johnson case. He seemed most upset by Morris's incendiary remark "that war ought to be immediately declared against Kentucky; that perfect non-intercourse should take place, and that every Kentuckian should be shot down as soon as he sets his foot on the Ohio side."[11]

Morris responded by writing a letter to Campbell and publishing it in the *Philanthropist*. He wrote that he had no recollection of advocating a border war with Kentucky. "The idea of Ohio declaring war on Kentucky," he continued, "is so perfectly ridiculous, comment is unnecessary. . . . I am not in the habit of indulging in expressions such as shooting down men on any occasion."[12]

Morris used the incident as an opportunity to articulate his "slaveocracy" theory.

The slave holding power is far more dangerous in the country than I ever anticipated; it is above the sovereignty of the states, if not that of the union. It will permit neither to recognize the colored person as a citizen enjoying certain rights, but as a thing when it can be done without a breach of the peace.[13]

The Johnson affair was another example of "the arrogance of the slaveholding power in their efforts to prostrate the constitution itself." Kentucky's action challenged the very sovereignty of Ohio as a free and independent state.

Senator Morris concluded,

A state which is unable to protect the person of individuals when found within its borders, from violence, has lost its sovereignty, and is unworthy the name of a free and independent state, and that between sovereign and independent nations the very act which took place near your town, though beginning in mere individual crime, yet if that crime was begun in one country and consumated in another, whose government should justify the act or make it her own—it would by the nation whose sovereignty was thus violated be considered just cause for WAR.[14]

John Rankin and his supporters successfully ginned up grass root support for a legislative resolution demanding Eliza Johnson's release from the Mason County, Kentucky, jail. On February 26, 1838, debate was held in the Ohio General Assembly on the following resolution:

Whereas it is represented in the General Assembly that Eliza Jane Johnson, a free woman of color, was lately carried by force, and without legal authority, from her home, in Brown County, Ohio, into Mason County, Kentucky, on the pretense of being a slave of Arthur Fox, of said County of Mason, and though the said Arthur Fox disdains any title to said Eliza, she is still detained in confinement in the said county: Therefore,

Resolved, That his excellency, The Governor, be, and is hereby requested to open correspondence with the Governor of Kentucky, in relation to the illegal seizure and forcible removal of said Eliza Jane Johnson, from Brown County, Ohio, to Mason County, Kentucky, where she is detained in prison, and that he respectfully insist on the restoration of said Eliza Jane Johnson to the enjoyment of freedom and friends.[15]

The resolution passed: thirty-seven in favor, twenty-three opposed. The resolution did not, however, receive the support of Rep. Thomas Buchanan of Batavia. Buchanan was unmoved by all of "the glowing descriptions of her being torn from her husband, children, pots and kettles." All of it existed only in the "imaginations of abolitionists," he wrote. If it was not for them "we should have heard nothing of it, she would have lain in prison till she died." "Blacks," he declared, "have no more right to petition than dogs have." He did concede, however, that blacks are human, "but of a lower order."[16]

Eliza was still in jail a month later, having been there for about five months. Finally, Judge Reid recognized that Eliza was not a slave. Incredibly, the judge actually thought about holding her in jail until she paid for the costs of her incarceration, as provided for under Kentucky law. Aside from the obvious injustice of the act, Eliza could not have come up with money. Either Rankin and his friends would have to pay, or Eliza would be sold into slavery for the costs. The judge wisely decided not to pursue the second option, and released Eliza. However, Rankin was not finished with the matter. He called upon the Commonwealth of Kentucky to compensate for Eliza's unlawful incarceration. He chided Mason County for their lack of charity.

Had the Mason court paid her reasonable damages, and discharged her before her case came before the legislature of Ohio, we should have had a higher sense both of their justice and humanity. Ought not the State of Ohio, through the executive, to demand full justice? Can the people of Mason County sustain a character for honesty, if they refuse to pay reasonable damages? The court by her discharge, acknowledged that she was unjustly imprisoned.[17]

Kentucky made criminals of John Rankin, Alexander Campbell, Dr. Isaac Beck, and John Mahan following the Johnson affair. Wanted posters were put up all over northern Kentucky offering twenty-five hundred dollars for the arrest of the four men from Brown County.[18]

The impact of the Johnson case cannot be underestimated. The incident was a boon for the newly born abolitionist movement. The abolitionists seized upon the excess of the slaveholding interests and translated the outrage into political success. By successfully involving the Ohio General Assembly in the matter, they were able to shift the entire antislavery movement into the political mainstream. To be sure, the incident was spun by the abolitionists into an assault upon Ohio's sovereignty rather than an opposition to slavery as an institution. The cagey abolitionists realized that Ohio was not ready for that tact just yet. The furor did gain new converts to the cause; however, it was mild in comparison to the eruption involving the Rev. John B. Mahan of Sardinia.

John B. Mahan

John Bennington Mahan was a second generation abolitionist. Both of his parents hated the institution. In 1804, when Mahan was three years old, they left Kentucky for the more accommodating environment of Bethel, Ohio. There, young Mahan drank in the antislavery passions of Thomas Morris, Obed Denham, and Dr. Isaac Beck. Mahan became a school teacher and a Methodist minister. After leaving Bethel for Sardinia in Brown County in the early 1830s, he switched his religious affiliation to the Presbyterian Church and began preaching. He operated a sawmill and a "temperance" tavern, and he also became an important link on the Underground Railroad.[19]

The Mason County, Kentucky Circuit Court indicted Mahan on August 13, 1838, upon the charges of slave stealing. Specifically, he was accused of assisting two slaves, John and Nelson, of escaping from their owner, William Greathouse, who lived in Mason County. The charges were based solely upon the affidavit of Greathouse, a convicted felon. In order to convict Mahan of the crime, the prosecution had to prove that he was within the state of Kentucky at the time the crime was committed.[20]

Mahan was physically in the state of Ohio at the time of the indictment. In order to legally bring him to Kentucky to stand trail, Kentucky had to extradite him from Ohio. James Clark, governor of Kentucky, began the process by sending a formal requisition to Joseph Vance, governor of Ohio. Clark's demand stated that "Mahan has fled from Justice and is now going at large in the State of Ohio."[21] Implicit within the statement was Mahan's presence in Kentucky at the time of the commission of the crime.

Governor Vance carelessly signed the extradition papers, giving the State of Kentucky the right to arrest Mahan. On September 17, 1838, David Wood, Kentucky's statutory agent; Vincent Crabb, deputy Brown County sheriff; and Greathouse arrested Mahan at his home. Soon thereafter, Dr. Isaac Beck appeared to advise Deputy Crabb that Mahan was entitled to a habeas corpus hearing to challenge the validity of the arrest. Mahan was escorted to Georgetown, the county seat, for that purpose. Mahan was taken to the law office of Thomas Hamer, a well-respected local attorney. Hamer, a proslavery advocate, refused to help. The posse sped on toward Kentucky. Just before crossing the Ohio River, Wood was served with a writ issued by a lawyer from Sardinia to give up Mahan. Wood refused to pay any attention to the order and proceeded on to Mason County. Mahan was clasped into irons and imprisoned to await trial in the same jail that held Eliza Johnson.[22]

While Mahan was languishing in jail, his support was gathering force. The first blow was struck by "Veritas," widely believed to be Rankin. He informed the *Philanthropist* of Mahan's arrest and the denial of a habeas corpus hearing. Veritas described Mahan as "one of the most upright and benevolent men in the State." He argued that the entire affair was "highly mysterious" and must have been based upon perjury because Mahan had not been in Kentucky for years. He concluded with this question: "What will not the protection of slavery lead men to do!"[23] The paper criticized Vance's hasty and unwise decision to extradite Mahan: "The conduct of Governor Vance in this affair must undergo the strictest scrutiny. . . . The demand having been made, he seems to have proceeded at once, without hesitation, to issue an order for the arrest of Mr. Mahan." Vance was also accused of undermining Ohio's sovereignty.

Let us, the people of Ohio, know, whether we are to be subjected to like grievances . . . be torn from home, from friends, from the free soil of Ohio . . . and cast into a slave-holding jail, to be arraigned before a slave-holding tribunal, tried by slave-holding laws.

If such be the fact, we call upon the citizens of Ohio to awake—they are slaves.

"And what occasioned all this distress?" asked the paper, "The answer is short. Mr. Mahan is charged with feeding the hungry and clothing the naked as they fled from the land of oppression to Canada. In short he was charged with doing what the Bible requires of every Christian, and indeed of every human being."[24]

These excerpts provide a glimpse of the theories that surfaced throughout the entire controversy. First, the charges were baseless because Mahan had not been within Kentucky for years; therefore, the court lacked jurisdiction to even file charges. Second, even if Mahan did assist the slaves to escape, he was merely following God's law and his Christian conscience. Third, the Mason County court exemplified the arrogance and excess of the proslavery faction. Fourth, Vance, by agreeing to extradite Mahan to Kentucky, abdicated his responsibilities as a governor of the sovereign State of Ohio.

Newspapers around the country weighed in on the case. William Lloyd Garrison's the *Liberator* wrote,

What will the people of Ohio think when they are told that the unfortunate Mahan is in irons. . . . Irons on a citizen of Ohio, the victim of perjury! . . . Have they any regard for the sovereignty of their state?[25]

The *Pennsylvania Freeman* called the extradition "One of the most disgraceful transactions ever recorded in the history of the United States." Mahan, "a minister of the gospel has been torn from his family and friends and delivered to the tender mercies of a slaveholding Jury exasperated and maddened by the loss of their property in human beings."[26] The *Christian Witness* argued that unless slavery was abolished "it will abolish us and our liberties with us. . . . Humanity is throttled by the bloody hand of despotism and unless rescued will die of strangulation."[27]

Closer to home, the *Cincinnati Gazette* framed the case within the larger political prism. The reporter indicated that the prosecution would try to sustain the charges by proving that Mahan had worked with another person in Kentucky, thus implicating Mahan under a theory of agency.

This mode of reaching citizens of a free state has been looked to for some time by the owners as one of vital importance to their security in slave property. It is not improbable that Mahan's may be a test case. Its importance in aiding a political revolution in Ohio may turn out to be a lesser influence upon the officers of the nation.[28]

Vance began to feel the heat. Unfortunately, for the first-term governor, the affair took place in the middle of his re-election bid. He tried to make amends. He wrote a letter to the Kentucky governor advising him that the evidence before him indicated that Mahan was innocent. He wrote that he had always tried to promote "peace and harmony" between the states, despite this, he could not "consent that a citizen of this state shall be taken to another state and be tried for an offense that . . . he did not commit within her jurisdiction."[29]

Vance then tried the personal approach. He sent an emissary to meet with Governor Clark of Kentucky. Vance's entreaties were rebuffed. The Democrats naturally pounced upon the Whig governor's misfortunes. The party's paper called on Vance to bring Mahan back to Ohio.

Ohio's voters rejected Vance. Whereas he had been elected with a six thousand vote margin only two years earlier, he was defeated by five thousand votes. Vance's hold as Ohio's first Whig governor may have been tenuous in traditionally Democratic Ohio, but the fallout from the Mahan fiasco must have been damaging.[30] The *Philanthropist* had no doubt as to the reason for Vance's defeat. It editorialized,

The intelligence of the arrest and delivery of Mahan thrilled, like an electric shock, through Ohio; and important results have followed. . . . The people of Ohio have thus given evidence of a keen sense of personal rights, and a wholesome regard for the honor of the state. . . . No Executive officer will venture to lay aside his reason, in administering a law which intrenches on state-sovereignty, and places the liberties of the citizens at his disposal.[31]

On November 12, 1838, fifty-three-year-old Judge Walker Reid called the case styled *Commonwealth v. Mahan* to order in the same Washington, Kentucky, courthouse in which he presided over the Eliza Jane Johnson case. As expected, the entire question of Mahan's guilt turned on whether Kentucky held jurisdiction to hear the question. The prosecution floated its theory of crime by agency: Mahan retained another in Kentucky to help the slaves escape. The evidence supporting this theory was weak at best. The defense argued that Mahan should be acquitted because Kentucky had no evidence placing Mahan in the state at the time the crime was committed.

Judge Reid then instructed the jurors. In order to convict, Reid explained,

the crime must have been committed here, in Kentucky, to give this court jurisdiction. It is so stated in the indictment and must be proved as stated. No after act will do. No aid and assistance given out of this state will do unless he was near enough at the time the escape was effected to receive information personally and aid in case of alarm by previous arrangement . . .

The result of the whole of my examination and deliberation is . . . that this court and jury have no jurisdiction of this case if from the evidence they are satisfied the prisoner is a citizen of Ohio and had not been in the state of Kentucky until brought here by legal process to answer this prosecution.[32]

The judge could have dismissed the case altogether because Mahan was not in Kentucky when the crime allegedly took place. To do so, however, the judge, a slaveowner and politician, would have put himself in political jeopardy. As an attorney, he had to know that the court did not have jurisdiction. He resolved his dilemma by giving the issue to the jury to decide with a clear instruction, ensuring they would arrive at the proper decision.

The jury retired to consider its verdict. Everyone expected a lengthy deliberation, but the jury came back quickly with a verdict of not guilty. Based upon this outcome, the second charge was dismissed. Mahan was released.[33]

The ten weeks he spent in jail were hard on Mahan. The irons placed on his wrists wore the flesh to the bone. Living in the dark cell probably caused him to contract tuberculosis, of which he later died. Just three months later, Greathouse sued Mahan in civil court for the monetary loss of his two slaves. The Kentucky court found in Greathouse's favor and ordered Mahan to pay twenty-four hundred dollars in damages. Mahan was forced to sell everything he owned to satisfy the judgment.[34]

The judicial system was not quite finished with Mahan. Brown County, Ohio, later charged him with criminal riot, alleging that Mahan and two others prohibited the arrest of a black man named Moses Cumberland. The lead prosecutor was Thomas Hamer, the same attorney who had earlier refused to help Mahan. Mahan was defended by the Clermont County "dream team": Senator Thomas Morris; former Clermont County prosecutor, John Jolliffe; and future Clermont County judge, Owen Fishback.

Upon the conclusion of four days and the testimony of fifteen witnesses, Mahan was convicted. He was sentenced to ten days in the Brown County jail on bread and water and a fifty dollar fine. Mahan appealed. The conviction was overturned by the Ohio Supreme Court because of an error in empaneling the jury.[35]

The trial of Mahan had an extraordinary reach beyond the courtroom. It brought down a governor. It nurtured the abolitionist movement by underscoring the hold that the slaveocracy had upon the country. The Commonwealth of Kentucky, alarmed by the acquittal of Mahan, further inflamed those concerned about the attack upon Ohio's sovereignty when it sent a high-level delegation to Columbus one year later to lobby for an Ohio fugitive slave law. The governor and the Ohio General Assembly, eager to repair the rupture of good will caused by the Mahan affair, acquiesced by passing the requested legislation. (This is discussed in greater detail in chapter 8.)

Margaret Garner

Margaret Garner was the twenty-two-year-old slave of Archibald Gaines. On the morning of January 28, 1856, Margaret, her husband Robert, their four children, and Robert's parents gathered for the eighteen-mile trip from Gaines's Maplewood farm in Richwood, Kentucky, to Cincinnati. Robert provided the transportation: A stolen sleigh and a team of horses. After reaching Covington, they abandoned the sleigh and crossed the frozen Ohio River on foot.[36]

The previous month had been the coldest on record in Cincinnati. With temperatures plunging to as low as twenty degrees below zero, the Ohio River froze solid. A Covington steel mill carted its products across the river by wagon. It was not uncommon to see herds of live-stock driven across the river to Cincinnati's slaughterhouses.[37]

The fugitives' destination was the home of Elijah Kite, a relative who lived along the Mill Creek. They were not able to find the house, and were forced to make inquiries. They were not aware that their escape had been discovered and that a posse was in pursuit.[38]

The slave hunters were tipped off as to their destination. They sur-rounded the home and demanded entry. The fugitives refused. A barred window was smashed in. A deputy U.S. marshall attempted to enter through the window but was shot in the arm by Robert Garner. The door was then battered down. Robert fired off several more rounds, wounding another deputy. He was then overpowered and arrested.[39] Margaret shouted, "Before my children shall be taken back to Kentucky I will kill every one of them." She grabbed up a butcher knife and ran to her two-year-old daughter Mary and with "a single stroke of the knife slashed her daughter's throat, nearly decapitating her."[40]

The proslavery *Cincinnati Enquirer* reported an eyewitness account of the scene:

A deed of horror had been committed, for weltering in its blood, the throat being cut from ear to ear and the head almost severed from the body. Upon the floor lay one of the children of the younger couple, a girl of three years old. While in a back room, crouched beneath the bed, two more of the chil-dren, boys, of two and five years, were moaning, the one having received two gashes in its throat, the other a cut upon the head. As the party entered the room the mother was wielding a heavy shovel, and before she could be secured she inflicted a heavy blow with it upon the face of the infant, which was lying upon the floor.[41]

Margaret was subdued, disarmed, and placed under arrest. Without the overlay of slavery, Margaret would have been charged with murder under state law. But this was not to be, Margaret's owner wanted his property back, not executed. Therefore, he sought to have her returned to Kentucky under the Fugitive Slave Act of 1850.

The Fugitive Slave Act of 1850 established a system for an expe-dited return of fugitive slaves. All that was necessary to gain the return of a fugitive was to present affidavits of identity and proof of ownership before a federal commissioner. The alleged fugitive was not even permitted to testify at the hearing. Further, the law established a financial incentive to return fugitives to slavery by paying a fee of ten dollars to any claimant, agent, or attorney if the slave was returned to his owner. Persons convicted of knowingly aiding a slave to escape could be fined up to one thousand dollars, jailed for six months, and ordered to pay up to one thousand dollars to the owner for each escaped slave.

The most galling provisions to Northerners were contained within Section V of the Act. Marshalls in local communities were required to aid slaveowners or their agents to capture runaways. If they did not, they could be subject to a one thousand dollar fine and ordered to compensate the owner for the value of the escaped slave. The marshalls also had the authority to call out a citizens' posse to chase down the fugitives. It further provided that "all good citizens are hereby commanded to aid and assist in the prompt and efficient execution of this law whenever their services may be required."[42]

Joshua Giddings, congressman from Ohio, denounced the law as the "vilest monument of infamy of the nineteenth century. Let the President . . . drench our land of freedom in blood, but he will never make us obey that law."[43] The law, according to the *New York Evening Post*, was "an act for the encouragement of kidnapping." The Chicago City Council resolved not "to aid or assist in the arrest of fugitives from oppression."[44]

Closer to home, the *Cincinnati Enquirer* questioned the constitutionality of the Act by opining, "We do not think the general government has any right to send out its officers into the states to carry out what good faith requires the states to do alone."[45] The *Clermont Courier* noted the "hubbub" the law prompted in New England and the stated intentions of some not to enforce it. If the law is so odious let the Congress repeal it or the Supreme Court nullify it, urged the paper, but until then "let it be respected." The editor was happy, though, that the Honorable Jonathan Morris, Clermont County's representative in Congress, had voted against the law.[46]

The Fugitive Slave Act, while delaying the War Between the States for a decade, perhaps did more to radicalize the North and polarize the sections than any other act passed by Congress.

In Margaret's court case, John Jolliffe signed on as her attorney. Jolliffe's involvement with this case was not surprising since he had previously defended thirty-three slaves charged under the Fugitive Slave Act. He lost every case, and had suffered for his passionately held beliefs. Three years before the Garner case, he was severely beaten and kicked by an intoxicated Cincinnati judge, Jacob Flin, who called him a "damned abolitionist."[47]

Fig. 6.2. *John Jolliffe, former Clermont County prosecuting attorney, became a well-known defender of fugitive slaves.*

Jolliffe was raised a Quaker in Virginia. After admission to the bar he moved, for reasons yet unknown, to Clermont County in 1827. He practiced law with Thomas Hamer of Brown County for six years. It must have been a strained relationship given the men's positions on slavery. Jolliffe was a staunch abolitionist and Hamer was a well-known Southern apologist.

Jolliffe struck out on his own in 1833 when he was elected Clermont County prosecuting attorney. He joined the Batavia Methodist Church and became an antislavery and temperance activist, joining the Clermont County Antislavery Society. He also ran unsuccessfully as an antislavery candidate for state senator and U.S. congressman.[48]

Months after losing an election for another term as Clermont County's prosecuting attorney, Jolliffe left for Cincinnati. By 1850 he had become, along with better-known Rutherford B. Hayes and Salmon P. Chase, a leading member of the antislavery bar in the Queen City.[49] Over the years Jolliffe developed a unique legal theory to attack slavery. He argued that slavery was a sin that all Christians had to oppose. He based his argument on several Biblical verses. Prominent among them was Matthew 19:18: "Thou shalt love thy neighbor as thyself." Slavery stole a slave's labor; therefore, slaveholders were thieves. He also attacked both the 1793 and 1850 fugitive laws as unconstitutional because they forced Christians, many of whom believed slavery to be a sin, to return the fugitives to slavery. Thus, the laws violated the freedom of religion clause of the First Amendment of the U.S. Constitution. He had one more arrow in his legal quiver—that Margaret was free because her master had taken her to Cincinnati sixteen years before.

The issue before the court was not Margaret's guilt or innocence for murder, but whether her master could claim her as property and take her back to Kentucky. The trial was set for the morning of January 30, 1856. Within the courtroom the legal wrangling droned on and on. What normally would take at most two days to resolve stretched into weeks. Despite Jolliffe's heroic efforts, Commissioner John Pendry was unmoved. He rendered his decision on February 26, 1856: Margaret Garner was the slave of Archibald Gaines. She was to be released to his custody.

Pendry ruled that Jolliffe's argument that Margaret Garner had become free when her owner brought her to Ohio was not well taken. He wrote that the intent of Ohio's Constitution preventing slavery in the state was "to prevent slavery as an institution within her limits, rather than execute the act of manumission upon foreign slaves temporarily upon our soil with the master's consent."[50]

The only question before the court, he continued,

is not one of humanity. . . . The laws of Kentucky and of the United States make it a question of property. It is not a question of feeling. . . . It is the essence of the institution that the slave does not possess equal rights with the free man. The abstract rights to life, liberty, and property are in this case replaced by statutes providing expressly for his condition.[51]

Two days later, Margaret and her family were transported across the river back into Kentucky and slavery.

Jolliffe's supporters treated their champion to dinner and gave him money to compensate him for his efforts on Margaret's behalf. They wrote a letter to the *Cincinnati Gazette* expressing their feelings about the case.

We have seen a child perishing by the hands of its mother: that tragedy gives to us an illustration of the ruin wrought by that system. . . . Such laws pour contempt upon the dictates of justice and humanity, and one calculated to harden the heart, and benumb the conscience of every man who assist in their execution. The great conflict between freedom and slavery must sooner or later come to a crisis. All neutral ground upon this subject will be unknown.[52]

There was one last act to play out in the legal drama. Indictments for murder in an Ohio state court were handed down against Margaret. This could have set up an interesting legal question, of which court, the federal or state, would have jurisdiction over this case. However, that question did not arise. The indictments were a desperate last measure. The hope was to hold Margaret in Ohio, convict her of murder, impose a light sentence, and then release her as a free woman. But Margaret was already in Kentucky when the indictments were issued.

There was one major question: Would Charles S. Morehead, governor of Kentucky, respect a request from Ohio to extradite her to the state? Salmon P. Chase, governor of Ohio, widely known as "The Attorney General of the Underground Railroad" for his strong antislavery views, took five days to draft a brief, arguing his case for Margaret's return. He attached the lengthy "brief" to the requisition. Morehead sarcastically rejected Chase's argument. Nevertheless, by then Margaret was on board a boat bound for the slave markets of New Orleans.[53]

Margaret lived just two years after the trial, succumbing to the rigors of the sugar fields and typhoid fever.[54]

Margaret's case forced the attention of the nation to focus upon the most elemental horror of the institution of slavery, driving a mother to commit infanticide. What could be more horrible than murdering your own child? This issue resonated with people who previously may have been ambivalent to the question. Apologists argued that one could not blame the institution for the tragedy. Margaret was responsible for the act, not the institution. There must be a flaw within the mother. Others suggested that revenge may have been the motive for the murder. They pointed out that Gaines, her owner, was most likely the father of the dead child. Margaret was wreaking her own personal vengeance just as Medea, her classic predecessor, had done.

Regardless of the cause or motivation, this case was a sensation. It was quickly seized upon by the abolitionists, who spun it to political advantage, but it was eclipsed one year later by the *Dred Scott* case, which concluded that slaves were not human beings worthy of the protections of the United States Constitution.

NOTES

1. Hagedorn, *Beyond the River*, 124; *Cincinnati Journal and Luminary*, September 30, 1837.
2. Adam Lowry Rankin, "Autobiography of Adam Lowry Rankin," ed. Michael Speer, *Ohio History* 79 (Winter 1970) 35–36.
3. *Cincinnati Journal and Luminary*, September 30, 1837.
4. Ibid.
5. Hagedorn, *Beyond the River*, 125.
6. Judge Walker Reid's opinion as reported in the *Maysville Eagle*, November 4, 1837.
7. "CCAS Resolution, January 5, 1838," *Clermont Courier*, January 20, 1838.
8. Ibid.
9. *Clermont Courier*, February 16, 1838.
10. Ibid.
11. *Maysville Eagle*, November 1837.
12. *Philanthropist*, December 26, 1837.
13. Ibid.
14. Ibid.
15. "Resolution of the Ohio General Assembly," *Clermont Courier*, March 17, 1838.
16. Ibid.
17. *Philanthropist*, March 20, 1838.
18. Hagedorn, *Beyond the River*, 143.
19. Ibid., 87–88; *Transactions of the McClean County Historical Society*, (Bloomington: Pantograph Printing, 1899) 1:397.
20. *Philanthropist*, October 9, 1838.
21. Ibid.
22. Hagedorn, *Beyond the River*, 154–56.
23. *Philanthropist*, October 2, 1838.
24. Ibid.
25. Garrison quoted in Hagedorn, *Beyond the River*, 159–160.
26. Ibid., 160.
27. Ibid., 161.
28. Ibid.
29. *Philanthropist*, October 23, 1838.

30. Ibid. In Clermont County Vance actually picked up 217 votes in 1838. Rockey and Bancroft, *Clermont County, Ohio*, 128.

31. *Philanthropist*, October 23, 1838.

32. *Commonwealth v. John B. Mahan*, Mason County Circuit Court, 1838. Kentucky Dept. of Archives.

33. Ibid.

34. *Transaction of the McClean County Historical Society*, 398–99.

35. *The State of Ohio v. John B. Mahan, et al.*, Wilcox, 232.

36. Steven Wiesenberger, *The Modern Medea* (New York: Hill and Wang, 1998) 59–60.

37. Ibid., 49.

38. Levi Coffin, *Reminiscences of Levi Coffin: The Reputed President of the Underground Railroad; being a Brief History of the Labors of a Lifetime in Behalf of the Slave, with the Stories of Numerous Fugitives, who gained their Freedom through his Instrumentality, and many other Incidents* (Cincinnati, Ohio: Western Tract Society, 1876) 558–59.

39. Ibid.

40. Wiesenberger, *Modern Medea*, 74.

41. As quoted in Wiesenberger, 73.

42. "The Fugitive Slave Act of 1850," the full text printed in the *Clermont Courier*, November 14, 1850.

43. Quoted in Boyer, *The Enduring Vision*, 411.

44. Both quotes from Hagedorn, *Beyond the River*, 241.

45. *Cincinnati Enquirer*, October 30, 1850.

46. *Clermont Courier*, October 24, 1850.

47. Wiesenberger, *Modern Medea*, 100, 95.

48. Ibid., 93; Rockey & Bancroft, *Clermont County, Ohio*, 126,138; *Clermont Courier*, October 19, 1840.

49. Wiesenberger, *Modern Medea*, 93.

50. Ibid., 190.

51. Ibid.

52. Ibid., 200–201.

53. Ibid., 211–20.

54. Ibid., 278.

Part Two

The Underground Railroad

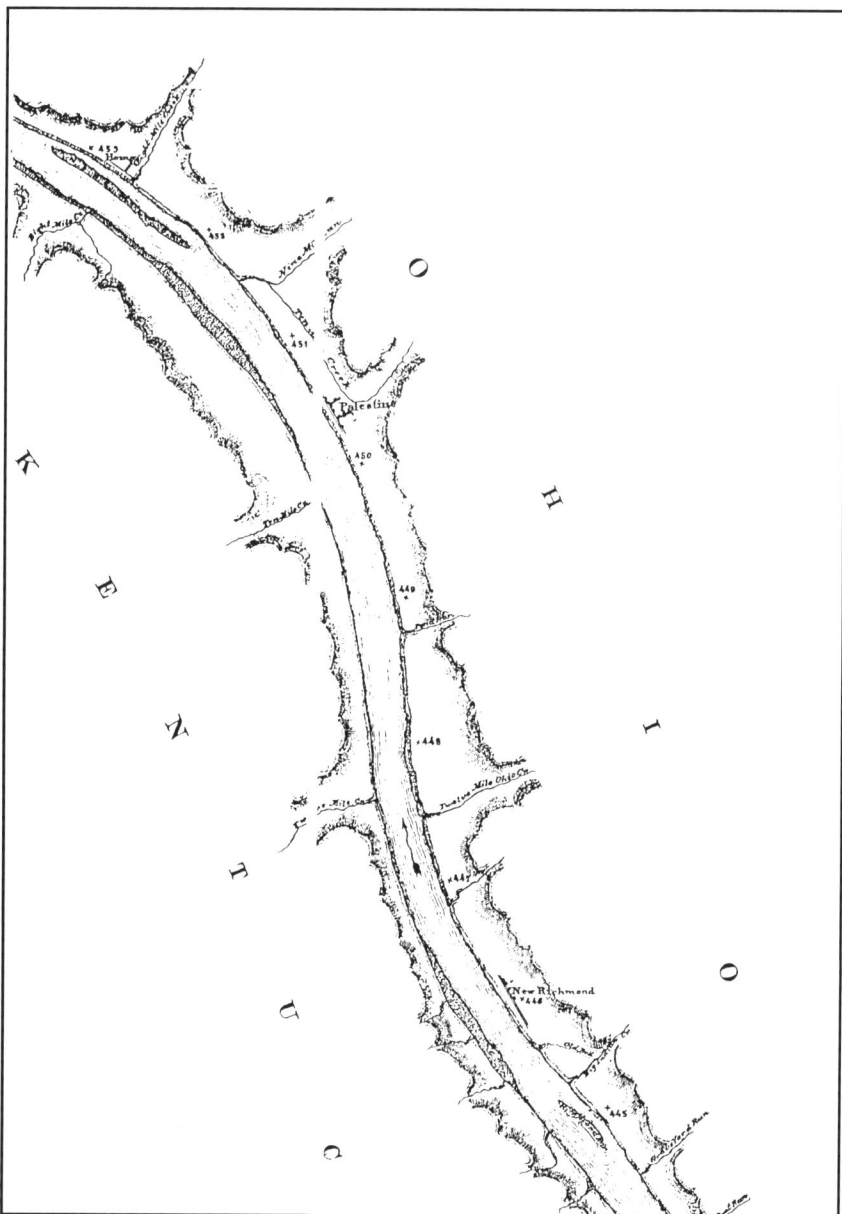

Fig. 6.1. *This map, circa 1870, shows the stretch of the Ohio River from New Palestine to New Richmond, Ohio. Note the islands, sand bars and the narrow width. All were flooded by the twentieth century dams constructed along the river.*

Introduction

THE UNDERGROUND RAILROAD WAS NEITHER underground nor a railroad. How, then, did this enterprise come to be called the Underground Railroad? There are many stories purporting to explain the origin of the term. The story of the escape of Tice Davids is the best.

Sometime in 1831, Tice Davids, a slave from Mason County, Kentucky, made a break for freedom. He ran toward the Ohio River in the direction of Ripley, Ohio, where he knew he would find help. His owner discovered the escape attempt and gave chase. Davids made it to the bank of the river and plunged in. The posse jumped into a skiff and began rowing after the fugitive. Tice left the river before his pursuers and ran down Front Street in Ripley. His owner gained a glimpse of his quarry, but suddenly lost sight of him. One of the pursuers exclaimed that the vanished Davids must have disappeared underground on a railroad.[1]

Fig. I-2. *A typical representation of the Underground Railroad in the 1840s.*

Traditionally, the Underground Railroad has referred to a loosely organized network of people, both black and white, who assisted slaves to freedom. The network consisted of routes and safe houses used by the "conductors," "engineers," and "station masters" for the work of moving the fugitives along the line. Until recently, researchers placed the Underground Railroad as operating from the early 1820s through the beginning of the Civil War. More contemporary scholars have extended this time frame through the enactment of the Thirteenth Amendment in 1865.

The National Park Service has expanded the definition even further. Their Network to Freedom program defines the Underground Railroad as "resistance to enslavement through flight." The emphasis has been placed upon the activities of those escaping slavery. Sites that may be included within the Network to Freedom program include natural landscape features such as caves, swamps, and river crossings. Church congregations that were active in the Underground Railroad, Maroon communities, kidnapping and slave rescue sites, and locations where legal challenges to slavery were made, may be included under this definition.[2]

Most fugitives entering Clermont County did so through the river portals of Palestine, New Richmond, and Moscow. One of the most popular south-to-north routes ran along the Bull Skin Trace, or Xenia Road. This road tracked north from the Ohio River at the mouth of the Bull Skin Creek in Franklin Township up through the inland villages of Felicity, Bethel, and Williamsburg. The trail exited Clermont County at Williamsburg. Most of the "passengers" were conveyed to the Quaker community of Martinsville in Clinton County.

The Bull Skin Trace was used by migrating eastern buffalo and later by Shawnee hunters from Old Town (Xenia) on trips into Kentucky. The name generally is thought to have been given to the trail by white hunters who saw a buffalo hide stretched on racks for drying near the mouth of the creek. The trace was improved in 1807 to permit wagon travel and was renamed Xenia Road. Later, it was extended to Detroit. Xenia Road was used to haul gunpowder to Sandusky, Ohio, during the War of 1812. Slaves, crossing over the Ohio River from Kentucky, most likely began using the trail to reach Canada some time after the conclusion of the War of 1812, when they heard veterans returning from the

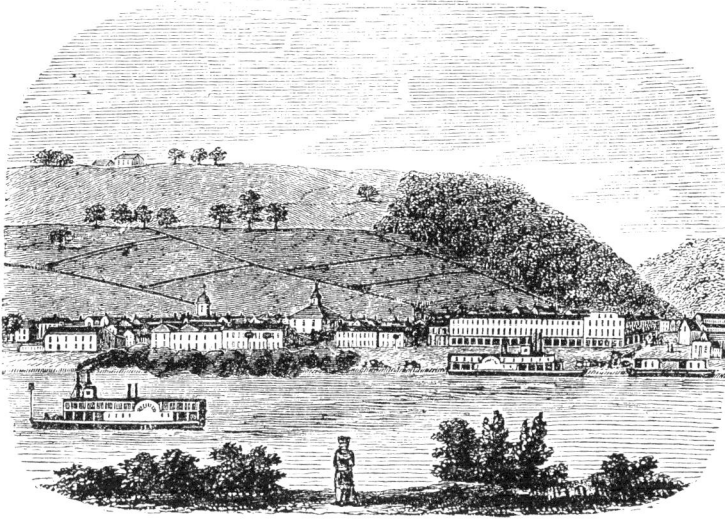

Fig. I-3. *This 1846 sketch drawn by Henry Howe shows the village of Ripley, Ohio, from the Kentucky shore. John Rankin's home can be seen on top of the hill.*

war tell stories of free blacks in Canada. Today the trail is known as State Route 133.

Another main spur ran from New Richmond, generally along the course of State Route 132, to the Andrew Coombs operation in Lindale. From there the escapees would be taken to Cincinnati via the Ohio Pike, now known as State Route 125. Another northward route went from the Ohio River through the Indian Creek Valley of Washington Township, through "Ricetown" to Bethel. From Bethel the fugitives could have proceeded, depending upon the circumstances, via State Route 125 to Cincinnati or to Williamsburg over State Route 133 or by smaller trails through the Elklick Creek Valley, now covered over by Harsha Lake.

The main east-to-west route, linking John Rankin's Ripley network to Levi Coffin's operation in Cincinnati, followed State Route 125. A secondary route led from Sardinia in Brown County to Williamsburg. This trail was utilized to send fugitives both ways, east and west, depending upon the circumstances.

The entire area of eastern Clermont County was laced with small trails, some of which have become roads that are still used today. Other trails have become overgrown through time and have become lost. No doubt these trails were used by escaping slaves when the main routes became too hot to use.

Fig. I-4. *The mouth of Bullskin Creek at the Ohio River—a popular crossing point for Kentucky slaves on their way to freedom.*

Fig. I-5. *The southern terminus of the Xenia Road, now known as State Route 133, used by fugitives passing through Clermont County soon after crossing the Ohio River from Kentucky.*

Clermont's Black Citizens

Blacks were present in southwestern Ohio before Clermont County was established in 1800. Most of the early blacks were freed slaves who came here when their former masters moved to escape slavery. The number of black citizens grew over time, but remained a very small percentage of the overall population. By 1850, the black population reached 380 out of a total population of 30,455. Within the next decade the numbers of blacks more than doubled to 792, accounting for 15 percent of the total population growth for the decade.[3]

Blacks tended to settle in several communities. The largest concentration lived in and near New Richmond. Other centers were Mt. Pisgah, Bethel, Felicity, Williamsburg, and Batavia. It should not be surprising that these villages were also centers of Underground Railroad activity. Many, but not all blacks, felt a sense of kindredness with fugitives. Escapees could, more or less, "hide in plain view" in these communities.

Of the 191 black household entries appearing in the 1860 census, 43 owned real estate. Some owned substantial real estate holdings valued at thousands of dollars. (There is a more complete analysis of the black community by township or village, where appropriate.) The occupations represented in the black census were diverse, with an emphasis on farming and river-related work.

Uncovering the history of black involvement in the Underground Railroad has been difficult. In fact, only one escape narrative has been found. Several factors have contributed to the lack of escape narratives. First, most of the fugitives simply passed through here on their way to Canada. Their connection may have lasted merely several hours to perhaps several days. Therefore, any written or oral recollections of the event are most likely located outside of the county. Until the advent of the internet, the likelihood of locating any of these records was very low. Second, black-generated records are scarce. Most of the fugitives were illiterate at that time because of laws prohibiting the education of slaves. Ohio's efforts at educating its black citizens were minimal. Third, since it was illegal to assist any of the fugitives to escape, keeping written records was tantamount to a confession. Fourth, blacks generally conveyed their family history orally from one generation to the next. Many of the nineteenth-century black Clermont County families have migrated out of the county, taking their family traditions with them. Thus, we are left with fragmentary accounts of their histories.

Fugitives

For many years scholars have been profiling the "typical" fugitive slave. They began by compiling advertisements for runaways, court documents, and newspaper articles. From that database, they have developed various categories of interest and applied statistical manipulations. In general, scholars have asserted that the typical fugitive was a young, biracial male, known as a "trusty" who had gained the confidence of his master.

Professor J. Blaine Hudson of the University of Louisville has compiled The Kentucky Fugitive Slave Database consisting of 801 cases representing 1,196 individuals. Based on his research, he drew a number of interesting conclusions about the fugitive slaves escaping from Kentucky. It should be noted that, while his conclusions are instructive in understanding what may have happened in Clermont County, they cannot be seen as conclusive.

According to Dr. Hudson, Kentucky fugitives were overwhelmingly male and generally were mulatto before 1850, but black after 1850. More slaves escaped during the decade of 1850s than any other decade of the period. The decade total was 630, or 52.6 percent of the entire 1,196 fugitives recorded.[4]

Kentucky was the home state of nearly 80 percent of those who escaped. Winter, defined as December through February, was the most popular season to escape and Sunday the most popular day. According to Hudson, nearly three-fourths of the escaped Kentucky slaves did so without assistance, though the numbers of those who received help more than doubled during the 1850s.[5]

A number of caveats must be mentioned. Professor Hudson's study is based primarily upon data collected from western Kentucky. Further, there were no newspapers of general circulation in Pendleton and Bracken counties, Kentucky, two of the three Kentucky counties directly facing Clermont County. Therefore, developing a profile of slaves escaping into Clermont County is statistically impossible. However, Dr. Hudson does include a few references from Mason County, Kentucky. Many, if not most, slaves escaping from Mason County entered Ripley in Brown County, Ohio, on their northward journey. However, there were an undetermined number of fugitives who were conveyed westward into Clermont County before going north. Substantive conclusions about the typical fugitive entering Clermont

County cannot be drawn because we simply lack statistically significant numbers of examples.

Palestine and Jacob Ebersole

Palestine, sometimes referred to as New Palestine, is the westernmost village in Clermont County, straddling the Hamilton County border. It was platted by Zachariah Chapman and Christian Ebersole in 1818 on land formerly owned by George Washington's nephew. The village's fifty-two lots were laid out into two streets that ran parallel to the Ohio River. These streets were bisected by five cross streets. The proprietors planned their village to be a riverport rivaling New Richmond several miles upstream.

Fig. I-6. *Jacob Ebersole.*

Christian's son, Jacob, was born in 1812. At age thirty-one he married Lydia Ann Rogers, the daughter of Dr. John Rogers and Julia Morris Rogers. Mrs. Rogers was the daughter of Clermont County's antislavery Senator Thomas Morris. The merging of these two antislavery families was not an uncommon practice in Clermont County. Indeed, Jacob's sister, Catherine, married Robert Fee of Moscow, one of Clermont County's most noted and documented Underground Railroad conductors.[6]

Jacob was reputed to have had "a generous . . . lively temperament," who was always "kind to the poor," and basically was a "good citizen." He was a member of the Baptist Church and, not surprisingly, he was a Conscience Whig who became a Free-Soiler and later a Republican. He was closely associated with all of the leading abolitionists of Clermont County such as Eben Ricker, Thomas Donaldson, and Dr. Rogers. These men were called the Liberty Chieftains.[7]

It is unclear when Jacob Ebersole became involved in the Underground Railroad. He kept a "fleet" of skiffs and other "small water craft" at the ready on the riverbank at Palestine. From his home on the hill overlooking the river he kept watch at night for lanterns on the Kentucky bank indicating he had "passengers" waiting to cross the river. He sent over the skiffs and ferried the escapees to the Ohio side. The fugitives were put into wagons for the eighteen-mile trip through the county northward to the Charles Huber station at Williamsburg.[8] Ebersole's death in 1861 came, unfortunately, four years before the slaves were freed.[9]

The Lindale Network

Lindale is a "small and pleasant hamlet," located astride State Route 132 near the northern boundary of Ohio Township. During the period, there was a collier and harness factory, a tannery, a cooperage, and several stores.[10]

One of the prominent families of the hamlet was the Coombs family. Andrew Coombs Jr. was born in Maine on Christmas Eve of 1805. He migrated to Ohio with his family in 1812 and settled in Lindale. The Coombs family became "an intimate friend" of Rev. John Rankin. Andrew attended Rankin's school in Ripley and later became an assistant teacher there. He married Kitty Shannon of Nicholsville, Ohio, and became a member of her church, the abolitionist Monroe Presbyterian Church.[11]

On August 18, 1835, Coombs transferred his membership to the

Fig. I-7. *The Lindale Baptist Church located at 3052 State Route 132 in Lindale, Ohio.*

Lindale Baptist Church and, nearly three years later, he became a licensed minister in the Baptist Church. The church was organized originally as the Second Ten Mile Baptist Church in Pierce Township. In 1829, his father had donated a lot in Lindale for the construction of a new Baptist church. A wood-frame church was built on the site in 1833. Twenty years later, a brick church was constructed.[12]

Coombs's first recorded venture into the abolitionist movement occurred in 1836 when he became the organizing secretary of the Mt. Gilead Antislavery Society. The society's constitution read, in part,

this society shall endeavor to elevate the character and condition of the colored people by encouraging their intellectual, moral, and religious improvement, but this Society will never encourage the colored people to assert their rights by force.[13]

John Rankin reported favorably that his former student was "a young Baptist preacher Zealous and efficient."[14] The president of the new society was the future U.S. congressman Dr. William Doan. Other officers included Walter Butler and E. T. Tibbets. The organization grew from its founding membership of forty to sixty within a year. Coombs wrote to the *Philanthropist* that before the founding of the society there were few abolitionists in the area but "now almost entirely abolitionist." The society formed a circulating library of antislavery tracts and newspapers.[15]

In February of 1839, the citizens of Lindale circulated three hand-written petitions calling for the abolition of slavery in the District of Columbia, denying the admission of Texas to the Union, and forbidding the admission of any other state that tolerated slavery. Coombs, his wife, and other members of his family signed the petitions. Seven of the twenty-seven signers were women, a most progressive statement. The petitions were sent to Thomas Morris, U.S. senator from Clermont County, for presentation to the Senate. Morris presented them, but they were tabled per the Senate's proslavery "Gag" rule.[16]

On August 10, 1844, Coombs drafted an antislavery memorial approved by the Lindale Church.

Resolved, That we regard slaveholding as contrary to the principles of the gospel and inconsistent with a profession of Christianity.

Resolved, That it is the duty of Christian churches and other religious bodies to express their disapprobation of the same and to use their influence for the removal of this great evil.[17]

At some point Coombs moved beyond abolitionist activism into involvement in the Underground Railroad. His home, located on a hill next to the Lindale Church, became a way station between the homes of John Rankin in Ripley and Levi Coffin in Cincinnati. It is also probable, given his location between New Richmond and Ohio Pike, that he moved fugitives from New Richmond. Wilbur Siebert writes that Coombs secreted slaves in "the back rooms and lower parts" of his house."[18] Andrew also used his general store as a cover for his Underground Railroad operations. At some point, he opened a store in Cincinnati at the corner of Third and John streets, reports Siebert.

Runaways from the Rankin station, at Ripley, were sent north and west to Lindale and there secreted in the Coombs store, his two large houses, and several tenements, from which they were conveyed twenty-five miles to Cincinnati in the grocery wagon and delivered in charge of Levi Coffin.[19]

Andrew and Kitty Coombs continued their efforts to free the slaves until Andrew's death on May 26, 1864. He is buried in lot no. 3 of the Lindale Baptist Church.

Andrew Coombs was not alone in his efforts at Lindale. He had help from another member of the Baptist church—John Tibbets. John was the son of Dr. Samuel Tibbets, Coombs's brother-in-law, who came from Maine to Clermont County in 1811.[20] John's first experience with the Underground Railroad occurred in 1838 when he was twenty years

Fig. I-8. *Andrew and Kitty Shannon Coombs, both of whom were ardent abolitionists and Underground Railroad operators.*

Fig. I-9. *The burial marker of Andrew and Kitty Coombs, located at the Lindale Baptist Church Cemetery, 3052 State Route 132, in Lindale, Ohio.*

old. A young black man presented himself to John and Thomas Coombs. They took the man by horseback to a Mr. Hoover living near Brounston in Clermont County, making the fifteen-mile trip at night because it "was very risky business."[21]

Two years later, John Tibbets was approached by John Oliver Butler, who came to his father's house to report that there was "a colored man and his Wife" at his house. The fugitives had been hiding out in the woods near his home but had been forced to come in because of hunger. Oliver didn't know what to do, so he came to the Tibbets because he knew they were abolitionists.

Young Tibbets agreed to help by taking the man and his wife to Deacon Harwood of Cincinnati. He had one problem though: he did not have a team to transport them. Mr. Butler offered his carriage and a horse for the trip. They planned to leave at 9:00 p.m. so that they could make the twenty-seven-mile trip and return before daylight.

They had three toll gates to go through on the Ohio Pike. Tibbets said that this was very risky because almost every toll tender was proslavery and opposed to "anything to aid our fellowman to obtain his God-given rights." The first gate in Amelia was passed without incident. He feared what might happen at the second gate in Withamsville because the gate tender was a man "not to be trusted." Tibbitts had some trouble getting the man to answer his call. The man tried to look in the buggy. He thrust the lantern closer, but the curtain was drawn all around. Tibbets next jumped in next to the man. The tender ran to the gate and let him through. They reached their destination without further incident, and the two fugitives were delivered to Harwood. Tibbets later moved to Jefferson County, Indiana, where he continued his Underground Railroad activities. He then moved on to Kansas and died in 1907.[22]

Fig. I-10. *The old tollhouse on State Route 125 in Amelia, Ohio.*

NOTES

1. Henrietta Buckmaster, *Let My People Go: The Story of the Underground Railroad and the Growth of the Abolition Movement* (New York: Harper Brothers, 1941) 43.
2. Application Instructions, National Underground Network to Freedom, National Park Service, September 30, 2002, 3.
3. *Clermont Courier*, December 26, 1851; Rockey and Bancroft, *Clermont County, Ohio*, 92; 1860 United States Census, Clermont County, Ohio.
4. J. Blaine Hudson, *Fugitive Slaves and the Underground Railroad in the Kentucky Borderland* (Jefferson, N.C.: McFarland & Co., 2002) 36, table 111-8; 37, table 111-9; 34, table 111-5.
5. Ibid., 35, table 111-7; 38, table 111-10, table 111-11; 39, table 111-12. It must be noted that the assistance received was from Kentucky and does not reference any help the fugitives received in the free states.
6. Rockey & Bancroft, *Clermont County, Ohio*, 441.
7. Ibid., 441–42.
8. W. P. Fishback to Wilbur Siebert, May 23, 1892; W. S. Fishback to Wilbur Siebert, September 3, 1898, Siebert Papers, Ohio Historical Society, Columbus, Ohio.
9. Rockey and Bancroft, *Clermont County, Ohio*, 442.
10. Ibid., 400.
11. Ibid., 401; William Carey Coombs, *The Story of Anthony Coombs and His Descendants* (Boston: A.C. Getchell & Son, printer, 1913) 75, 92. Aileen M. Whitt, *Monroe*

Presbyterian Church Nicholsville, Clermont County, Ohio, 1831–1850 (New Richmond, Ohio: A. M. Whitt, 1996) 5.

12. Lindale Baptist Church (Lindale, Ohio), Minutes, 1:104; Clifford Hughes, et al., *The 181 Year History of the Lindale Baptist Church, Clermont County, Ohio Bicentennial 1800–2000* (Batavia, Ohio: Clermont County Historical Society, 2000) 12; Rockey and Bancroft, *Clermont County, Ohio*, 422.

13. Coombs, *Story of Anthony Coombs*, 76.

14. John Rankin to the *Emancipator*, September 13, 1836, printed September 29, 1836.

15. Coombs, *Story of Anthony Coombs*, 75; *Philanthropist*, September 9, 1837.

16. Antislavery petitions presented to Senator Thomas Morris, February 28, 1839; series SEN 25A-H5 (Slavery), box 13, 25th Congress; Records of the Senate, Record Group 46; National Archives, Washington, D.C. Those who signed the petition include the following: Samuel Tibbets, Andrew Coombs, Thomas M. Lewis, Horace Hayford, Robert A. Tibbets, Daniel L. Stinchfield, Thomas M. Coombs, Andrew Coombs Jr., Kitty Ann Coombs, Angelina Lovelace, Silas Dolin, R. Hubbard, William Hayford, Emily Conklin, Vinton[?] Bonner, Walter Cutter[?] Jr., Thomas Sheldon, Abbigail Conklin, Silas[?] Tibbets, Elizabeth Coombs, Rachel Hayford, William Dolan, Reliance Dolan, Earl T. Tibbets, and Abraham Hune.

17. Lindale Baptist Church (Lindale, Ohio), Minutes, August 10, 1844, 1:169–170.

18. Wilbur Siebert, *The Mysteries of Ohio's Underground Railroad* (Columbus: Long's College Book Co., 1951) 64.

19. Ibid., 64–65.

20. Rockey and Bancroft, *Clermont County, Ohio*, 107, 401, 422.

21. This could have been a mistranscription or a misreference to Charles Huber as "Hoover." However, they also state "Hoover" of Williamsburg. There is a Braunsville, a town in Tate Township, near Bethel, which would have been a logical stop. A David Hoover, known to have had abolitionist sentiments, lived in that place. Herman Fagley interview, July 22, 2003.

22. John Tibbets, *Reminiscences of Slavery Times*, written by Grandfather Tibbets in his 70th year, transcribed 1878, original personal collection of Michael Tibbets.

CHAPTER 7

New Richmond

NEW RICHMOND WAS THE HEART AND SOUL of Clermont County's abolitionist movement. The village, once the most populous in the county, is located twenty miles upstream from Cincinnati. It is situated on the northern bank of the Ohio River at the base of a long, sloping hill. Directly across from the village lies Campbell County, Kentucky.

New Richmond became a prosperous riverport city soon after its founding in 1814. Farmers in the hinterlands of southern Clermont County brought their agricultural products to New Richmond for shipment, first by flatboat and later by steamboats, to distant markets. Mills, mercantile establishments, a tannery, distillery, and other smaller concerns were founded. In 1826 a small stern-wheeler named *Alegheny* was launched from the New Richmond boatyards, ushering in an industry that lasted for forty years.[1]

In 1816 Englishman Thomas Ashburn laid out a rival town adjacent to New Richmond. The new village, named Susanna after Ashburn's wife, featured a one-hundred-foot-wide promenade facing the Ohio River. Land was set aside for a large public market, schools, a circulating library, and churches. The towns contended with each other for twelve years before the Ohio General Assembly ended the rivalry by ordering the villages to merge. New Richmond was the Clermont County seat from January 25, 1823, until February 24, 1824. By 1837 there were eighty-four individual property owners in New Richmond.[2]

The Abolitionist Heritage

The First Presbyterian Church of New Richmond, now known as the

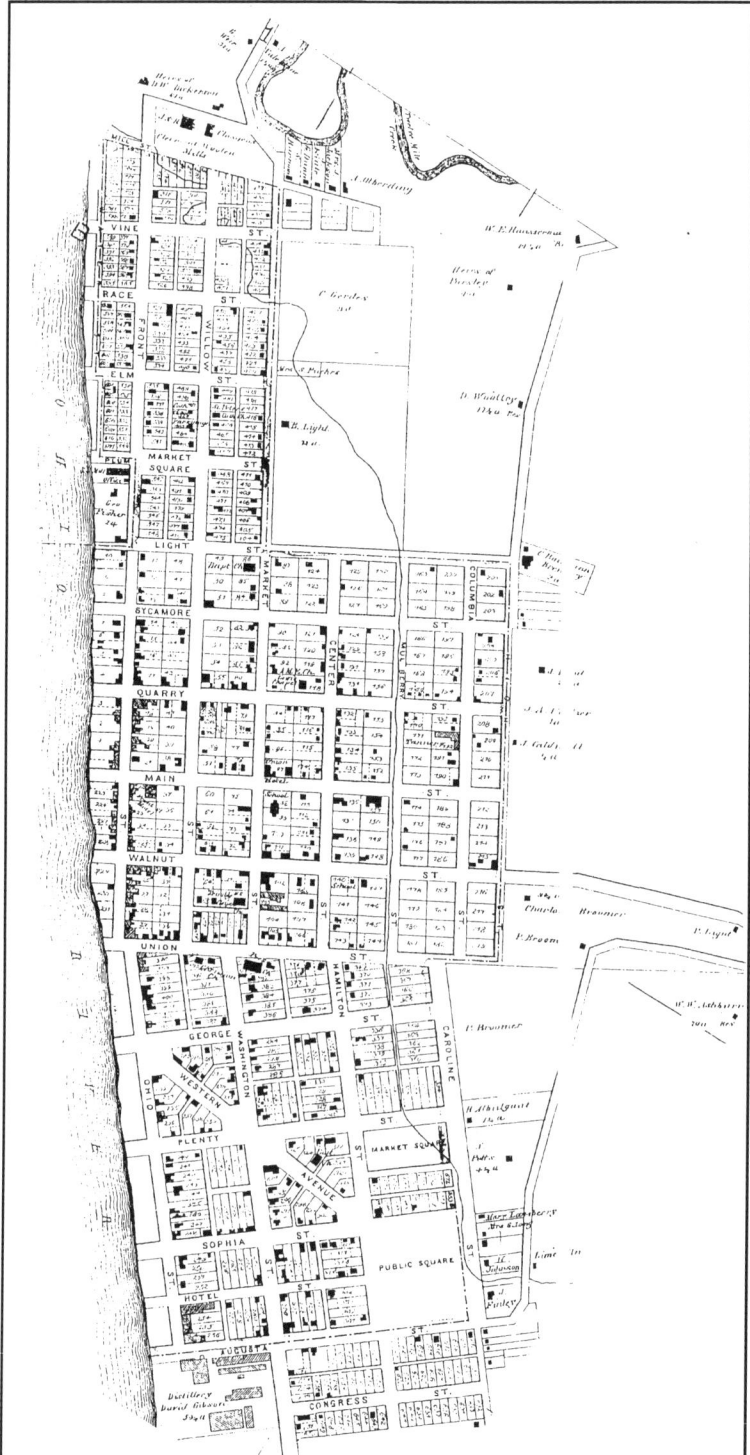

Fig. 7.1. *Plat of New Richmond*

Cranston Memorial Presbyterian Church, was the center of the village's abolitionist movement. The church was formally organized on June 15, 1821, and less than two years later, a church building was constructed on land donated by Thomas Ashburn.[3]

The congregation took an early and uncompromising stand against slavery. Among the antislavery notables who spoke, preached, or moderated sessions at the church were James Birney, publisher of the *Philanthropist* newspaper; Calvin Stowe; George Beecher; and John and Alexander Rankin. John Gregg Fee, the Kentucky abolitionist and founder of Berea College, most likely spoke here as well during his forced exiles from Kentucky. The church had several black members who were elected to leadership positions. On January 2, 1836, the church hosted the organizational meeting of the New Richmond Antislavery Society.[4]

The church issued two strongly worded antislavery statements. The first statement was written during a session moderated by Rev. George Beecher, brother of Harriet Beecher Stowe. That statement condemned slavery as a "horrid violation of the commandments of the Lord our God." It urged the Cincinnati Presbytery to withhold communion from all who own slaves. The more conservative Cincinnati Presbytery disavowed New Richmond's pronouncement, expunging it from their official records.[5]

There is no better barometer with which to gauge the antislavery sentiment of the congregation than by examining the life of Amos Dresser, the man appointed pastor in December of 1842. Born in Peru, Massachusetts, in 1812, Dresser began his religious studies at the Oneida Institute in New York before coming to Lane Theological Seminary in Cincinnati. Dresser left the seminary with seventy other students known as the Lane Rebels. He studied medicine to better prepare himself for foreign missionary service. In the summer of 1835 he planned a trip to Mississippi to visit an ill uncle.[6]

Along the way to Mississippi, Dresser sold Bibles and a few antislavery pamphlets. He arrived in Nashville, Tennessee, on July 18, 1835. A workman who he had hired to repair his carriage found several antislavery pamphlets in the carriage. Rumors flew that Dresser was in Nashville to foment a slave insurrection by distributing the pamphlets.

Dresser was set upon and hauled before a "star chamber" of sixty "respectable" citizens of Nashville convened to hear evidence of Dresser's transgressions. He was found guilty on all three charges:

"being a member of an antislavery society in Ohio, . . . possession of antislavery tracts," and of "circulating these tracts in the community." The criminal was sentenced to receive twenty lashes of a cowskin whip upon his naked back.

Dresser was taken into a ring formed by the citizens. Before the sentence was carried out, a motion to forgo the punishment was heard. According to Dresser,

this brought many and furious imprecations on the mover's head, and created a commotion which was opposed only by the sound of the instrument of torture and disgrace upon my naked body.

I knelt to receive the punishment, which was inflicted by Mr. Braughton, the city officer; with a heavy cowskin. When the infliction ceased an involuntary feeling of Thanksgiving to God for the fortitude which I had been enabled to endure it arose on my soul, to which for a moment, was suddenly broken with loud exclamations, 'G——d d——n him, stop his praying! I was raised to my feet by Mr. Braughton, conducted by him to my lodging, where it was thought safe for me to remain for a few moments.[7]

Word of Dresser's ordeal reached Cincinnati before he did. His story was widely repeated; he soon became a national celebrity and one of the first martyrs of the abolitionist movement. One can only imagine the crackling intensity of this man, the depth of his commitment forged by his suffering and indignity. He must have swept up into his whirlwind everyone with whom he came in contact.

The second antislavery statement made by the First Presbyterian Church on March 13, 1842, was drafted by Reverend Dresser and Dr. John Rogers. This statement declared that slavery was "a flagrant sin against God and man, and is in every form it assumes diametrically opposed to every principle of the Gospel of Christ."[8]

New Richmond's Abolitionists

New Richmond hosted a significant population of abolitionists. Contrary to conventional wisdom, they did not live at society's margins. They served in local government, were prominent church leaders, and were successful businessmen. Unfortunately, extensive biographical information is not available for many.

Fig. 7.2. Dr. John Rogers, an ardent abolitionist and member of New Richmond's Vigilance Committee.

DR. JOHN ROGERS

Dr. John Rogers, the second of seven children, was born on April 29, 1797, in Camden, New Jersey. The family moved to Clermont County in 1804, first settling in Williamsburg. Rogers' father, Levi, was a renaissance man. He was a Methodist minister, doctor, lawyer, state legislator, Clermont's sheriff, and prosecutor. John's father taught him the rudiments of the medical arts, such as pulling teeth, performing minor surgery, and bleeding. When John was fourteen, a local farmer was severely cut in the back and shoulder by a scythe. A friend sought Dr. Levi Rogers for treatment. The doctor was out, so the teenaged Rogers treated the man. Dr. Rogers subsequently examined the man, and was quite pleased with his son's work.

Levi died while John was still only a teenager. He studied under several local doctors until June 11, 1818, when he opened his own medical office in New Richmond. He practiced for seven years before he temporarily closed his office to attend the Medical College of Ohio. He graduated one year later and resumed his practice.

Dr. John Rogers married Julia Morris, daughter of Senator Thomas Morris, on October 19, 1820. The ceremony was officiated by Rev. George C. Light, agent of the American Colonization Society and a Methodist minister of local repute. Hannah Simpson, the future mother of Ulysses S. Grant, was a bridesmaid at the wedding. The marriage to the daughter of Senator Morris, the country's first antislavery U.S. senator, underscored the doctor's commitment to the antislavery cause.[9]

Fig. 7.3. *The home and office of Dr. John Rogers, located at 305–307 Front Street, New Richmond, Ohio, is being restored.*

Rogers practiced medicine in the New Richmond community for sixty years. He is best remembered for delivering Ulysses S. Grant on April 27, 1822. Henry Corbin relates the details of that morning in his memoirs. According to this account, Rogers was called to the Clark residence in Monroe Township to attend to Mrs. Clark, who had gone into labor. Shortly after the birth of Henry Corbin's mother, Jesse Grant arrived, looking for Rogers. Grant's wife was in labor with their first child. Rogers mounted his horse and motioned for Grant to come with him. "Uncle" Jesse told the doctor to go without him because he had some matters to discuss with Mr. Clark. Rogers rode onto Point Pleasant and delivered the ten-pound boy. Jesse showed up several hours later.[10]

Rogers was an ardent abolitionist. His evolution within the movement mirrored that of the nation. He was a member of the First Pres-

Fig. 7.4. *Dr. John Rogers in front of the Ulysses S. Grant cottage in Point Pleasant, Ohio. On April 27, 1822, Rogers delivered the ten-pound boy who grew up to be the eighteenth president of the United States.*

byterian Church and assisted Amos Dresser in drafting the church's second antislavery memorial. He entered the secular realm when he was elected the first president of the Clermont County Antislavery Society in 1836. Rogers left Andrew Jackson's Democratic Party because of its unflinching support of slavery. In 1845 he ran for state senator and in 1846 for state representative on the Liberty Party ticket, though he was soundly defeated both times. With the demise of the Liberty Party, he migrated to the Free-Soil Party and later to the Republican Party. A close friend and supporter of James Birney, who published the *Philanthropist* newspaper in New Richmond, Rogers and others stood guard at the paper's office to protect it from destruction by proslavers who threatened to destroy it.[11]

Dr. P. F. Greene wrote, "Dr. John Rogers set about doing all he could do to help runaway slaves safely on their way. He, together with his son-in-law Jacob Ebersole, Eben Ricker, and Thomas Donaldson formed the nucleus of the New Richmond station of the 'Underground Railroad.' The local people referred to them as the four 'Liberty Chieftains.'"[12]

THE DONALDSON FAMILY

Fig. 7.5. *The Donaldsons.*

The Donaldsons, of Scottish decent, immigrated to New Richmond in 1816 where they established two well-known residences: Frandon, named after the family patriarch; and Penmaen, Welsh for "brow of the hill." The family immediately made their presence known. They opened a large retail store, built the village's first wharf, operated the St. Charles Hotel, and owned several rental properties.[13]

Thomas Donaldson, who was born in Wales, was a prominent agriculturalist. He introduced blooded stock into Clermont County. He also engaged in the cultivation of various fruits, a rather unusual interest at the time. Donaldson's products were frequently seen at agricultural exhibits around southwest Ohio.[14]

Donaldson was a temperance Baptist who left the church because of its lukewarm antislavery attitude; he later drifted into the Unitarian denomination. After his second marriage in 1837 to Susanna Parker, the daughter of the Reverend Daniel and Priscilla Parker of Clermontville, Donaldson became an abolitionist. Because of his convictions and wealth he became associated with most of the movement's leading lights: William Lloyd Garrison, Joshua Giddings, James Birney, Gamaliel Bailey, and Parker Pillsbury. These men often stayed in his home

Fig. 7.6. *The home of Rev. Caleb Walker, located on Front Street in New Richmond, Ohio.*

on their visits to the area. Politically, Donaldson was an early supporter of the Liberty Party and, later, the Free-Soil and Republican parties. He helped Thomas Morris escape an egg-throwing mob in Dayton, Ohio, in 1843 when the latter tried to make an antislavery speech.[15]

Donaldson invited James Birney to come to New Richmond to publish the *Philanthropist*, a more secure venue than Danville, Kentucky. The family also advanced Birney the start up costs for the newspaper.[16]

CALEB S. WALKER

Caleb Swan Walker came to New Richmond in 1816 at age twenty-three. He promptly married Ann Ashburn, the daughter of Susanna's founder. Walker opened a general store at the corner of Union and Front streets in 1827. He expanded his business interests by establishing a carding operation at the southwest corner of Union and Willow streets. Later, he profitably raised Catawba grapes. Not all of his business ventures were profitable. He lost a fifteen-hundred-dollar investment in the ill-fated riverboat, *William Tell*, which was built in New Richmond.[17]

Walker was a member of the New Richmond Methodist Church and later became a Methodist circuit rider. He, along with the other riders of the Clough District, were "both outspoken opposers of human slavery, believing it a sin . . . that should be condemned publicly at all suitable occasions." Walker was also a Temperance activist. He, like other New Richmond men, was not marginalized by his antislavery sentiment. He was elected mayor of the village in 1829, township assessor, and Ohio township trustee.[18]

Reverend Walker was elected president of the New Richmond Antislavery Society in 1837. He met privately with individuals and converted them to the antislavery cause. He preached antislavery sermons and spoke at antislavery rallies.[19]

On July 3, 1836, Walker delivered a "True Freedom" homily based upon John 8:36: "If the son, therefore shall make you free, ye shall be free indeed." He spoke of the "need for social, civil, and political liberty"; the implications for black freedom were clearly drawn on the eve of Independence Day. He admitted that the sermon was "rather political" but it was well received. He felt compelled to speak because "the revolting scenes that summer demanded it."[20]

Walker attended a general conference meeting of the Methodist Church on May 6, 1836, in Cincinnati where the growing tensions of the slavery issue became apparent. New England delegates attempted to pass an antislavery resolution, but Southerners outmaneuvered the Yankees. Three delegates attended a meeting of the Cincinnati Antislavery Society held at the same time as the conference. The Southerners were outraged. They drafted a resolution declaring the act of attending the Antislavery Society to be "immoral," opening the conference to debate the slavery issue.

One frustrated Southern delegate yelled, in response to a strong denunciation of slavery, "I wish that brother was in heaven." Everyone was shocked at the implications contained within the statement.[21] William Gaspers delivered a tearful testimonial. He stated that only those who live with slavery can understand it. Continued agitation by the ignorant abolitionists will result in slave insurrections complete with "bloody slaves" of murder perpetrated by emboldened slaves. Walker observed, despite Gaspers's emotional and eloquent discourse, that it failed "to convince many of the justice and expediency of the system or the kindness and philanthropy of one man holding another in lifetime bondage for his benefit; however intellectual he might be if his skin was shaded with the fatal colour."[22]

Walker continued to "agitate" for the antislavery cause. Dave Roberts, a descendent of Walker, claimed that the reverend was active in the

Underground Railroad and probably used the six houses on Western Avenue he built for six former slave families as safe houses.[23] Walker does not claim any involvement in the enterprise in his diary, nor are there any other sources supporting Roberts's claim.

Walker, at age sixty-six, volunteered for service in the Eighty-ninth Ohio Volunteer Infantry during the siege of Cincinnati in 1862. He later worked as a hospital steward at the Camp Dennison General Military Hospital. Walker's "pilgrimage" ended in 1874. He is buried in Watkins Hill Cemetery in New Richmond.[24]

James G. Birney and the Philanthropist

James Gillespie Birney's influence upon the antislavery movement was significant. He was, at times, attorney, state legislator, agent of the American Colonization and Antislavery societies, newspaper publisher, and presidential candidate. Born in Danville, Kentucky, on February 4, 1792, he first attended college at the prestigious Transylvania University in Lexington, Kentucky, and later graduated from the College of New Jersey (now known as Princeton University). He was admitted to the practice of law in 1814. He became a slaveowner as the result of his marriage to Agatha McDowell in 1816 and was elected to the Kentucky House of Representatives the same year. In 1818 he moved to Alabama. It appears that he was influential in introducing measures into the Alabama Constitution providing for the emancipation of slaves and the banning of the importation of slaves into the state for sale. In addition to political influence, Birney was recognized as a rising attorney, acting as counsel for the Cherokee Nation for several years. His political career was derailed when he opposed the renomination of Andrew Jackson for president.[25]

In time Birney became disillusioned with slavery. He, along with many others in the 1820s, drifted toward the Colonization Society as an answer to the "slavery problem." He became the Southwest agent for the Colonization Society in 1833. Birney freed his six slaves the following year.[26]

Birney eventually became dissatisfied with the American Colonization Society; he publicly renounced the organization in 1835. Soon afterwards, he became an agent of the rival American Antislavery Society. He and the society wanted to publish an antislavery newspaper somewhere in the West. Birney's first choice was to publish his paper in his hometown of Danville, Kentucky. Danville residents were definitely hostile to the idea. Birney described the reaction in Danville to his plans for the paper, as follows:

As soon as my Prospectus was republished in Kentucky, it was the signal for rousing up the apparently great Spirit of Slaveholders in this part of the country. . . . A public meeting was held as the citizens and the people of the neighborhood, and they passed sundry resolutions against me and the paper, etc.[27]

If not Danville, then where was he to publish the paper? He wanted to be able to safely print the paper, yet be close to "the enemy." The logical choice became Cincinnati, the Queen City, just across from slaveholding Kentucky. But in many ways Cincinnati was a Southern city. Would the slaveholding interest and their apologists permit an anti-slavery paper to be published in the city?

Word of the proposed publication leaked out and the reaction was hostile. Thought was given to moving the paper to the safety of New England. But Birney was adamant. He wanted to give the paper a Western voice.[28] If Cincinnati was not safe, perhaps another location nearby could be found. By November of 1835 Birney was reasonably confident that the paper could be safely published in New Richmond.[29] He could then turn to the more mundane start-up concerns. He wrote the following to Gerrit Smith:

Now, my greatest stress will be in getting ready for the printing, in buying Press materials etc. etc. Moreover I shall commence the paper in a small village about twenty miles up the river from this place—or if not there, at one about 50 miles above where I can print with out being mobbed.[30]

It seems that Birney's plan was to get the paper started in New Richmond and after a few months, presumably after things cooled down, move it to Cincinnati. His target date for publication was January 1, 1836.[31]

The office site had to be, by necessity, close to the river so that the heavy printing stock could be conveyed easily from the river to the office. Birney chose an office about one block from the wharf at the corner of Market and Willow streets. As was the custom of the day, there was no more detailed address than the street names. Birney purchased a building at this location, lot no. 33, on April 2, 1836, for four hundred dollars.[32]

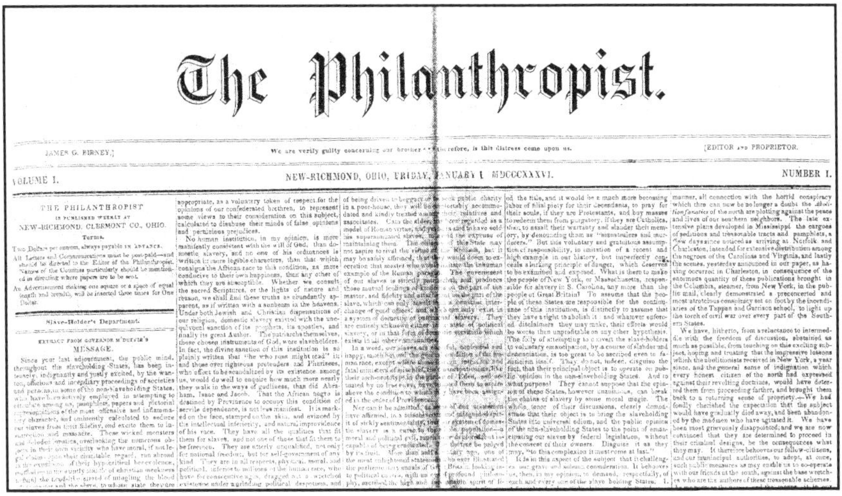

The Philanthropist.

JAMES G. BIRNEY,] We are verily guilty concerning our brother ... therefore, is this distress come upon us. [EDITOR AND PROPRIETOR.

VOLUME I. NEW-RICHMOND, OHIO, FRIDAY, JANUARY 1, MDCCCXXXVI. NUMBER I.

THE PHILANTHROPIST IS PUBLISHED WEEKLY AT NEW-RICHMOND, CLERMONT CO., OHIO.

Slave-Holder's Department.

EXTRACT FROM GOVERNOR M'DUFFIE'S MESSAGE.

Fig. 7.7. *The first issue of the* Philanthropist *newspaper.*

The *Philanthropist* made its debut on January 1, 1836. The paper's purpose was "to make the *Philanthropist* a repository of facts and arguments on the subject of slavery as connected with Emancipation." Liberty and slavery are "antagonistic elements, only one, liberty or slavery will survive," he wrote, "Either liberty will stand on its lifeless body, rejoicing in the everlasting overthrow of her great enemy, with its chains and its scourges, its woes, its curses, and its tears will overspread our favored land."[33]

He then explained why he chose to publish the paper in New Richmond.

After long delay, occasioned by difficulties which we have not been slow to overcome, we are enabled to issue our first number. It may be satisfying to our friends to give them—though we shall do it very briefly and in very personal terms—the reasons for issuing our paper at New Richmond, rather than at Cincinnati, where we reside.

When the opposition of slave holders had succeeded in defeating our *first* purpose of publishing the *Philanthropist* in Kentucky, and in virtually expelling us from the very village in which we had our birth, by rendering our residence in its neighborhood disagreeable, if not dangerous, to our self and our family, our attention was turned to this city;—not only as a pleasant place to dwell in, to a person who could find inducements in the intelligence of those around them, and in the religious influence which, it was supposed, prevailed in it—but as a town of safety, to any one engaged in the pursuit of truth, and who might be disposed to make publication of its results.[34]

For many years some local historians have claimed that Birney made his home in New Richmond. His statement that he resides in Cincinnati should resolve that claim. He clearly liked New Richmond and invested in it. Property records indicate that he owned numerous rental lots over the years and hired Mark Strickland as his agent to manage them. But he never lived in New Richmond.

The paper was a one-piece, eight-sided broadsheet, which sold at an annual subscription rate of two dollars, "always payable in advance." The paper accepted advertisements of one "square" for one dollar per three rows. The first edition contained an antislavery poem, a long letter from New York abolitionist Gerrit Smith, a column entitled "Antislavery Ecclesiastics," a very long letter from Birney, an obituary, and two announcements. One of the announcements contained details of a meeting of the New Richmond Antislavery Society, to be held at the Presbyterian Church "at an early candle-lighting."[35]

The publication of the paper at New Richmond elicited scornful editorials from Cincinnati papers. The *Cincinnati Whig* noted Birney's failure at Danville and his hostile reception at Cincinnati. It reported, "he has at length settled himself on the border of Kentucky, and so near Cincinnati as to make the pestiferous breath of the paper spread contagion among our citizens."[36]

Throughout its publication life, the *Philanthropist* printed scathing opposition to slavery. In reference to the trial of John Mahan, the paper commented,

Mr. Mahan is charged with feeding the hungry and clothing the naked as they fled the land of oppression to Canada. In short, he was charged with doing just what the Bible requires of every Christian and indeed of every human being.[37]

The paper was critical of Kentucky's efforts to compel Ohio's General Assembly to pass a state fugitive slave act in 1839. The editor wrote,

The truth is slaves are men; though slave holders seem to have forgotten it. Human nature loves liberty and abhors slavery . . . slaves are men and have legs. They have the motives and locomotives to make their escape.[38]

Although the paper found a safe haven in New Richmond, outsiders did make threats to destroy the office on several occasions. In response, a citizens' vigilance committee was formed to patrol the village streets to protect the paper. Among the committee members was

Dr. John Rogers. When the committee received intelligence of a specific threat, the alarm went out. The members mustered at the public market place, and then stood guard at the paper's office.[39]

Information was received that a group of men from Mason County, Kentucky, was planning an operation to "put down" the paper. Birney interviewed one member of the group. He assured the unnamed conspirator that such an attack against the paper "would be the consumption of impudence" and, further, it would "be a hazardous enterprise to themselves personally."[40]

Was Birney bluffing the Kentuckians with words of bravado? Or was he giving them fair warning of the consequences of their actions based upon the assurances of the vigilance committee? Birney's warnings were most likely rooted in his knowledge of the fortitude of his New Richmond supporters.

The winter of 1836 was foul: rain, sleet, snow, and prolonged frigid temperatures. The Ohio River froze over, forcing Birney to abandon the relative comfort of the commuter packet boat for the misery of riding horseback to and from New Richmond. After continued horseback commutes, Birney decided to move the paper's office to Cincinnati.[41] Cincinnatians were not pleased with the decision. A committee, composed largely of businessmen with commercial ties to the South, was formed to protest. Soon afterward, a mob formed on the evening of July 30, 1836. It broke into the paper's office, "scattered the type into the streets, tore down the presses and completely dismantled the office." The mob then went onto the home of Achilles Pugh, the printer; to the home of Christian Donaldson; and finally, on to the home of Birney, who was in Highland County, Ohio, on a speaking tour.[42] Despite the violence and threats, the paper was soon back in print, issuing its trademark denunciations of slavery.

A specific threat against New Richmond was received on August 1, 1836, soon after the destruction of the paper in Cincinnati. A group of rioters was planning a raid on the village "to wreak vengeance" on some of the early supporters of the *Philanthropist*. Caleb Walker called the citizens to convene at the Market House. He exhorted the residents to defend themselves, arguing that it was not only their "right" but their "duty" to resist the mob in defense of freedom of speech. The community, with but one vote opposed, decided to defend their First Amendment rights "to the bitter end and even death if need be."[43] Fortunately, calmer heads prevailed and the Cincinnatians stayed home.

New Richmond's Black Community—1860

New Richmond was the center of Clermont County's largest and most prosperous black community. During the decade of the 1850s the population of Ohio Township, of which New Richmond was the largest village, swelled from 225 to 574.[44] This robust growth can be attributed to both immigration and natural increase. Of the sixty-one black households recorded in the 1860 census, thirty-three owned real estate, a figure higher than in most current urban settings. The value of the real property fell into a range of $100 to $5,000, with the average being $1,530. Most of the black-owned real estate in New Richmond was concentrated in a quadrant bounded by Light Street in the west, Mulberry Street in the north, Main Street in the east, and Willow Street on the south. Another area was on the north and south side of Columbia bordered by Quarry Street.[45]

By examining the 1860 census, we can obtain a demographic snapshot of New Richmond's black population. The occupational pursuits of the black community were varied, with more working as rivermen and as laborers than any other occupation. Fifty-nine residents claimed Ohio as their state of origin. Of these fifty-nine, fifty-two were minors, most of whose parents were born in other states.[46] It seems apparent that most of the parents who moved to Ohio from other, mostly Southern, states did so in the decade of the 1850s. Mississippi was the home state of forty-two of the residents. At first glance it might seem odd that so many people migrated such a distance from home. Ohio, however, was the closest free state to Mississippi. New Richmond's location on the Ohio River made transportation easy. Further, there was plenty of work for those who had experience working the river trade. Finally, the agricultural areas surrounding New Richmond provided work opportunities to those with farming experience.

In the early 1850s, the Mississippi legislature passed restrictive emancipation laws making it very difficult for owners to free their slaves. As a consequence, many of the owners who wanted to free their slaves either retained attorneys in Cincinnati to complete the paperwork in Ohio or merely drafted manumission papers and instructed their former slaves to register the papers in the county probate courts where they intended to live.[47]

Elizabeth Rucker and her three children were freed by Jonathan and William Rucker of Natchez, Mississippi. The manumission paper was found in the Clermont County Probate Court. It describes Elizabeth as "a certain Negro woman slave named Elizabeth of light brown complexion about twenty-four years old." The document further stated that she was "with our consent residing in New Richmond in the State of Ohio."[48] Elizabeth made a living as a washer woman. She gave birth to a child, Lanora, who was described as a mulatto, after her arrival in New Richmond. Was one of the Rucker brothers the father of Elizabeth's child? It seems likely. One of her other children was named Peter, the name of the Rucker family patriarch.[49]

Mulattoes, or persons of mixed racial heritage, have been an ongoing topic of discussion among scholars. Generally speaking, mulattoes born of unions in the upper South or border areas were from whites and blacks of lower socioeconomic status. Those born in the lower South tended to have resulted from relations between black women and white plantation-owning fathers. Mulattoes were placed into a higher social status than were blacks. Those with white plantation-owner fathers stood at the apex of the "colored" social hierarchy. Gradations of color, with the lightest as the most favored, were also recognized.[50] Mulattoes were generally freed at a higher rate than blacks, probably because of their white blood. They also possessed better job skills, were more literate, and were wealthier.

In New Richmond there were 305 people of color of whom 146 were black and 88 mulatto. Of the ten wealthiest colored households, 5 were black and 5 were mulatto. The mulattoes were from Virginia, North Carolina, Mississippi, Alabama, and Tennessee. The blacks were from Virginia, South Carolina, and Alabama.[51] On the opposite end of the scale were the poor households that did not own real estate. Twenty-two households fell into this category. Of these twenty-two, 13 were black and 9 were mulatto.

There were 269 people of color living in Ohio Township, outside of New Richmond. Of these, 160 were classified as mulatto and 109 were listed as black. The black/mulatto ratio among the ten wealthiest colored households in Ohio Township was exactly the same as in the village—one to one. As with New Richmond, laborers, farmers, and rivermen framed the nucleus of the black labor force. Ohio was the state of origin of most, followed by Virginia and Kentucky. Many of the residents were children.

An unnamed Southerner came to New Richmond in the spring of 1860 to purchase a farm for his two mulatto sons. An account of his visit appeared in the *Clermont Courier*. He wrote,

My boys seem highly elated at the idea of being set free and having no master to dictate to them. . . . I have some fears in regard to their having judgment enough to make a good living for themselves, but having bought a good and comfortable farm, which I intend to furnish with ample stock and implements for working, I intend that they shall try their hand at their living.

The father explains his motivation for coming to the North to set up his sons.

I shall at last be rid of the trouble and tormenting thought that beings whom I have caused to come into existence, and in whose veins runs a current of my own blood, are not, and will not again be subject to the foul cause of slavery.

The man arrived at the New Richmond dock around 2:00 p.m. He noted that at least three-quarters of the people he saw at the wharf were mulattoes. He was told that most of the mulattoes then living in New Richmond were brought there by their white fathers or had come there on their own. Very few had been born there.[52]

The black community actively developed its own institutions. Around 1850, Elder Sachell formed a "Baptist society of colored persons" consisting of fifteen people. By 1861 the congregation built a simple one-story brick church on Market Street. The African Methodist Church was formed at roughly the same time. They met at the schoolhouse and at the Universalist Church until they built their meeting hall in 1865 at the corner of Center and Quarry streets.[53]

A remarkable organization called "The Union Association for the Advancement of the Colored Men of New Richmond" was formed in 1857. This organization was formed fifty-three years before the National Association for the Advancement of Colored People. The twenty-three founding members believed

that in union there is strength, and being desirous of employing all the means in our power for the elevation of ourselves and community and more, do hereby ascribe to the following bylaws.

The men stated,

The object of this Association shall be to aid and abet every means calculated to improve our condition, socially and politically, to foster in our youth a love of intelligence and business habits and further the interests of whatever tends to improve the happiness and glory of race.[54]

The organization established branches in Felicity and Ripley. A women's auxiliary, known as the Daughters Union Aid Society was formed in 1864 and existed until 1870.[55]

Despite the tolerant, if not benign, environment for blacks in the New Richmond area, they faced a threat common to other free blacks in the border lands—kidnapping. Kidnapping in this context refers to the forceful abduction of free blacks to be sold into slavery.[56] Kidnappers used a variety of methods to accomplish their goal. Many used force. Others used deception to lure the unsuspecting target into their grasp. Still others used the offer of a job.[57] Some kidnappers were unorganized, taking advantage of a last-minute opportunity. Others, such as the notorious Blackbirders of New York City, made a living from the activity. Both whites and blacks were involved in the enterprise. No one knows for sure how many free blacks were enslaved by the kidnappers. Carol Wilson writes, "The prevalence of kidnapping, however, demonstrates that free blacks could rapidly and easily become property. Just as slaves could become free by way of the Underground Railroad, so did free people become slaves by what Julie Winch has termed 'the other Underground Railroad.' And once free blacks were enslaved, it was likely that they would remain so."[58]

Three documented cases of black kidnappings in New Richmond occurred over three decades. Three white men were arrested in the village on January 30, 1837. Of the three, John Asbury and a Mr. Rollins were from Kentucky. Lewis Zeigler was from Ohio. All three were charged with kidnapping Moses Hawkins, a free black resident of New Richmond. Zeigler offered Hawkins, a fiddler of some renown, a job playing at a dance in Kentucky. Asbury and Rollins crossed over to Kentucky by ferry, leaving their horses at an inn in New Richmond. Hawkins was seized. When Rollins returned to New Richmond for their horses, a Mr. McCallister[59] overheard the conversation and swore out a warrant against the trio. Zeigler was arrested immediately. Rollins was picked up soon thereafter when he came back to the village to get the horses. Rollins then sent word to Asbury to return, whereupon Asbury was arrested.

Asbury haughtily "displayed the true spirit of a southern knight of the order of the cowhide." He was surprised that so many villagers expressed interest in his plot. His arrogance disappeared when he realized how serious the people were: "the color fled down his face, and he stood before them a pale, guilty, cowering thing."[60] Bond was set at one thousand dollars and the three were ordered to stand trial in Batavia. They were held overnight, giving them a chance to raise their bail. The *Philanthropist* declared that the kidnappers quaked "because their liberty was justly suspended for a time never once thinking of poor Hawkins who they attempted to reduce to endless bondage." The three offered to forfeit their horses to end the prosecution. Their offer was accepted, whereupon they were released. The *Philanthropist* continued,

How different was the conduct of the people of New Richmond, where nearly all are abolitionists, from what we have lately seen in the South. No lynching, no abuse—nothing unlawful was done. The law was to be enforced—they did it firmly yet mildly.[61]

Hawkins apparently escaped from those holding them.

A second documented kidnapping attempt occurred in November of 1850 when three Kentucky men—William Read, William McMillen, and Ferdinand Kirkham—seized a black man named Hubbard Cable, claiming he was a fugitive. Read produced a power of attorney stating that Cable was the property of five heirs who wanted their property returned. The three Kentuckians thought that they could simply take Cable back to Kentucky without due process. However, Cable had for some time been employed by Martin Ryan as a teamster for Ryan's New Richmond lumber business.[62] Seeing that the people from New Richmond would not allow them to take Cable with them, the men gave up. Meanwhile, two men in Ripley were telegraphed and inquiries were made about Cable; they learned that Cable was a free man.

The Kentuckians were arrested and brought before Mayor Noble Prebble on charges of attempted kidnapping. After hearing the evidence, the mayor discharged the men because of a lack of proof. The *New Richmond Age* newspaper commented,

We are very confident that these men were thoroughly satisfied that New Richmond is the wrong place to arrest even a slave, without paying strict attention to all the dry formalities of the law.

The paper added,

the excitement amongst our colored population was tremendous—but resulted in nothing but the excitement. No breach of the peace was committed.[63]

In a third case, Emily Medal of New Richmond, based upon the sworn affidavit of Levi Coffin, was charged with kidnapping a seven-year-old boy, Levi, who was named after the famous Quaker abolitionist. The mulatto woman was accused of taking the young Levi from the Cincinnati Colored Orphan Asylum. Cincinnati's Marshall Good personally served the warrant upon Emily in November of 1857. The marshall searched the home, but did not find the boy. He suspected that Emily sold the boy into slavery. Emily denied the accusation, saying that the boy was given to her in Arkansas and that she was his legal guardian.

Emily asked Marshall Good if she could change her clothes and he agreed. She went into the other room. After waiting a long time, the marshall went into the room where Emily had gone. She was not there. After a close examination, a trap door leading to an underground tunnel was found. Although Emily had a fifteen-minute head start, Good was able to catch her about two miles from her home. She was placed into custody and taken to Cincinnati to stand trial. Emily was held on a five hundred dollar bond. She repeated her story to the judge that she was the boy's legal guardian. She agreed to give up the boy in exchange for her freedom and payment of nearly forty dollars in court costs. The boy was returned to the orphanage.[64]

New Richmond and the Underground Railroad

New Richmond, with its location on the Ohio River across from Kentucky, its rich abolitionist heritage, and large, vibrant black population, was a logical center of Underground Railroad activity. Unfortunately, evidence documenting such activity is limited. We do know that Kentuckians looked to New Richmond as a destination to escape slavery.

On July 2, 1859, William Green, a German laborer, tried to help two slave women—Anny, Hagar, and Hagar's two children—to flee from a Pendleton County farm to New Richmond. On that day Green, Anny, Hagar, and Hagar's two children made a break for New Richmond. They did not get far as they were "treed" by hounds hunting them. Green was held on a two thousand dollar bond and was charged with two counts of enticing a slave to flee. He was convicted on both counts and sentenced to prison for two to twenty years on both counts.[65]

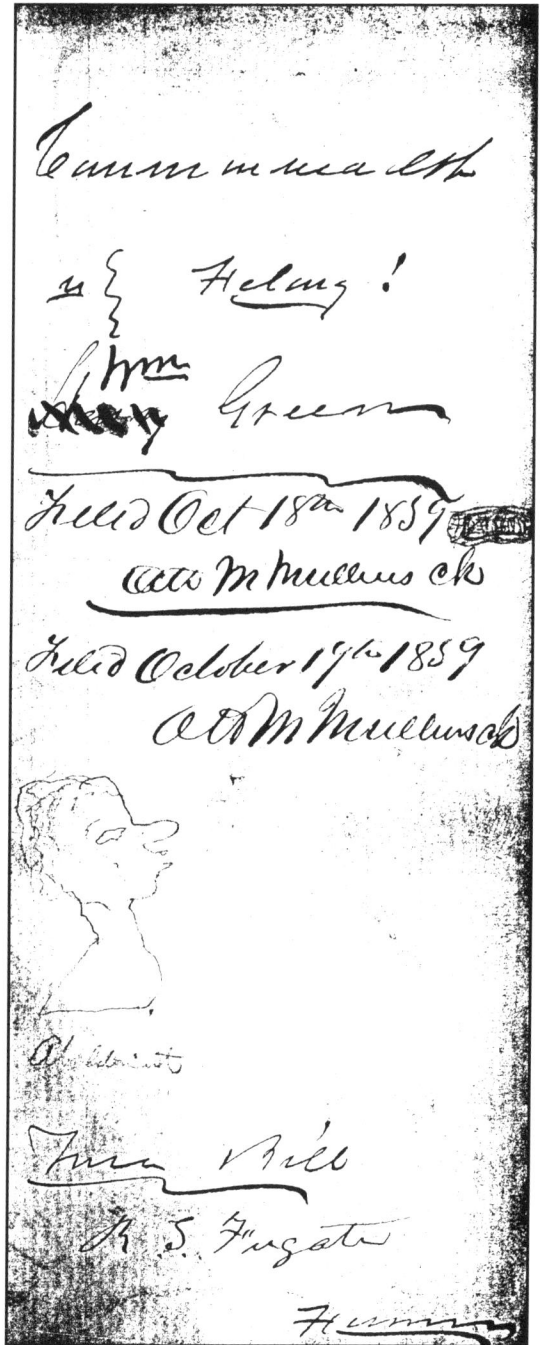

Fig. 7.8. *An unknown artist sketched this caricature of an abolitionist on the case jacket of* Commonwealth of Kentucky v. Green.

JIM AND JOE

Jim and Joe were best friends. Both lived in Louisville, Kentucky. Both were slaves. Jim's master was indulgent while Joe's was cruel. Joe decided that he had to escape and left his master to hide with friends in the city of Louisville. He asked Jim for help.

Jim built a shipping crate and hid Joe within. He took the box with Joe inside to the Louisville wharf and paid to ship the box to New Richmond, where Jim's parents lived. The "cargo" was consigned to Jim's father. Jim accompanied the box on the trip. It was off-loaded in Cincinnati.

When Jim was sure that no one listening he checked on Joe. He asked, "Joe, is you dar?" Joe replied, "I's hyer all right." The loading dock for the boat bound for New Richmond was several blocks away. Joe hired a wagon to transport the box. It then sat for several hours in the hot sun until the boat arrived. They reached New Richmond by sunset of the second day. The box was taken to Jim's parent's home on the outskirts of the village and Joe was finally released after thirty-six hours of confinement into the freedom of New Richmond.

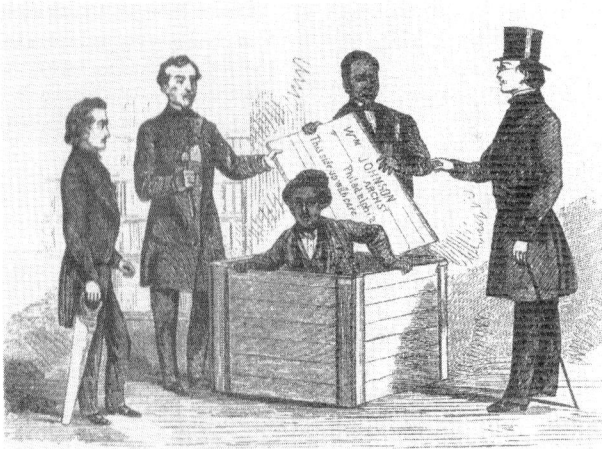

Fig. 7.9. *Sometimes slaves were shipped in boxes to aid in their escape.*

Several white abolitionists were taken to Jim's parents' home and asked if they could help take Joe to the next stop. They decided it was best to take Joe to Levi Coffin's home twenty miles away in Cincinnati. One of the white men knew Coffin and volunteered to make the trip.

They left in the early evening and arrived at Coffin's by 10:00 p.m. Coffin purchased a ticket for Joe on the night train for Sandusky, Ohio, where boat passage was secured for the trip across Lake Erie to Canada. Jim told Coffin about his desire to flee to Canada also. Sometime later Jim arrived at Coffin's for his train ticket to Sandusky. A few months later Jim's wife made the same trip.[66]

LeRoy Lee

It was October 1862, three months before President Abraham Lincoln issued the Emancipation Proclamation.[67] Young LeRoy Lee was owned by the Anderson family of northern Kentucky. Lee fled the farm for Cincinnati but was captured within one week of his escape. The slave hunters clasped the fugitive in manacles and dragged him behind a horse down Front Street, New Richmond, toward the ferry. The slave hunters were well aware of New Richmond's abolitionist reputation. So why did they come to New Richmond? There were other less dangerous places for slave hunters to bring home their quarry. We can only surmise that they intentionally came to the "abolitionist hell hole" as an in-your-face gesture. They soon found out that they badly underestimated the New Richmonders.

A "low murmur of disapproval" passed through the village as "little knots of men" gathered in the streets. They quickly "swelled to crowds" which soon grew to "an army standing in a solid phalanx across the street." The Kentuckians drew their guns. The villagers "laughed them to scorn" shouting "release your man."[68] Tense moments passed as both sides stared down the other. The slavers realized they were outnumbered by the stalwart townsmen and released Lee. Lee was cared for by his rescuers. Within two weeks he enlisted in the army, returning after the war to live in New Richmond.

The *Clermont Sun* wrote of the incident years later. The paper said this about the citizens of New Richmond:

The temper of the citizens of New Richmond, when stirred up is well known, having been made manifest upon several occasions. They are not to be trodden upon; their disposition is quiet, law abiding, and their individual and municipal government is of the best. Living upon the borders of a slave state, and being brought into intimate acquaintance with the peculiar workings of the institution, they were by no means in love with it, though depending largely for trade upon the planters from the opposite side of the river.[69]

THE CLERMONT ACADEMY

In the spring of 1846, Rev. Daniel Parker boarded a river boat at his home in Clermontville, Ohio, for New Orleans. Parker was a committed abolitionist who, seven years earlier, started a private academy open to all students regardless of color. Despite his obvious dislike of slavery, this trip to New Orleans was probably his first exposure to the institution in the deep South.

On May 15 he passed by a large Mississippi plantation. His disdain of slavery is palpable in his words. The buildings he saw were "residences of slaves and therefore not like white sepulchers full of dead men's bones, for they enclose living bones and muscles driven to toil for the luxurious support of others on whom the creator has seen fit to bestow a fair complexion and different features."[70] He believed that

southern and northern philosophy must have originated from different sources. If this be the way to make the colored race happy, the advocates of universal freedom must be sadly mistaken.[71]

He thought that slavery's influence over Southern society was so pervasive that one was either an advocate or an apologist for it as they were "thrown over the whole face of society as an almost impenetrable shield in which the arrows of truth can not penetrate."[72]

Parker was born in Massachusetts, immigrated first to Pennsylvania, and then to Gallipolis, Ohio. He was "converted" to Evangelical Christianity in 1805 and immediately began one of his many preaching missions. In the fall of 1816 he met a young widow named Priscilla King and began a whirlwind courtship, culminating in marriage in the same year.[73] On one of his ministerial trips, he passed by a hill overlooking the Ohio River near Boat Run in Monroe Township. He became almost mystically bonded with the land. His wife described the event. As he

slowly descended the hill to Boat Run his imaginative mind dwelt on the thought that there was a theater for good from which should spread imagination in some inexplicable manner connected with his destiny.[74]

He immediately purchased the property, calling it Mt. Hygiene. He later built his home there.

Parker was attracted to the American Colonization Society, as were many who saw it as the "answer" to the slavery problem. He raised money for the organization and spoke on its behalf. His ardor for the organization cooled "when he saw the proslavery hate and the spite

Fig. 7.10. *The home of Rev. Daniel Parker, perched atop Mt. Hygiene, located on U.S. 52 in Monroe Township.*

with which the abolitionists were assigned, he was convinced that he should take the side of the mobbed."[75] He heard John Rankin lecture and read his works. Though he agreed with Rankin's sentiments, he could not sanction Rankin's advocacy of force.

Parker's destined link with his land manifested itself in 1839. The family, dissatisfied with the educational opportunities available in the area, decided to send their son, James Kennedy Parker, to Hanover College so that he could come back to teach his younger brothers and sisters. The family thought that perhaps other families would want a quality education for their children as well. They faced two problems: how to raise the initial capital to build a schoolhouse and what kind of school it would be.

Parker sought spiritual assistance years before about how he might find his calling. Prayer told him to keep all of the money that he received from side jobs and when the amount reached two hundred dollars he would know his calling. He hoarded his money, but never counted it. While he was thinking about starting his school he decided to count the money. Much to his surprise and reassurance he found that his cache totaled two hundred dollars, the amount he needed to build a twenty-by-forty-foot brick school building.[76] The Parkers wanted to open the school to students of all races, but they questioned what the reaction to that approach would be within their neighborhood. Mrs. Parker recalled the debate as follows:

Opposition to our views was very strong in our neighborhood yet many opposite views from us have been our friends and patrons of the school—Shaws, Fergusons, Nichols. Oberlin was the only school we knew in the world where no distinction was made on account of color. . . . But could we admit colored students here? Would it be tolerated? These were puzzling questions for awhile.[77]

They sought guidance from their friend, Josiah Denham, a Baptist minister and teacher. He was unequivocally supportive.

You have now an opportunity to act out your principles. You are independent—you can do this thing. Set your school without distinction on account of color. If such a school cannot be maintained you can live without it.[78]

That settled it. The Parkers decided to open their doors to "all whose behavior accorded with good order." November 4, 1839, was the first day of school; seven students enrolled.[79] The Clermont Academy, also known locally as the Parker Academy, became the educational home of the children of many of the county's abolitionists. Among those who attended were Gerard Polycarp Riley of Bethel; Frances Strickland, son of Mark Strickland of New Richmond; John Porter, son of Mark Porter of New Richmond; Samuel Walker, son of Caleb Walker of New Richmond; and the children of Andrew Coombs of Lindale. John Jolliffe enrolled Catherine Flinn over whom he held a guardianship.[80]

Free blacks frequently enrolled. The first black student to enroll at the school was Edwin Matthews, the former slave of James Birney. Matthews was apprenticed to Mark Strickland, who also acted as Birney's New Richmond business agent. Samuel Wilkins, described as "a pious old colored man" and former slave attended the school to learn how to read the Bible.[81]

William, Oliver, Virginia, and Almeda Harding were brought to the school from Texas by their white father. Their mother was a slave. Their father, according to Mrs. Sarah Parker, was "tender hearted who couldn't sell his children." Unfortunately, Almeda hanged herself in a barn at the school.[82]

Fig. 7.11. *The Clermont Academy, also known as the Parker Academy, opened to educate both boys and girls and students of all races. The classroom is on the right of the picture. The building to the left, known as "Bach Row," was where the male boarding students lived.*

The attendance of black and mulatto children at the school was not without controversy. In the fall of 1847, Milton Taylor of Maysville, Kentucky, brought his three mulatto children, John, Phoebe, and Mary Jane, to the school. All three of the Taylor children were "comely, polite, and well dressed." They had previously attended John Rankin's school in Ripley and were, therefore, well schooled. John was a very good mathematician and was soon tutoring others in algebra. One young Kentuckian, John Adams, was very upset by the Taylors' presence at the school. One day he exclaimed, "I could kill that man and all of his children and be glad of it." Adams wanted to go home, but could not because the Ohio River was in flood. "Warm debates" over "the earnest struggle" took place in the school during the month it took for the Ohio River to return to its banks. Adam's father came to the school and told his son to stay put. Some of the other Kentucky students, however, did leave the school, as did a few from Ohio. All of the Taylor children completed their studies. Phoebe later married Robert Duncanson, the noted black painter.[83]

In 1857 James Parker, Reverend Parker's son and the headmaster of the school, was asked to take a similar position at Wilberforce, a new school being established for blacks in Xenia. Parker accepted the one-year appointment and he and his family moved to Xenia. During his

Fig. 7.12. *The headmaster's home of the Clermont/Parker Academy. The female students who boarded at the school stayed here.*

absence, the Clermont Academy was shut down, but reopened after his return.

Most of the people in Xenia supported the school. Others opposed it. Fannie Parker, James's daughter, recalled that some of the residents threatened to burn them out. "These threats," wrote Fannie many years later, "frightened me, so that often at night, before going to sleep I would plan how I might get out of the house in case it should be set on fire. I was relieved when it rained at night, for I thought then, that the wicked men from Xenia would not come, in the rain, to burn us out."[84]

The outbreak of the Civil War greatly affected the academy. "It was all excitement," recalled Sarah Parker, "It is very difficult to carry out the daily round of school room activities."[85] Nine of the twenty-one boys left for the war.

As with many of the religious abolitionists, Mrs. Parker saw the Civil War as divine retribution for the evils of slavery. She described the war as follows:

The cup of our iniquity as a nation is full. God's wrath pours down upon us. None can stay His hand. We had professed to believe in Freedom and we supported the vilest style of slavery upon the earth. We did this with our eyes fully open to all the abomination that was in it. God came quickly, suddenly as a Thunder bolt in a clear sky. We trembled, but aroused ourselves and the north sprang into the arms at the first sound of alarm.[86]

Fig. 7.13. *Rev. John Gregg Fee, a second cousin to the Clermont County Fees. The Kentucky fireband abolitionist and Underground Railroad conductor was twice exiled from Kentucky. During one of the exiles, he and his family lived with the Parkers. He later founded Berea College.*

The Parkers' home was a place of refuge for John Gregg Fee during the Civil War. Fee, the great Kentucky abolitionist, was accused of preaching a sermon calling for more "John Browns" and for ordering a box of Sharpe's rifles to arm Kentucky slaves. Fee denied the charges. Nevertheless, a committee of wealthy Kentuckians exiled him from the state. He found refuge with the Parkers. Arnold Gragsdon, a black Underground Railroad conductor from northern Kentucky, wrote that Fee was involved with Underground Railroad activities before his exile to Ohio. Did Fee continue his Underground Railroad activities while living at the Parkers'? There is no documented evidence that he did. His children did attend the academy for several months and Fee was known to have preached at the academy and at local churches. Later he moved to Camp Nelson in Kentucky and ministered to contraband slaves there.[87]

The academy remained open during the war. By the time it closed in 1889, it had educated fifteen hundred students.[88]

Was the academy a station on the Underground Railroad? Local stories state that it was. A "secret closet" near the fireplace in the head-master's home is cited as proof of the story. Although there is a closet or room-like structure next to the fireplace, it is extremely small and could not provide refuge for any but the smallest person.

Lucie Parker Cranston, Reverend Parker's granddaughter, wrote that "all of the family homes were stations on the Underground Rail-road and the sons had many exciting experiences driving all night with fugitives northward to a relay station toward Lake Erie and Free-dom."[89] Mrs. Cranston unequivocally states that the family homes were stations, but does not state her belief about the school.

Lt. Gen. Henry Clark Corbin, a former academy student, wrote in his autobiography that the academy was a station. He recalled an incident in 1858 when slave hunters came to the school one night in pursuit of a specific fugi-tive. Daniel Parker replied that there was no slave by that name at the academy. They accepted Parker at his word and left.[90] Did Parker answer truthfully, but not completely, to the very specific question regarding a particular individ-ual? Could there have been other fugi-tives there? Corbin does not address those intriguing possibilities.

Fig. 7.14. *United States Army Lt. Gen. Henry Clark Corbin was a student at the academy in the 1840s.*

The strongest statement denying connections to the Underground Railroad came from James K. Parker. In response to an inquiry from Wilbur Siebert in 1892, Parker replied, "Although an old time abolition-ist, living in full view of the 'Dark and Bloody Ground' I never was in any way connected with the road. . . . Our home was not a safe place for fugitives being connected with a school with numerous students always about."[91]

The question remains unanswered.

NOTES

1. Rockey & Bancroft, *Clermont County, Ohio*, 410–414.

2. Ibid., 406–408, 66–67.

3. Ibid., 420; Whitt, *Cranston Memorial Presbyterian Church*, 13.

4. Whitt, *Cranston Memorial Presbyterian Church*, 16–17; *Philanthropist*, January 1, 1836. Aileen Whitt, the church historian, indicates that the church records from January 1844 to March 1869 are missing. It seems almost inconceivable that Fee, a fiery abolitionist, would not have spoken here.

5. Whitt, *Cranston Memorial Presbyterian Church*, 153.

6. Amos Dresser, *Family History*, http://members.aol.com/wardiary/dresser.html, 1–7.

7. The *Anti-slavery Record*, November 1835, no. 11, 1:1–7.

8. Whitt, *Cranston Memorial Presbyterian Church*, 153.

9. Rockey & Bancroft, *Clermont County, Ohio*, 414.A.

10. Henry Corbin, *The Autobiography of Henry Clark Corbin*, ed. Gary L. Knepp (Batavia, Ohio: Cragburn Press, 2003) 8.

11. *Clermont Courier*, December 31, 1836; October 17, 1845; and October 16, 1846; Rockey & Bancroft, *Clermont County, Ohio*, 414A.

12. P. F. Greene, M.D. "John Rogers, M.D. A Biography of the Man Who Delivered President Grant." *The Ohio State Medical Journal*, vol. 59, Jan–Feb, 1963. Unfortunately, Dr. Greene does not cite his sources for Dr. Rogers's involvement in the Underground Railroad. It certainly seems likely that, considering Rogers's extraordinary commitment to the antislavery cause, he was involved in the enterprise. Dr. Greene's statement is the only source, to date, which supports the claim.

13. Rockey & Bancroft, *Clermont County, Ohio*, 423–24; Pat Donaldson Mills, "New Richmond: A Center for Abolitionists," *Clermont County Bicentennial*, 36.

14. Rockey & Bancroft, *Clermont County, Ohio*, 424.

15. Ibid., 424.

16. Ibid.; Mills, "New Richmond: A Center for Abolitionists," 36.

17. Caleb S. Walker, *Autobiography*, Walker Family Papers, mss 168, Ohio Historical Society (OHS), Columbus, Ohio, 128–130; Claude Walker, *Walker Family Tree*, Walker Family papers, mss 168, OHS.

18. Rockey & Bancroft, *Clermont County, Ohio*, 404, 409, 419; Walker, *Autobiography*, 199, 172.

19. Walker, *Autobiography*, 215, 197.

20. Ibid., 195. Walker was speaking of the increasing anti-abolitionist mob violence, including an attack on the *Philanthropist* offices in Cincinnati.

21. Ibid., 186–87

22. Ibid., 191.

23. Dave Roberts, travel ed., "New Richmond Landmark Razed," *Cincinnati Enquirer*, date unknown.

24. Walker, *Autobiography*, 313, 316; Polly Staley to Gary Knepp, June 20, 2006; Daughters of the American Revolution, Ohio, Beech Forest Chapter, Williamsburg, *Monument Inscriptions Prior to 1900 from Cemeteries in Clermont County, Ohio. Copied by Beech Forest Chapter, D.A.R., Williamsburg, Ohio* ([Evansville, Ind., Reproduction by Unigraphic, Inc.], 1952 [i.e. 1974]) 10:3.

25. *Dictionary of American Biography*, ed. Allen Johnson, et al. (New York: Scribner, 1957) 1:291–92.

26. Ibid., 292. One of his former slaves was Edwin Matthews. The young man was apprenticed to Mark Strickland, a New Richmond abolitionist. Matthews also became the first black student at the Clermont Academy; James Birney to Jacob Barker, July 12, 1845, *Letters of James Birney . . .* , Dwight Lowell Dumond, ed., (New York: D. Appleton-Century, 1938) 2:953–54.

27. James Birney to Joseph Healy, October 2, 1835, *Letters of James Birney*, 1:249.

28. Elizur Wright Jr. to Birney, November 5, 1835; Ibid., 1:255.

29. Rockey & Bancroft, *Clermont County, Ohio*, 158.

30. Birney to Gerrit Smith, November 25, 1835; *Letters of James Birney*, 1:273–74. The reference to a village "50 miles above," was probably to Ripley.

31. Ibid.

32. Rockey & Bancroft, *Clermont County, Ohio*, 159; Clermont County Property Records, Deed Book 135, 405–06.

33. *Philanthropist*, January 1, 1836.

34. Ibid.

35. Ibid.

36. *Cincinnati Whig*, December 21, 1835.

37. *Philanthropist*, October 2, 1838.

38. Ibid., February 12, 1839.

39. Rockey & Bancroft, *Clermont County, Ohio*, 414A, 159.

40. *Philanthropist*, February 12, 1836.

41. Ibid., March 1, 1836.

42. *Cincinnati Gazette*, July 31, 1836.

43. Walker, *Autobiography*, 198. Rockey & Bancroft offers a slightly different version. It writes that Walker did indeed make a spirited speech in defense of the paper, but it was made before the paper left for Cincinnati; Rockey & Bancroft, *Clermont County, Ohio*, 159.

44. *Clermont Courier*, December 26, 1851 The paper was reporting results from the 1850 Census. 1860 Census.

45. Ibid.; Steve Gordon, New Richmond Village Form, Miami Purchase Association, 1981.

46. Ibid.

47. Mimi Miller interview, Natchez, Mississippi Historical Foundation, April 18, 2000.

48. Manumission papers of Elizabeth Rucker, June 4, 1859, Clermont County, Ohio Probate Court, Misc. Papers, Batavia, Ohio.

49. 1860 Census; Mimi Miller interview.

50. James Oliver Horton, *Free People of Color: Inside the African American Community* (Washington: Smithsonian Institute Press, 1993) 124–25, 135.

51. 1860 Census.

52. *Clermont Courier*, June 1, 1860.

53. Rockey & Bancroft, *Clermont County, Ohio*, 472.

54. Whitt, "Outstanding Black People of New Richmond," *Clermont County Bicentennial*, 17. The twenty-three founding members were Delvan Mathews, Benjamin Goins, Henry Fox, Whitfield Early, William Hasty, William Casey, Andrew Tone, William Layton, George Taylor, Alexander McCoul, Howell Boone, Thornton Smith, George Cooper, Jesse Orritt, Turner Wilson, Thomas Ruglan, John Arnold, William McDaul, P. L. Colomon, Albert Chapman, John Taylor, Tobias Peoples, and William Smith.

55. Ibid.

56. See Carol Wilson, *Freedom at Risk: The Kidnapping of Free Blacks in America 1780–1865* (Lexington, Ky.: University Press of Kentucky, 1994) 4.

57. Ibid., 10–11

58. Ibid., 118

59. A Robert McCallister served as New Richmond town marshall in 1842. Rockey & Bancroft, *Clermont County, Ohio*, 410.

60. *Philanthropist*, February 10, 1837.

61. Ibid.

62. Rockey & Bancroft, *Clermont County, Ohio*, 424A.

63. "The New Richmond Age," reprinted in *The Ripley Bee*, November 30, 1850.

64. *Cincinnati Commercial*, November 28–29, 1857, *Albany Journal*, December 1, 1857.

65. *Commonwealth v. William Green*. Pendleton County Circuit Court. October 1859. Kentucky Department for Libraries and Archives. Public Records Division. Frankfort, Kentucky. On the outside of the case jacket someone drew a man with Negro features and wrote the word "abolitionist" beneath.

66. Levi Coffin, *Reminiscences* (New York: Arno Press (reprint) 1968) 412–418.

67. The Emancipation Proclamation freed the slaves in areas not controlled by the government of the United States. Kentucky was brought into the Union fold soon after the start of the war. Therefore, Kentucky slaves were not freed until the ratification of the Thirteenth Amendment in 1865.

68. *Clermont Sun*, July 6, 1898.

69. Ibid.

70. Reverend Parker could have been referring to Matthew 23:27 which likened the Pharisees to "white washed tombs, which outwardly appear beautiful but within are full of dead men's bones and all uncleanness."

71. Ibid.

72. Ibid.

73. Rockey & Bancroft, *Clermont County, Ohio*, 171.

74. Priscilla Parker, "A History of the Clermont Academy," *Clermont Sun*, May 16, 1861.

75. Ibid.

76. Rockey & Bancroft, *Clermont County, Ohio*, 171–72; Parker, "A History of the Clermont Academy"; *Clermont Sun*, May 16, 1861.

77. Parker, "A History of the Clermont Academy."

78. Ibid.

79. Ibid.

80. Sarah Preston Parker, *Brief History of Clermont Academy, Together with a Few Items from the Lives of its Founder & Principal*, Ohio Historical Society, transcribed copy at Batavia Branch Library, 13, 14, 30, 70.

81. Ibid., 12, 131, 144, 146.

82. Ibid., 117–18

83. Ibid., 43–45

84. One night the barn and stable did burn, but not by arsonists. Fannie Parker to Wilberforce University, March 1916. Stokes Library, Wilberforce University, trans. J. Mulhern. Greene County Public Library. Xenia, Ohio.

85. Parker, *Brief History of Clermont Academy*, 145–46.

86. Ibid., 155.

87. John Gregg Fee, *Autobiography of John G. Fee, Berea, Kentucky* (Chicago: National Christian Association, 1891) 147–48; Arnold Gragsdon, *Bullwhip Days: The Slaves Remembered*, ed. James Mellon (New York: Weidenfeld & Nicolson, 1988) 268.

88. Parker, "A History of the Clermont Academy"; *Clermont Sun*, May 16, 1861.

89. Lucie Parker Cranston to Harper Brothers Co., June 1917, typewritten copy at the Clermont County Public Library, Batavia, Ohio.

90. Corbin, *Autobiography*, 20.

91. James K. Parker to Wilbur Siebert, March 30, 1892, Siebert Papers, OHS.

CHAPTER 8

Moscow and Washington Township

Robert Fee and the Clermont Outrage

Six armed men crashed through the door of Vincent and Fanny Wig-glesworth's Washington Township home at 2:00 a.m. on the morning of October 30, 1842. The Kentuckians quickly subdued Vincent and bound him. Two of the men, intent on reclaiming their "property," forcibly removed the forty-five-year-old Fanny and her four children from their home. The gang, with its quarry in tow, struck out for the Ohio River over the back country roads of Clermont County. An alarm was raised in the community. A citizen's posse was formed, and chase was given. Despite the community's best efforts, the abductors, with Fanny and her children, slipped away into Kentucky.[1]

A large group of outraged Washington Township citizens gathered at the Calvary Methodist Church to discuss the Wigglesworth abductions. A committee of local luminaries, including the state senator Dowty Utter and the future United States congressman David Fisher, was formed to express the sentiments of the residents and "to take such steps for the apprehension of the family stolen."[2] The committee resolved,

Whereas: We the citizens of Clermont County have ever been and ever will be, ready to maintain and support the law provided for the reclaiming of fugitive slaves, escaping from the State of Kentucky into our own, when taken in a legal manner, as pointed out by an act of our Legislature made at the special solicitation of the State of Kentucky . . .

Whereas: Not withstanding the often manifested willingness of our citizens to do every thing just and honorable for the protection of the rights and property of our sister State, a number of the citizens of Kentucky . . .

Fig. 8.3. *The Wigglesworth home was located along the banks of Indian Creek in Washington Township.*

invaded the dwelling of Vincent Wigglesworth, a free colored resident of Ohio, bound him, and with relentless cruelty and barbarity, unworthy of the character and dignity of men, kidnapped his Wife, who has been a peaceable resident of our county for sixteen years and four children born in our state, and stole them away into Kentucky, without the least demand for them or right [to] them under our law . . .

Resolved, That as citizens of Ohio, we feel it our duty to refrain from intermeddling with any of the laws or institutions of Kentucky, and more especially with that of slavery . . . and when slaves so escaping are sought to be reclaimed in a lawful manner we have never interfered, nor will we, to thwart or prevent the due execution of the law.

Resolved, That kidnapping is a daring offense and heinous crime in the contemplation of our laws . . . and that without the prompt execution of the Statute in such case made and provided, we have no security for the liberty of the free colored, native residents of their State, or even our own.[3]

Further, the resolution proclaimed that Fanny Wigglesworth and her children were free and were entitled to the protections of Ohio law. The actions of the kidnappers, it continued, was "an outrage, and an insult to all law," and demanded "immediate and satisfactory redress."[4]

The committee made one last assertion that the people of Ohio were law abiding, never failing to help return fugitive slaves. The committee, therefore, expected the people of Kentucky to do the same:

bring the kidnappers to justice and return the Wigglesworth family home to freedom. It is quite obvious that the committee went to great lengths to state that its members were law-abiding citizens, not lawless abolitionists. There was no moralizing here, no attack upon the institution of slavery. The resolution pointed out that Ohio favorably responded to Kentucky's request to criminalize Underground Railroad activities. This statement was probably inserted by committee member Dowty Utter, who voted for the law three years earlier.[5] They drew one final distinction: Fanny Wigglesworth and her children were free, and by virtue thereof, the men who took them were criminals.

The *Philanthropist* ran the resolution under the headline "The Clermont Outrage." It is difficult to tell from the tenor of the accompanying editorial what it considered more outrageous—the kidnappings or the committee's response. The paper excoriated the committee's resolution as being disgraceful and blasphemous because it practically conceded that slaves were property not men. Further, the committee's statement reeked of "exquisite morality" because it equated "kidnapping and aiding innocent men to escape bondage in the same category." The paper concluded that the church gathering was "far from an abolitionist meeting."[6]

The *Cincinnati Daily Gazette*, the Queen City's Whig newspaper, was angered by the incident. It noted the growing numbers of slave cases between Ohio and Kentucky that had "excited blood shed" between the people of the two neighboring states. "There is no sympathy," wrote the editor, "felt among us for slavery; but there is a settled purpose to give to the slaveowner all the rights which the law guarantees." However, "the rash and unwise conduct of Kentuckians" will change that attitude. The editorial warned Kentucky slaveowners not to use force because the people of Ohio will never submit to it.[7]

Clermont County's Thomas Morris, formerly a U.S. senator abandoned by the Democratic Party for his antislavery viewpoints, weighed in on the kidnapping. He called it an assault upon Ohio's sovereignty, an issue of great interest in the state's rights-conscious country. He declared that had this kidnapping been "between nations such an action might have been a good cause of war." He asked,

Will the time never come when we shall wake up to the preservation of our rights and all the sovereignty of our state? Broadcloth gentlemen from the slave states come here to instruct us in our legal duties . . . while the Negro hunting tribe, like the hyena, break open our dwellings and steal our people.

Morris called upon the governor of Kentucky to return the family to their home.[8]

While political issues surrounding the incident were being debated, legal issues remained unanswered. Were Fanny Wigglesworth and her children the victims of a criminal kidnapping? To answer that question, we must first determine their legal status. Were they free or slaves? Details of Fanny's life are sketchy. What we do know is that she was forty-five years old at the time of the abduction, was born into slavery in the state of Maryland, had been given to an unnamed Maryland woman by will as a life estate, had come into the state of Ohio sometime in 1826, and had remained in the state ever since.[9]

What is a life estate? A life estate occurs when someone gives property to another for the duration of the recipient's life. After the recipient dies, the property goes to another who is known as a future interest holder. Thus, when the unnamed Maryland woman died, Fanny would pass to the people named in the will as the future owners. In this case, the future interest holders were William Moore and William Middletown (sometimes found as Middleton), who were identified as the leaders of the gang who took Fanny and the children.[10] Could Moore and Middletown be guilty of kidnapping their own property?

Thomas Morris, a preeminent attorney, argued that the two were guilty of kidnapping because Fanny had been freed after she came to Ohio. He claimed that manumission papers had been registered in the offices of the Clermont County Probate Court.[11]

Morris did not indicate that Fanny was a life estate. Her status is critical in determining whether a kidnapping had occurred. The life estate holder could not have freed Fanny because she did not own her. What are we to make of Morris's assertions? Was he ignoring an inconvenient fact or did he not know that she was a life estate?

If Moore and Middletown were innocent of kidnapping Fanny, were they guilty of kidnapping the children? All of the evidence presented supports that the children were born in Ohio. Under the law of the day, any child born in Ohio was free regardless of the legal status of the parents. So it did not matter if Fanny was a slave; the children were free. Therefore, Moore and Middletown did commit a crime when they took the children.

Assuming that Fanny was a slave, did Moore and Middletown act properly when they seized her and took her to Kentucky? The common law frequently permitted owners to engage in "self-help" in retrieving property illegally held by others. This did not apply to slaves. The Federal Fugitive Slave Act of 1793 permitted slaveowners or their agents to cross state lines to recover fugitive slaves. However, they had to appear before a state or federal judge, or a local magistrate, to present evidence of ownership and positive identification of the specific slave in question. If sufficient evidence was presented, the claimant was issued a "certificate of removal," after which they could leave the jurisdiction with their property.[12]

Why didn't Moore and Middletown invoke the Fugitive Slave Act and legally recover their property? Unfortunately, we do not have that answer. It was probably just a matter of expediency. Or perhaps the two were aware of a legal theory gaining ground in Ohio that threatened the state's traditional support for the slaveholding interest. The theory's proponents argued that slaves, accompanying their masters, became free the moment they touched Ohio's soil. The argument was based upon a provision in Ohio's constitution that read, "There shall be neither slavery nor involuntary servitude in the state."[13]

The theory gained traction when an Ohio appeals court ruled in an 1841 Warren County case known as *State v. Farr* that it was immaterial whether a black man was free or slave in his home state "because if a slave there he became free when brought to this state by his master." The court made it clear, however, that this did not apply to fugitive slaves—they remained in bondage. The evidence we have thus far indicates that Fanny was brought to Ohio by her master. The question of whether this case would apply is left unanswered.[14]

Moore and Middletown may also have been wary of pressing their claim in the Clermont County Court of Common Pleas. The judge was Owen T. Fishback. Fishback was an abolitionist who regularly attended antislavery conventions, was married to the sister of Clermont County's most outspoken Underground Railroad conductor and, along with John Jolliffe and Thomas Morris, defended Underground Railroad conductor, John Mahan.[15]

Soon after the abductions, Vincent Wigglesworth moved to Lebanon, Ohio. His story caught the attention of Governor Thomas Corwin and his brother, Robert. A meeting was convened at the Lebanon Town Hall for the purpose of raising money for the recovery of the family. Vincent "gave a brief and touching history of the wrongs and outrages inflicted" upon his family.[16] The Corwin brothers succeeded in raising "a considerable sum" for his rescue efforts. Vincent retained Robert Fee as his agent to bring his family home.

Robert Fee, of Moscow, Ohio, was a forty-five-year-old merchant. His family immigrated to Kentucky from Pennsylvania in 1790. Six years later, they crossed over the Ohio River into Clermont County. The Fees were devout Methodists and ardent supporters of the temperance movement.

The Fees were also abolitionists, as was their Kentucky cousin John Gregg Fee, the founder of Berea College. Robert's father, Thomas, harbored fugitives in their Washington Township home as early as the 1820s. The Fees moved over time to the inland communities of Felicity, Bethel, and Williamsburg, where they formed the nodes of the Underground Railroad network in Clermont County.[17]

The Fees married into other Underground Railroad families, forming strategic alliances. Robert's sister, Nancy, married Dr. L. T. Pease of Williamsburg, who became that community's Underground Railroad station manager in the 1850s.[18] Fee, himself, married into another Underground Railroad family just before the abductions. Fee's second wife was Catherine Ebersole, whose brother, Jacob, was actively involved in the Underground Railroad in Palestine, down river from Moscow.[19]

Fee was able to trace the movements of the Wigglesworth family across the state of Kentucky to Independence, Missouri. He felt that, with this knowledge and with the money raised by the people of Lebanon and Clermont County, he could go to Missouri and try to negotiate with Moore and Middletown for the family's release.[20] Fee was armed with a detailed description of each member of the Wigglesworth family.

Fanny, the Wife, is about 45 years of age, dark color, has a remarkable bump about the size of a cherry on her forehead in the edge of her hair—Maryann aged 15 years well grown, dark color, Eliza, aged 10 years has a scar on the forehead running from about the left eyebrow down to the right, also dark color—Josiah aged 5 has a remarkable natural mark on one side of his face and running across his face and . . . the tail on the other, he is quick spoken and lisps—the other a female infant about 10 days old when taken.[21]

The descriptions were probably not needed, since it is likely that Fee knew the family. His home was less than ten miles from the Indian Creek home of Benjamin Penn on whose property the Wigglesworth family lived. Further, Robert's brother, Thomas, married Benjamin

Penn's daughter. In such a small world as Clermont County in the 1840s and with the family connections, Fee probably did know the Wigglesworth family. This and his family's connections to the abolitionist movement most likely explain his involvement in this matter.[22]

Fee left for Independence, Missouri, on January 15, 1843. He traveled the first leg of his journey in the comfort of a riverboat. However, by the time he reached St. Louis, the Missouri River froze over. He was forced to hire out a horse for the 250-mile overland trip to Independence.[23]

Fee located Fanny and her children in Independence. He opened negotiations for their "purchase." A deal was struck. The family would be released upon the payment of $150.[24] Fee made a $20 down payment and agreed to return within sixty days to complete the transaction. To hedge his bets, Fee also retained an attorney to bring proceedings against Moore and Middletown in Independence. Fee was hesitant to leave Missouri without the family, but he had exhausted his funds. Before leaving, he wrote a letter to Vincent explaining what he had done. Since Vincent could not read, he asked Robert Corwin to read Fee's letter to him. As Corwin began to read, Vincent started to cry, shouting "Thanks to God."[25]

Robert returned to Ohio and began another round of fundraising. Soon after the initiation of the lawsuit, Moore and Middletown skipped town. Fee learned that the two had taken the family to Platte County, Missouri, located approximately forty miles north of Kansas City.[26]

By now, Fee had had enough of Moore and Middletown. He decided to deploy the full strength of the State of Ohio on behalf of the family. Indictments for kidnapping were obtained against the men. A requisition, or order, upon John Cummins Edwards, governor of Missouri, for the extradition of the two men was issued. Thomas H. Mosley was appointed as Ohio's agent on February 10, 1845. Another agent, William Russell of Fulton, Missouri, was also appointed two months later. Fulton was to be paid only if he safely delivered the charged to Clermont County.[27]

Fee did not wait for the agents to bring the kidnappers back to Clermont County. Armed with the indictments and the extradition papers, Fee, accompanied by a deputy marshall, set off on the nearly seven-hundred-mile trek to Platte County. They arrived in Platte City some time in March 1845.[28]

Moore and Middletown were arrested, but were soon released. The proceedings created "quite an excitement" in Platte City. A mob gathered to "persuade" Fee to leave their fair city. The vigilantes pursued Fee to his hotel. They nearly caught him, passing through the room where he was hiding.[29] The *Weston Journal* urged Fee to leave the area quickly less he "get a coat of feathers or something worse." Fee left the area and returned to Clermont County. After April 8, 1845, nothing more of the family is known.[30]

The *Western Star* newspaper of Lebanon was quite upset with the events in Platte City. It asserted that, had the kidnapped been the family of an influential white man, the public would have been outraged.

Instead of apathy and inactivity, all would be excitement, indignation, and vengeance, and the insolent Missourians, instead of talking about a coat of tar and feathers for the back of an agent sent to recover, by legal process, the stolen enslaved family would be called upon to defend their own dastardly carcasses from the bristling bayonets of an insulted and outraged people. How hard to comprehend and act upon naked, abstract right!—how difficult to understand that justice knows no color, cast, or condition!—that the poor black man has the same claim upon our sympathy, and the protection of his legal rights as the proudest name in our great state.[31]

The Missouri experience turned Fee into a committed Underground Railroad operative. His large, two-story brick home, perched atop a hill overlooking the Ohio River became a well-known stopover. Fee kept lighted candles in the windows at night, facing the river, as a beacon for escaping slaves. Slave hunters frequently surrounded the home. They brandished torches and threatened to burn him out if he did not turn over their property. So real were the threats that each member of the family kept loaded pistols by the bedside each night.[32]

On June 20, 1852, Fee traveled to Falmouth, Kentucky, though the purpose of this trip to the Pendleton County village is not clear. It was probably to visit with Sarah Wilcoxen, an old family friend.[33] Wilcoxen, a widow, had fallen on hard times. She wanted to free her four slaves, but depended upon the income she earned by hiring them out. She did, however, draft a will freeing them upon her death.[34]

One of Sarah's slaves was Mariah, a forty-two-year-old woman who was married to Bob. Bob was owned by John H. Barker, whose farm was nearby. Together, Mariah and Bob had several children. Robert Fee knew Mariah well, as he had hired her as a domestic servant in his Moscow home.[35]

Sarah Wilcoxen had a son who was described as "a drunken, good-

Fig. 8.4. *Robert E. Fee's stately mansion was located on the outskirts of Moscow, overlooking the Ohio River. The home was razed after years of neglect.*

Fig. 8.5. *The location of the Robert E. Fee home on a hill overlooking the Ohio River. The site is now a park in the village of Moscow, Ohio.*

for-nothing physician."[36] Upon learning of his mother's plan to free Mariah and her children, Dr. Wilcoxen conspired to sell them to a slave trader named Johnson. John Barker, Dr. Wilcoxen's father-in-law and Bob's owner, and the Pendleton County sheriff were in on the scheme. One of Mariah's children and a grandchild were taken in furtherance of the plot. Mariah and another child refused to go and began screaming. It was at this point that Fee became involved. He heard Mariah's screams and learned of the plot. Bob came by, and together he and Mariah escaped to Moscow. They probably crossed the Ohio River on a ferry owned by Robert Fee.[37]

From the account of the incident chronicled in the newspaper, it appears that Fee was only tangentially involved in the affair. The paper insisted that Fee had no knowledge of the escape. He is "among the most respectable and best citizens of Clermont County" and "is every inch a kind, benevolent, Christian gentleman."[38] Of course, with that reputation, Fee could not possibly have been involved with anything as disreputable as slave stealing. The Pendleton County grand jury thought otherwise. It indicted Fee for "slave stealing" and "slave enticing" based upon the events of June 20, 1852.

The indictment claimed that Fee did

feloniously steal a Negro man slave named Bob, the property of John H. Barker and a Negro woman named Mariah, the property of Sarah Wilcoxen. The said Bob of the value of five hundred dollars and said Mariah the value of four hundred dollars.

On the second count of the indictment, Fee was charged with feloniously attempting

to persuade away and entice away a Negro man named Bob . . . from the service and employment of John H. Barker and . . . did feloniously attempt to persuade away and entice away a Negro woman slaved named Mariah from the service and employment of Sarah Wilcoxen . . . being the lawful owner of said Negro woman slave.[39]

A warrant for Fee's arrest was issued. Kentucky requested that Clermont County sheriff George W. Richards arrest and extradite Fee to Kentucky to stand trial on the charges.[40] The *Ripley Bee* reported that Fee had not been arrested as of its publication date of November 26, 1853—fifteen days after the requisition had been filed with the Governor's Office.[41] In fact, Fee never was arrested. William Medill, governor of Ohio, did not seem to have the stomach for the matter. He probably remembered the furor that greeted his predecessor, Joseph Vance, who turned over Rev. John Mahan for the prosecution of similar charges fifteen years earlier. Vance was turned out of office. Mahan was released after ten months of captivity because it was found that Kentucky did not have jurisdiction to try the case.[42]

Fee lived for eighteen months under the threat of arrest until June 5, 1855, when the Commonwealth's attorney dismissed the case. The court entry said simply "it is so ordered that this case be filed away with leave to reinstate."[43]

There was no explanation for the order. The case was probably dismissed because John H. Barker, described as the "instigator" of the charges, died in 1854, leaving no one interested in pursuing the matter.[44]

Robert Fee lived for fourteen years after the enactment of the Thirteenth Amendment outlawing slavery. He died on October 4, 1879, at his home in Moscow. He was eulogized as a man who loved his fellow man. "He sought the suffering," reads his obituary, "and the lowly, gave of his means to the calls of charity, and never seemed to feel himself more profitably engaged than when ministering to the necessities of his fellow man."[45] The old lion rests with his family in the Moscow, Ohio, Cemetery.[46]

Fig. 8.6. *The burial marker of Robert Fee, located in the Moscow Cemetery.*

The Fee Villa

For many years a story has circulated that a building in Moscow, known as the Fee Villa, was associated with the Underground Railroad. Local historian Richard Crawford has gone even further; he has written that the Fee Villa was "the center of the Underground Railroad activity in

Fig. 8.7. *The Fee Villa was once the home of Thomas Fee. It is located at 110 Water Street, Moscow, Ohio.*

Clermont County." These are the elements of the story. The Fee family kept a candle burning in a window, facing the Ohio River and Kentucky, as a beacon for escaping slaves. Once the slaves crossed over the river, they came to the Fee home where they were given clothes and food from the general store located on the site. If necessary, they were hidden in the basement until it was safe to transport them inland. A tunnel in the basement, which extended across Broadway into another building known as the Spaeth House, was used to harbor the fugitives.[47]

There are no references to any specific events tying the building to the Underground Railroad. And there is no documentary evidence linking the Fee Villa to the Underground Railroad. The circumstantial evidence is, at times, contradictory. We will examine the evidence, both pro and con, in the following paragraphs.

The strongest evidence in support of the story is the family connection. The Fees were prominent abolitionists and Underground Railroad conductors. We have previously discussed the activities of Thomas Fee Sr., his son, Robert, and his daughter, Nancy. Other family members connected with the activity include Arthur and Oliver Perry Spencer Fee of Felicity.

Thomas Fee Jr., Robert and Nancy's brother, purchased the Spaeth house from the United States Bank in 1832. Thomas and another brother, Enos, opened a store in the building shortly thereafter.[48] The building was constructed upon a limestone foundation on lot no. 1 by John Payne, Moscow's founder, in 1817. It is a large, two-story brick building that, along with a similar building, was raised to attract potential investors to the river community. Moscow never lived up to its founders' dreams of becoming a major riverport city.[49]

At the foot of the lot upon which the Fee Villa was built lay the landing for the ferry that operated between Moscow and Pendleton County, Kentucky. Robert Fee was granted a license for the ferry. Alonzo Judd ran the ferry for many years. Interestingly, Judd was an antislavery man. He had lived in Nashville, Tennessee, for a year, but came back to Clermont County because of his disgust for slavery.[50] An antislavery ferry owner would have been a great asset in operating an Underground Railroad station on the river across from Kentucky.

Thomas Ryan, who owned the home in the 1970s, told Randy McNutt, formerly of the *Cincinnati Enquirer*, that the house had "secret rooms" that were used to hide slaves. According to Ryan, these rooms were destroyed by fire sometime before the Civil War.[51] Kathy Barre, a later owner, was asked about the secret rooms and the fire that destroyed them. She replied that they had completely gutted the home when they purchased it, and had not found any evidence of a fire.[52]

Ryan also mentioned that two Catholic priests, who had previously lived in the house, found shackles in the basement. The implication is that the shackles had been removed from an escaping slave and left behind. The priests took the shackles and other implements and made a decorative arrangement that was placed on the wall. The shackles were stolen from the house in 1978. Fortunately, Richard Crawford took a picture of the wall decoration before the shackles were stolen.[53]

A copy of the photo was sent to Jerry Gore, a slave artifact expert, for review. Mr. Gore reported that one of the items depicted in the photo was a shackle. He cautioned that the shackles used in this period were dual use, both slave and penal. There were no known penal institutions located in the area.[54]

A popular oral tradition describes a tunnel between the Fee Villa and the Spaeth house. A recessed, bricked-up structure is located on the eastern basement wall of the building next to Broadway Street. The

Fig. 8.8. *This building, known as the Spaeth House, was purchased by Thomas Fee. It was allegedly a gambling house for rivermen and, according to legend, was used as a stop on the Underground Railroad.*

Fig. 8.9. *The Moscow landing. Robert Fee operated a ferry between Moscow and Pendleton County, Kentucky, across the Ohio River.*

Fig. 8.10. *An earlier photo of the Fee Villa in the background and a cart awaiting transport across the Ohio River by the Moscow Ferry.*

Fig. 8.11. *The bricked-up structure in the basement of the Fee Villa which legend claims is an entrance to a tunnel connected to the Spaeth House across the street used by fugitive slaves.*

structure is below ground level. Approximately twenty feet away on the opposite side of Broadway stands the Spaeth House. A similar recessed bricked structure exists in the basement of that house. It lies in perfect alignment with the one in the Fee Villa, forming the tunnel in the story. Historical archaeologist, Jeanaine Krienbrink, examined the structure in the Fee Villa during a recent FEMA (Federal Emergency Management Agency) mitigation study. She believes that the structure is most likely a former entrance to the basement that had been covered up over time.[55]

Stories about tunnels and secret passageways are popular in Underground Railroad lore and must be approached with great caution. Digging underground structures was a very time-consuming and expensive undertaking at that time. It seems unlikely that people would have engaged in such activities for Underground Railroad use only.[56]

Slaveowners across the Ohio River from Fee's home in Pendleton County, Kentucky, were very concerned about the number of slaves they were losing each year to Ohio. Samuel T. Hauser, who owned twelve slaves, was given a possessory interest in five additional slaves.[57] A date for their sale was set. Until that time, Hauser was given permission to use the slaves so long as he did not remove them from the county without permission of the court. On the evening of August 24, 1850, Essex, one of the slaves entrusted to Hauser, escaped from Foster's Landing into Clermont County near Neville.[58]

Hauser hired agents Reuben McCarty and William Wilson to bring Essex back. They tracked Essex to Sandusky, Ohio, but were unable to apprehend him, primarily because Ohio officials refused to help.[59]

Following Essex's escape, Hauser took the other slaves to Lexington, Kentucky, as a precautionary measure. The court conducted an official inquiry into the matter. Hauser told the court that he removed the other slaves because he believed that they might run as well. He pointed out that many Pendleton County slaves had recently escaped into Ohio without recapture. He explained the reasons for the exodus: there were many well-constructed public roads throughout the county leading to the Ohio River, making it easy for slaves to make a quick getaway, and there were many abolitionists in Pendleton County who were ready to help escaping slaves. Once at the river, the slaves had no trouble finding "skiffs and other watercraft" at the river's bank to convey them across. In addition, there were "abolitionists in abundance upon the other and adjacent bank" to help them onto Canada.[60]

William C. Naylor, commissioner of the court, exonerated Hauser of any liability related to the loss of Essex. He further ruled that Hauser's actions in removing the other slaves from the jurisdiction were justified. Essex's loss, he added, was due to the "adverse sentiments" of Ohioans and not to Hauser's negligence.[61]

Was Hauser's claim that Pendleton County was losing significant numbers of slaves to Ohio accurate? Or was he merely hyping the numbers to mitigate his own negligence? Unfortunately, no newspapers existed in Pendleton at the time, so we cannot scan the papers for fugitive slave advertisements to determine numbers of fugitive slaves.

However, the slave schedule in the 1850 U.S. census for Pendleton County indicates that county residents owned 268 slaves. Of these, 38 or 14 percent were reported as fugitives. One of the 38 belonged to Hauser. Based upon this record, it is understandable that owners would be concerned.[62]

The question still remains: Was the Fee Villa an Underground Railroad station? There is insufficient evidence to support the claim that it was a major center of operation. There is a body of circumstantial evidence to sift through. We know that Robert Fee, whose home was less than one-quarter of a mile away, was active in aiding runaway slaves. Fee's family—his father, brother, sister, and extended members—were active as well. It is disconcerting that nothing has been found in the family history linking Thomas Fee to the enterprise. The evidence regarding the tunnel has been largely discounted by the archaeologist's opinion that the bricked-up structure was most likely a former entrance to the basement. There is no way to prove or disprove the claim that the basement was used as a hideaway. The claim that the house contained secret rooms that were burned at some time before the Civil War was severely compromised by the statement of Kathy Barre that she did not notice any signs of fire in the home when they remodeled it. However, the persistence and widespread distribution of the story must be given some weight. The possibility that the tellers of the story confused the brothers and really meant Robert instead of Thomas must also be given some credence. In the final analysis, there seems to be an insufficient body of credible evidence to verify the story.

Dowty Utter

Dowty Utter was the caricature of the nineteenth-century "westerner"—crude, tobacco-spitting, card-playing Jacksonian Democrat. But appearances could be deceiving. Utter was a skilled politician who prowled the halls of Ohio's legislature for twenty years, coming within one vote of receiving the Democratic nomination for governor in 1844. And, according to some accounts, he was the basis for one of the characters in *Uncle Tom's Cabin*, the best-selling American novel of the nineteenth century.

Utter, of Washington Township, was largely unschooled, yet "he was deeply read in the great work of nature, and with it came a knowledge of men."[63] He was a spellbinding public speaker, even though he occasionally "murdered the King's English."[64] He entered the Ohio State House of Representatives in 1835 and was elected to the state Senate two years later. Utter earned the moniker of the "Democrat Meat-Axe" for his bare-knuckled, no-holds-barred brand of politics, and yet it was said "a kinder heart never beat in a man's bosom."[65]

In his public acts he appeared to support his party's proslavery positions. He opposed a bill incorporating a school for blacks. One month later he voted for Ohio's Fugitive Slave Act.[66] On the other hand, J. L. Rockey and R. J. Bancroft, Utter's contemporaries, portray the senator as a closet Underground Railroader. They wrote that he "was never deaf to the entreaties of a person in distress—black or white." While a state senator, he "kept and succored in his house overnight a poor and bleeding fugitive slave, and filled his purse the next morning, to continue his journey northward." According to Rockey and Bancroft, this incident became the basis for a scene in *Uncle Tom's Cabin.*[67]

Fletcher Day, editor of the *Felicity Times,* iterated a similar conclusion about Senator Utter, but went further. He wrote that Utter's home, near the mouth of Bear Creek, "also formed a safe asylum for the fugitive slave while awaiting transportation to this point"—Felicity. "That home," he added, "unmistakably figures in Mrs. Stowe's never-dying story known throughout civilization as 'Uncle Tom's Cabin'!"[68]

Mary Harrison Games wrote in 1937, "Dowty Utter, who was at one time a state senator, gave Fee valiant assistance." She was probably referring to Robert Fee of Moscow. Games's most likely source for this information was Dr. William E. Thompson, himself an Underground

Railroad conductor from Bethel, to whom her book was dedicated.[69]

Did Harriet Beecher Stowe base a character in *Uncle Tom's Cabin* upon Dowty Utter? As with many questions involving the Underground Railroad, the answer is not clear cut. There are no references to Dowty Utter in the novel. Nor is there any mention of him in Stowe's companion text titled *The Key. The Key* was Stowe's response to critics who questioned the authenticity of the characters in the story. Scholars still debate the identity of the characters today.

There is but one character in the book who could be Dowty Utter, and that is Senator John Bird. The scene involving Bird, found in chapter nine, is entitled, "In Which it Appears that a Senator is But A Man." The scene opens with Senator John Bird and his wife Mary sitting in the parlor of their Ohio home located near the Ohio River. Mary asks the senator what was going on in the Senate. He replies, "not much." The senator is surprised at his wife's sudden interest in politics. Mary asks,

Well; but is it true that they have been passing a law forbidding people to give meat and drink to those poor colored folks that come along? I have heard they are talking of some such law, but I didn't think any Christian Legislature would pass it.[70]

The senator answered,

There has been a law passed forbidding people to help the slaves that come over from Kentucky, my dear; so much of that thing has been done by the reckless Abolitionists that our brethren in Kentucky are very strongly excited, and it seems necessary, and no more than Christian and kind that something should be done by our state to quiet the excitement.[71]

They continue their conversation with the usually subdued and apolitical Mrs. Bird becoming very excited. She directly confronts her husband.

"You didn't vote for it?" she asks.

"Even so, my fair politician," he replies.[72]

"You ought to be ashamed, John! Poor homeless creatures! It is a shameful, wicked abominable law. I'll break it, for one the first time I get a chance; . . ." she chastises.[73]

He tries to reason with her. "These are matters of great state importance," he argues. "So much so that we must put aside our personal feelings."

She would have none of it. "Obeying God never brings on public evils. I know it can't," Mary counters.[74]

John sputters a reply, but Mary interrupts before he finishes.

Oh nonsense John! You can talk all night but you wouldn't do it. I put it to you John. Would you now, turn away a poor, shivering, hungry creature from your door because he was a runaway? Would you now?[75]

The senator fumbles for a reply. During the pause the author reveals that the senator "had the misfortune to be a man who had a particularly humane and accessible nature, and turning away anybody that was in need never had been his forte."[76]

Soon after this exchange there is a knock at the door and as fate would have it, Eliza, the heroine of the tale, appears. What was the senator to do—obey the law, conform to the demands of the state, or follow the dictates of his heart? The senator followed his heart. He clothed and fed Eliza. He then took her and her child to the home of a former slaveowner, whom he knew was involved with the Underground Railroad. As he was about to leave the man's home, which was located further up the creek, he slipped ten dollars to the farmer to help Eliza along the "road."

Why did Bird change from being "as bold as a lion" in favor of the new law to helping Eliza? Stowe explains that prior to the chance encounter that night, Bird could not understand how anyone could "put the welfare of a few miserable fugitives before great state interests." But that was before Bird had seen "the imploring human eye, the frail trembling hand, the despairing appeal of helpless agony."[77]

We come back to the question: Was Dowty Utter the historical basis for Senator John Bird? We will probably never know the answer for sure. However, there are a number of arguments supporting the case. First, we have the statements of three respected reporters that Bird was Utter. The family of Fletcher Day, editor of the *Felicity Times*, was reportedly involved in the Underground Railroad. Rockey and Bancroft, contemporaries of Utter, also wrote that he was the basis for Bird and that Utter was involved with the Underground Railroad. Dr. William Thompson, a documented conductor, reported that Utter was associated with Fee. Second, there are a number of details of Utter's life and personality traits that correspond to those of Bird. Utter was an Ohio state senator, as was Bird. Both lived on the Ohio River. Utter was reported by Rockey and Bancroft to be big-hearted and sympa-

Fig. 8.12. *The home of Brice Blair, president of the Clermont County Antislavery Society. George Beecher stayed with Blair when he preached at the Batavia Presbyterian Church. According to church history, Beecher's sister Harriet Beecher Stowe, visited here as well, giving her the opportunity to learn details about Clermont County's Underground Railroad. It is located at 123 North Street, Batavia, Ohio, and is now the office of the Clermont County Prosecuting Attorney.*

thetic to those, both black and white, who were in need; Stowe portrays Bird as being "particularly humane."

Third, Harriet Beecher Stowe had the opportunity to know Utter. Her brother, George, was a Presbyterian minister in Clermont County during the 1830s. Harriet came to Batavia to visit with her brother when he was pastoring to the Batavia Presbyterian Church. Stowe's husband, Calvin, spoke to the New Richmond Presbyterian Church. It is entirely plausible that she would have known someone with Utter's political stature in the county.

What about the law that Bird and his wife were discussing? Was there a historical basis for that discussion? There was. In the aftermath of the *Mahan* case, Kentucky sent a high-level delegation to Ohio to lobby the state legislature for the enactment of an Ohio fugitive slave act. Kentucky realized that it could not close its porous borders by trying to prosecute Ohioans who helped escaping slaves under its state law. The *Mahan* case told them that the only way to prosecute Ohioans successfully was to prove that the defendant was in Kentucky at the time he aided the slave. No right-thinking Ohioan would take the risk. They would simply wait for the fugitive to cross the river and then help him with virtual immunity from the Kentucky statute. Their only hope was to convince the Ohio General Assembly to pass an Ohio fugitive slave act, which would criminalize the act of helping a slave who had escaped from Kentucky.

Two commissioners arrived in Columbus in 1839 to present to Governor Wilson Shannon the formal request for the new law. The Kentuckians claimed that the passage of the new law was necessary to "preserve and perpetuate the union" and to guarantee "perfect comity and good feeling between neighboring states." Shannon acted with alacrity to the request. In his letter of transmittal to the General Assembly, the governor characterized those who helped fugitives within Ohio as "evil disposed persons."[78]

The governor and the legislature literally fell over themselves to accommodate the Kentuckians. The legislation was put on the fast track. Twenty-six Ohio senators, including Utter, voted for the law. Only two opposed it.[79]

It is easy to see why Utter and his colleagues voted for this law. They were presented with the "great state interest" of "preserving the union" and of guaranteeing good relations between two sister states. How could they choose the interests of a "handful of miserable fugitives" over that?

If we are to believe that Utter and Bird are one we must believe that something happened to change Utter's mind on the issue. Perhaps before the vote in 1839 he had not been presented with the great moral choice of freedom or state interest. Or, as Stowe more eloquently put it, he had not seen the "imploring human eye, the fail trembling hand."

In some respects, Utter/Bird may be seen as a metaphor for many Americans of the age who, when confronted by an escaping slave, had to make a choice between freedom and humanity or duty to obey the law. Utter must have chosen the former. As Stowe put it, "if our good Senator was a political sinner, he was in a fair way to expiate it by his night's penance."[80]

NOTES

1. *Clermont Courier*, December 3, 1842; *Cincinnati Daily Gazette*, December 6, 1842; the *Western Star*, May 9, 1845.
2. *Clermont Courier*, December 3, 1842.
3. Ibid.
4. Ibid.
5. The State of Kentucky sent a high-level delegation to Columbus to request that Ohio enact a fugitive slave act. This request followed the dismissal of charges of slave stealing brought against John Mahan of Sardinia, Ohio. The Mason County, Kentucky Circuit Court jury found that Kentucky did not have jurisdiction over Mahan because he had not been in Kentucky for twenty years before the crime allegedly took place. It was apparent to Kentucky that it did not have authority to stop Ohioans from helping slaves to escape once the fugitives crossed into Ohio. The bill quickly passed the Ohio General Assembly in 1839 with Dowty Utter's support. C. B. Galbreath, "Ohio's Fugitive Slave Law," *Ohio Archaeological and Historical Quarterly*, 34, no. 2 (April 1925): 216–240.
6. *Philanthropist*, December 21, 1842.
7. *Cincinnati Daily Gazette*, December 6, 1842; *Philanthropist*, November 19, 1842.
8. Morris was born in Pennsylvania on January 3, 1776. He immigrated to Ohio in 1795. Five years later he settled in Williamsburg, Ohio, the county seat of Clermont County, with his wife. After serving a stint in debtor's prison, Morris began the study of law, becoming the first resident of Clermont to be admitted to the bar. In 1806 he was elected to the Ohio General Assembly and became a staunch Jacksonian Democrat. The Ohio legislature selected Morris as its newest United States senator in 1833. Morris became involved in the antislavery movement when he presented antislavery petitions to the Senate, earning him the ire of Senator John C. Calhoun. He moved consistently toward the antislavery position and became the first person to articulate the "slave power" theory. The Ohio legislature, incensed with his antislavery rhetoric, chose Benjamin Tapp to replace him in 1838. Morris delivered a powerful antislavery valedictory speech declaring, "I conclude that the Negro will yet be free." In August 1843 the Liberty Party chose Morris to be its vice-presidential candidate. Morris died in his Bethel home on December 7, 1844. Gary L. Knepp, *Nine who made a Difference* (Batavia, Ohio: Cragburn, 2000) 18–21.
9. *Clermont Courier*, December 3, 1842; *Western Star*, May 5, 1845.
10. Ibid.
11. T. Morris to *Philanthropist*, November 19, 1842. A search of the probate court records was conducted. However, no manumission papers were found.
12. Paul Finkelman, *Slavery and the Founders: Race and Liberty in the age of Jefferson* (Armonk, N.Y.: M. E. Sharpe, 1996) 99.
13. Ohio's constitutional convention was convened on November 1, 1802, at Chillicothe. The delegates were closely divided over the issue of slavery. Democrats of

eastern Ohio, largely emigrants from Virginia, favored legalization while those from western Ohio opposed. Clermont's delegates, Philip Gatch and James Sargent, opposed. Despite President Jefferson's letter urging legalization, the measure failed by one vote. Donald J. Ratcliffe, *Party Spirit in a Frontier Republic: Democratic Politics in Ohio 1793–1821* (Columbus: Ohio State University, 1998) 70–71; Ohio Constitution of 1802, art. 8, sec. 2.

14. This statement has been erroneously reported as a ruling from the Ohio Supreme Court. It is, however, an opinion of the Appeals Court on a Warren County Court of Common Pleas case known as *State v. Farr*. The case, as reported by the *Western Star*, arose from a confrontation in November of 1839 near the village of Springborough. Bennet Rains, his family, and an unspecified number of blacks were traveling from Virginia to Missouri. They had settled in for the night when as many as eighteen people including Farr and a Dr. Brooke, approached the campsite with the intention of rescuing the blacks. The defendants, some of whom were armed, went into the tent, pulling out several of the tent stakes. Another defendant took a black child from the arms of one of the Rains' family.

The defendant's were acquitted of violating the Fugitive Slave Act because the prosecution failed to prove that the blacks were slaves. Fourteen of the defendants were convicted of criminal riot for collapsing the tent and taking the child.

It was under these circumstances that Judges Hitchcock and Lane, reversed the common pleas decision and issued their statement regarding the freedom of slaves brought into the state of Ohio by their masters.

The *Western Star* framed the statement properly when it wrote, "The much vexed question, therefore, whether the owners of slaves in Virginia, or other slave state, can carry them through Ohio, in removing them to another slave state has been settled in the negative, so far as the opinion of two of the Supreme Judges can settle any point." *Cincinnati Daily Gazette*, May 19 & June 1, 1841; *Western Star*, May 14, May 28, and June 1, 1841.

15. Rockey & Bancroft, *Clermont County, Ohio*, 111; Josiah Morrow, *History of Brown County, Ohio* . . . (Chicago: W. H. Beers & Co., 1883) 315.

16. *Western Star*, May 9, 1845.

17. Rockey and Bancroft, *Clermont County, Ohio*, 135; Ralph Pearson, *A History of the Fee Family*, (1969) 331, 354–356. Oliver Perry Spencer Fee of Felicity was described as the "High Priest" of the Felicity network. An antislavery Democrat, Fee was a merchant who publicly castigated the abolitionists, thereby gaining the trust of slaveholders. He was often consulted by slave catchers. Fee directed them away from the fugitives. Arthur Fee, also of Felicity, harbored fugitives in the fruit cellar of his home. Fletcher Day, "Its Tracks were Crowded," *The Felicity Times*, July 6, 1893; Mary Kate Liming, interview, July 17, 2001.

18. Rockey and Bancroft, *Clermont County, Ohio*, 308A, 298; Louise Abbott to Wilbur Siebert, November 27, 1915, Wilbur Siebert Papers, Ohio Historical Society, Columbus, Ohio.

19. Rockey and Bancroft, *Clermont County, Ohio*, 441; W. P. Fishback to Wilbur Siebert, May 23, 1892, Siebert Papers; *Clermont Courier*, October 22, 1879.

20. *Western Star*, May 2, 1845.

21. *Clermont Courier*, December 3, 1842.

22. Thomas Morris to the *Philanthropist*, November 19, 1842; Pearson, *Fee Family*, 353.

23. Robert Fee to Vincent Wigglesworth as printed in the *Philanthropist*, April 12, 1843.

24. This figure sounds quite low and may have been a transcription error.

25. Robert Corwin to *Philanthropist*, April 12, 1843.

26. *The Western Star*, May 9, 1845.

27. Ohio Governor's General Record, vol. 6, 1841–1856, February 10, 1845, and April 12, 1845, Ohio Historical Society, Columbus, Ohio.

28. *St. Louis Republican*, April 8, 1845.

29. Ibid.; Rockey and Bancroft, *Clermont County, Ohio*, 135; Henry Howe, *Historical Collections of Ohio* (Cincinnati: C. J. Krehbiel & Co. printer,1904) 1:419–420.

30. *St. Louis Republican*, April 8, 1845. A search for the Wigglesworths was conducted. A local historian/genealogist was hired to research local records. Nothing was found. Slave sale records and records of the Freedman's Bureau were also examined with the same result.

31. *Western Star*, May 9, 1845.

32. Rockey & Bancroft, *Clermont County, Ohio*, 135; Howe, *Historical Collections of Ohio*, 1:419–420.

33. "Cincinnati Columbian," *Ripley Bee*, November 12, 1853; *Commonwealth v. Robert Fee*, Pendleton County, Kentucky Circuit Court. Ky. Dept. of Library & Archives, Frankfort, Ky.

34. *Ripley Bee*, November 26, 1853; 1850 Pendleton County, Kentucky Slave Schedule.

35. *Ripley Bee*, November 26, 1853.

36. Ibid.

37. Ibid.; Robert Fee was first licensed to operate the ferry at Moscow in 1845 for a yearly fee of $2.50. He was authorized to charge $0.12 per person, $0.25 for a man and a horse, and $1.00 for a wagon and a horse. Clermont County, Ohio, Common Pleas Court, Minutes Book, 1842–1845 Batavia, Ohio, 188–89.

38. *Ripley Bee*, November 26, 1853.

39. Commonwealth v. Robert Fee

40. Ohio Governor's Record, vol. 6, 1841–1856, November 11, 1853, 237, Ohio Historical Society, Columbus, Ohio.

41. *Ripley Bee*, November 26, 1853.

42. The court specifically found that it could not prosecute Mahan because he had not been in the state during the commission of the "crime." Mahan maintained that he did nothing to aid the fugitive to escape from the state. *Commonwealth v. John B. Mahan*, Mason County, Kentucky, Circuit Court, November 12, 1838, Ky. Department of Library & Archives.

43. Pendleton County, Kentucky Circuit Court Order Books, June 5, 1855, 534, Kentucky Department of Library & Archives.

44. Barker's will was probated on September 4, 1854. No slaves appeared in the inventory. Pendleton County, Kentucky, Will Book, 1841–1871; Janet K. Pease, comp., "Pendleton County Wills 1799–1871," *Kentucky Court Records: Grant-Harrison-Pendleton* (Williamstown, Ky.: Grant County Historical Society, 1986) (Also found as *Abstracted Court Records*, 3:242.

45. *Clermont Courier*, October 22, 1879.

46. The research upon which this article is based was generated by the Clermont County, Ohio, Underground Railroad Research Project sponsored by the Clermont County Convention and Visitors Bureau. The author chaired the project. The Clermont County, Ohio Freedom Trail, consisting of thirty Clermont County sites associated with the Underground Railroad and the abolitionist movement, is an outgrowth of that project. Nineteen sites have been accepted into the National Park Service National Underground Railroad Network to Freedom Program, the most in the country. Robert Fee's home and burial site, the Old Cavalry Methodist Church, and the *Philanthropist* office site are all designated sites. The author's guided tour and public education program are accredited by the National Park Service. Copies of the Clermont County, Ohio, Freedom Trail self-guided driving tour may be obtained by contacting the Convention and Visitors Bureau at 1-800-796-4282.

47. Kathy Bare (owner of Fee Villa) interview, March 3, 1999; Richard Crawford, photo caption, *Clermont County Bicentennial 1800–2000*, 68.

48. Mary Liming interview, February 17, 2000. *Felicity Times*, July 6, 1893; Clermont County, Ohio, Tax Duplicates 1832; Rockey & Bancroft, *Clermont County, Ohio,* 373.

49. Rockey & Bancroft, *Clermont County, Ohio,* 313.

50. Williams, *History of Clermont and Brown Counties,* 2:106–07; Clermont County Court of Common Pleas Record Books, 1825.

51. Randy McNutt, "Moscow Future Reawakens Past," *Cincinnati Enquirer,* spring 1976. The article was found reproduced without a date attached. Mr. McNutt stated that the article was published in the spring of 1976, though the original has been destroyed. Randy McNutt interview, June 26,2001.

52. Kathy Bare interview, March 3, 1999.

53. Ibid; Richard Crawford interview, August 8, 2000.

54. Jerry Gore interview, August 8, 2000.

55. Jeannine Kreinbrink interview, May 25, 2001.

56. Carl N. Thompson, comp., *Historical Collections of Brown County* (Piqua, Ohio: Printed by Hammer Graphics, 1969) 284; Letter of Isaac Beck.

57. Affidavit of Samuel T. Hauser, September 30, 1850., *Owen T. Sharp, et al. v. Jennetta Sharp*, Pendleton County, Kentucky, Circuit Court, 126, Kentucky Department of Library Archives, Frankfort, Kentucky.

58. *Sharp v. Sharp.*

59. Affidavits of Reuben McCarty and Wilson Sharp, September 23, 1850; *Sharp v. Sharp.*

60. Affidavit of Samuel T. Hauser, September 23, 1850; *Sharp v. Sharp.*

61. Opinion of William C. Naylor, October 12, 1850; *Sharp v. Sharp.*

62. 1850 Pendleton County, Kentucky, Slave Schedule, transcribed by Sherida Daugherty, http://www.rootsweb.com/kypendle/black1850slave.htm.

63. Rockey & Bancroft, *Clermont County, Ohio*, 191.

64. Ibid, 192.

65. Ibid.

66. *Clermont Courier*, January 26, 1839; Galbreath, "Ohio's Fugitive Slave Act," 216.

67. Rockey & Bancroft, *Clermont County, Ohio*, 193.

68. Fletcher Day, "Its Tracks were Clouded," *Felicity Times*, July 6, 1893. J. N. Altman of Felicity wrote to Wilbur Siebert stating that Fletcher Day's father, friends, and other relatives "were connected with the enterprise" and "knows more of the subject than any other man in Southern Ohio"; J. N. Altman to Wilbur Siebert, August 31, 1894, Siebert Papers.

69. Mary Harrison Games, *The Underground Railroad in Ohio* (Wilmington, Ohio: 1937) 70.

70. Harriet Beecher Stowe, *Uncle Tom's Cabin* (New York: Bantam Books, 1981) 91.

71. Ibid.

72. Ibid.

73. Ibid., 92.

74. Ibid.

75. Ibid., 93.

76. Ibid.

77. Ibid., 102.

78. Ohio Documents of the Thirty-seventh General Assembly, vol. 4, pt. 2, 1838–39, 1.

79. C. B. Galbreath, "Ohio's Fugitive Slave Act," 216-240-219.

80. Stowe, *Uncle Tom's Cabin*, 103.

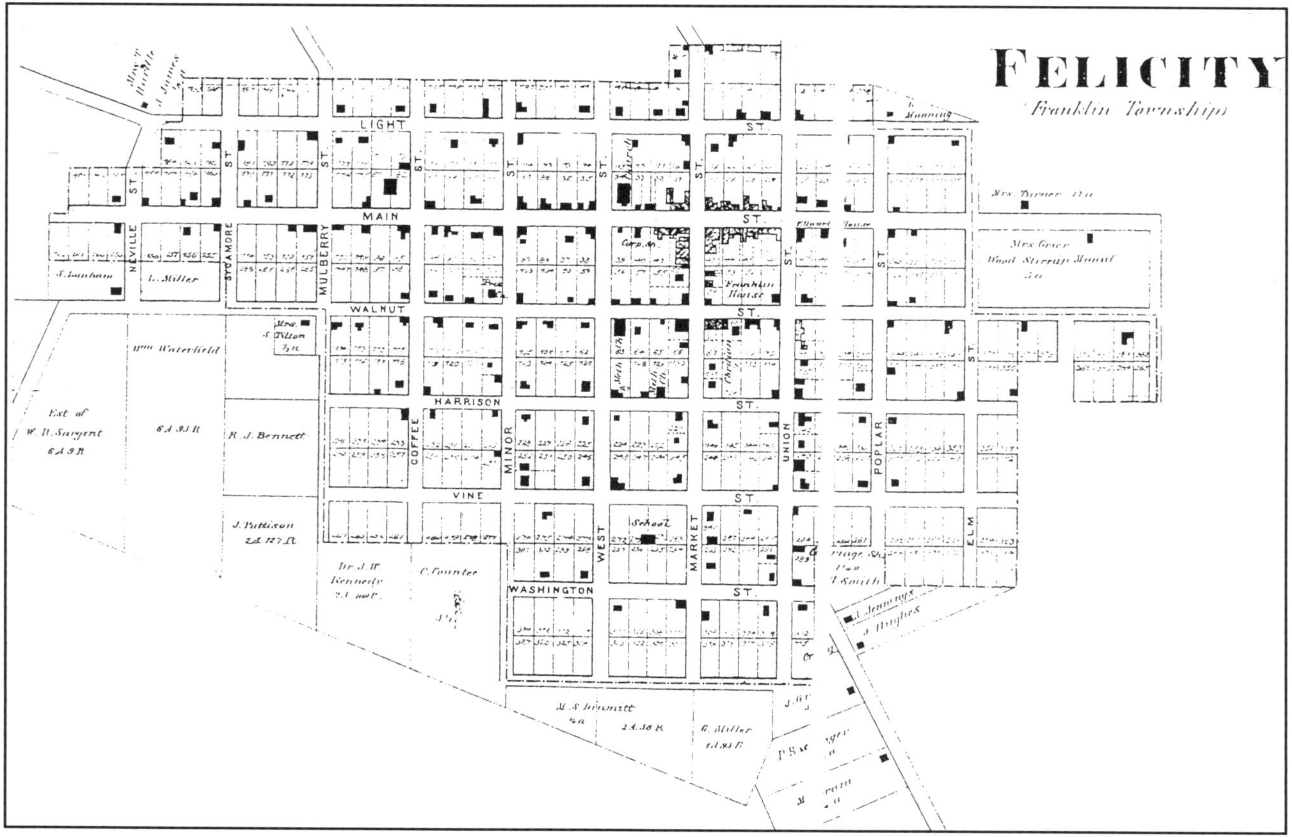

Fig. 9.1. Felicity, Ohio, a bustling agricultural and manufacturing center, was a very tolerant community.

CHAPTER 9

Felicity and Franklin Township

FOR MANY FUGITIVES RIDING Clermont's Underground Railroad, Felicity was their first stop. The pleasant village, founded in 1817 by William Fee and Peter Hastings, is located four miles north of the Ohio River on the tablelands of southern Ohio. By the mid years of the nineteenth century, Felicity was the second most populous village in Clermont County, surpassed by only New Richmond.[1] One enthusiast painted the following endearing portrait of the village in 1857:

Our town from the very first of its existence has been growing in wealth and population till it now contains 1200 to 1500 inhabitants. We have 7 Dry Good stores, 3 drug stores, 4 groceries, several clothing stores and tailoring establishments, five shoe shops, one tin shop, two hat stores, four carriage and wagon stores, one saddle shop, five blacksmith shops, 3 silversmith shops, two meat establishments, one bakery & confectionary. The Messers. Fallen & Fee have a large Pork House, where several thousand Hogs are eventually cut and packaged; There are five physicians and 2 or 3 rx's. There are four full grown lawyers, and 2 or 3 more in the bud; perhaps by the opening of next spring their Judicial leaves will begin to unfold . . .

There are many buildings, both business and private dwellings, a large proportion of which have a fresh and a new appearance, and presents a pleasing aspect to the eye of the passing traveller.

As . . . however, for want of roads, we have the underground office here, and it is not every town that can obtain intelligence sooner from the most distant parts without the use of lightening . . .

. . . The health of our inhabitants is almost proverbial. Desirable thus as a place of residence on the scope of health, the attraction is equally and decidedly on account of the beauty of the location. . . . We venture to say that a more enchanting inland town cannot be found in the West, surrounding it a fine fertile and well cultivated section of the country as Ohio can boast.[2]

The Presbyterians and the Methodists dominated the religious landscape in Felicity. The Felicity Presbyterian Church was organized as the Smyrna Presbyterian Church in 1808; the congregation left the log meetinghouse in 1828 and moved to the schoolhouse in Felicity. Rev. John Rankin of Ripley was pastor of the church for one year. His brother Alexander replaced him. A social activist, Alexander was involved in both the temperance and abolitionist movements. Alexander remained in Felicity for eight years before accepting a position in Fort Wayne, Indiana.[3]

In 1847 the Felicity Presbyterian Church fractured into two segments: Old School and New School. While there were other doctrinal issues, the primary reason for the split in the Presbyterian Church was slavery, with the New Schoolers actively opposing the institution. The New Schoolers built a new church building in 1854; soon after, the Old School church sued for possession of the new building. The Old Schoolers won the legal battle in the Clermont County Court of Common Pleas. John Rankin wrote a letter on behalf of the losers, whom he called Free Presbyterians. He claimed that the antislavery congregation was "robbed of its house" by a "few villains of the neighborhood." He closed the letter by asking for money to help his dispossessed former parishioners.[4]

The Methodists and the Wesleyans

The first Methodist class in Franklin Township was organized in 1805. It met in a large, two-story log building located one mile west of Felicity and was known as the Old Hopewell Church. In its day the church hosted many of the early Methodist leaders, including Bishop Asbury. Twenty years later, the Felicity Methodist Church was founded. Among its members were the Fee and Hasting families. As with many other Methodist churches of the day, the Felicity church was torn apart by the slavery issue.[5]

In 1847 nine persons, mostly Methodists, formed the Felicity Wesleyan Church. It essentially became an antislavery version of the Methodist Church. Despite this it was "looked upon as a degraded portion of the community."[6] A small, white brick church building was erected at the corner of Market and Walnut streets in 1848.[7]

One of the earliest members of the breakaway church was Dr. Matthew Gibson. Dr. Gibson came to Felicity with his two brothers from

Fig. 9.2. *Dr. Matthew Gibson, a member of the Felecity Wesleyan Church and an Underground Railroad conductor.*

Fig. 9.3. *The burial marker of Nelson Gibson, brother of Dr. Gibson and Underground Railroad conductor, is located at the Tate Township Cemetery in Bethel, Ohio.*

Tennessee. A graduate of Tusculum College in Grenville, Tennessee, he received a medical degree from the same institution one year later. Dr. Gibson served as president of Hiawassie College in Madisonville, Tennessee, for three years. He was always highly regarded for his scientific knowledge and his proficiency in making medical instruments and measuring devices. He even crafted a telescope that he used in Felicity. He developed a widespread reputation for using electricity as a medical treatment and for addressing "female complaints."[8]

Dr. Gibson and his brothers left Tennessee specifically because of their antislavery sentiment. The brothers felt that "the proslavery character of that church," (Methodist South) did not suit them, "and the antislavery character of the Church North, they thought no better." As a result, they left the Methodists to unite with the Wesleyans in 1848.[9]

A conversation between Rev. Wesley Rowe and Mifflin Harker about slavery at Robert Chalfant's store sparked a community-wide debate that dramatically altered Felicity's religious landscape. The conversation took place in front of others and became quite heated.

A short time afterward Harker wrote a letter to the *True Wesleyan* newspaper relating his version of the conversation. According to Harker, an unnamed Methodist minister admitted that under certain circumstances he would own slaves as an act of Christian benevolence. He stated that he would hold those slaves who were "too young or too old, to take care of themselves," until his death at which time he would free them. "How strange," Harker exclaimed, "that men would perceive that the only proper way to exercise benevolence towards those unable to supply their own wants, should be to hold them by the same tenure they hold their horses and cattle!"[10]

Harker unleashed another salvo in the early fall of 1849. This time he attacked churches that did not sufficiently condemn slavery. He wrote the following:

I know that those Churches who endorse slavery by endorsing the character of the slave holders; give to slavery the strongest support. This they do when they admit slave holders to Church Fellowship. Now, to support such churches is to support slavery. Can those persons whose minds are enlightened by antislavery truth, love their neighbor as themselves while they help to bind their neighbor, in the character of a bleeding slave, in the galling chains of slavery?[11]

Rowe responded one week later. He identified himself as the Methodist minister alluded to in Harker's first letter. He contended that

Harker "grossly misrepresented" his statements. He further alleged that Harker asked him a very specific question: "Could a man under any circumstances hold slaves and be a Christian?" He responded in the following way:

Suppose I lived in Kentucky, or some slave state, where the laws forbid emancipation without giving security for the maintenance of the slaves emancipated, and by inheritance or some other act of law, slaves are cast upon me—some too young, and others too old to support themselves, I believe I might sustain the relation of master towards them for their own benefit, to educate the young and to support the aged; it would be my duty to make for provision for their emancipation in case of my death.[12]

He also asserted that he voted for a rule denying membership in the Methodist Church to anyone who held slaves. Accompanying his rebuttal were "certificates" from bystanders attesting to the accuracy of his version of the conversation.[13]

Rowe and Harker traded barbs through February of 1850. Rowe presented additional certificates of accuracy. Harker spoke the last word in the personal duel when he questioned the recollections and veracity of Rowe's supporters. The people of Felicity took all of this very seriously. "Great interest has been manifested, by professors of all denominations, and the citizen in general," wrote one observer about the weekly debate carried out in the pages of the *True Wesleyan*. To answer these and other puzzling questions regarding slavery, the community decided to schedule a debate at the Free Presbyterian Church.[14]

The debate focused on three questions: Should churches be opened for the discussion of slavery? Should ministers preach against it? And should slaveholding be made a test of Christian fellowship? The three weekly discussions were well attended. "The distant muttering, and pealing thunders of God's wrath upon the oppressor, and his abettors have been sounded, echoed, and reverberated. Through its spacious halls, from time to time, with a degree of firmness, and eloquence, that would have added laurels to the fame of Cicero."[15] The proslavers or those abettors seemed, according to the writer, to have conceded the high ground by arguing not the morality of slavery, but the dire consequences of abolishing it. The writer continued,

While those of the negative side, have been attempted from the very 'mountains brow' of sublimity, to portray in lurid colors, the direful and sanguinary effects, that must result, from such base and unnatural proceedings, as would stand up in judgment against it, condemn, and unchristianize the majority of

Christiandom, and thereby rob heaven of earth's most noble tenants.[16]

The results of the debate, according to another observer, "led many members of the proslavery churches to give serious reflection."[17] This was particularly true in the Methodist Church where, after "mature reflection," many "concluded that the M. E. Church cherished and nourished this abomination."[18]

Forty-nine members of the church, led by businessman Joseph Parrish, bolted and joined the fledgling Wesleyan Church. The Parrish defection was important for several reasons. At its simplest, forty-nine new members, must have been an incredible boost to the new church. Many of the defectors were prominent citizens and long-time Methodist church leaders. They brought social respectability to the Wesleyans.[19]

Momentum was clearly with the Wesleyans. In just under six months following the debate, the church grew from 20 members to 112. A Sabbath School was established and a Female Benevolent Society was organized. Its primary purpose was to aid fugitive families in Canada.[20]

The church continued to grow throughout the 1850s. John O'Neill

Fig. 9.4. *The home of Joseph Parrish, located at Main Street in Felicity, Ohio. Parrish was an important supporter of the Felicity Wesleyan Church and a business associate of Jesse Grant— Ulysses Grant's father.*

reported in 1854: "Sixty-four have been added to the church. Some from the M. E. Church. Some from the Christian Church, some from the Baptist Church, but most from the world."[21] O'Neill predicted that the congregation would soon outgrow its small building. He continued,

We have a church in this place of two hundred good and true. We shall soon have to pull down our comfortable house of worship, and build up larger to accommodate the eager listeners that attend our ministry. And so we go down with a rush.[22]

Joseph Parrish took charge of the construction project which began in the spring of 1856. The large brick building with a one-hundred-foot steeple was adorned with a five-hundred-dollar clock, the total cost of the new church topped nine thousand dollars.[23] The church became a node of the Felicity Underground Railroad network. Among its members who were active in the Underground Railroad were Nelson and Matthew Gibson, Silas Chase, and James Parrish. Undoubtedly, there were others among its two-hundred-member congregation who were involved in the enterprise.[24]

Felicity was perfectly situated for the Underground Railroad. It was just four miles from the Ohio River and sat astride the Bull Skin Trace, the main south-to-north escape route through the county. There can be little doubt that fugitives passed through the village well before whites became active in the Underground Railroad. There are, however, no written accounts of Underground Railroad activity in Felicity before the 1850s.

The winter of 1856 was a very busy time for the Underground Railroad in Felicity. The winter was extremely cold and of long duration. The Ohio River froze over for nearly ten weeks. "During this freeze," wrote John O'Neill, "perhaps hundreds of slaves have made their escape. About one year's continual weather as we have had and Kentucky would be depopulated of its slaves. One poor fellow was taken with his feet and legs badly frozen."[25]

Another resident, new to Felicity, wrote about the weather and crops on June 30, 1858. It was quite warm—ninety-two degrees—and rainy. The corn crop did not look promising because of the heavy rains. He was disappointed that the Underground Railroad was quite slow recently, but had been very busy in the past. Perhaps this was because there were fewer slaves in Kentucky to escape, he thought. The writer

Fig. 9.5. *The Felicity Wesleyan Church, located at 305 Main Street in Felicity, Ohio, was a strongly abolitionist church with Underground Railroad connections.*

likened the enterprise to a railroad constructed to haul off timber.

When the timber is all cut off, the road must sink into disuse, and grass will grow upon its tracks, and the rails will get rusty. As the only articles transported upon the Underground Railroad come from Kentucky over the river, we are dependent on them for business, which has failed. There is no more of the article along the River on the border, all having been removed, and as goods from the interior find other roots, our business is ruined here.[26]

Fletcher Day, editor of the *Felicity Times*, wrote that the village was "both famous and infamous as an abolitionist town." It was both blessed by the enslaved and "accursed, anathematized, and threatened by slave owners." He claimed that slaves knew that if they could make it to Felicity they were safe and "ready to be ticketed and transferred by comparatively easy stages to Canadian soil."

The operations did not abate during the Civil War, but actually became bolder. Male fugitives were often enlisted in the army and sent back South. Activity picked up after the Emancipation Proclamation. "They were all sizes kinds and colors," wrote Day, "from the strong limbed and muscled field hand, to the good old 'aunty' and 'mammy.'"[27]

Fig. 9.6. *Fletcher Day was the editor of the* Felicity Times *newspaper and wrote about Felicity's involvement in the Underground Railroad, reportedly based upon his family's personal experiences.*

Felicity's Black Community and the Underground Railroad

As with other communities in Clermont County, Felicity witnessed a tremendous growth in its black population during the 1850s. In all of Franklin Township there were but twenty-one black residents in 1850. This number more than tripled by 1860 to sixty-eight, fifty-nine of whom lived in the Village of Felicity.[28]

By 1860 Felicity and Franklin Township had the second-largest black population in the county. The black population in the Felicity area was far less diverse than that of the New Richmond area. Thirty-five people listed their state of origin as Kentucky, twenty as Ohio, eight as Virginia, and the rest scattered among five other states. Eighty percent of those listing Ohio as their state of origin were minors, indicating a recent move to the state. Standing in stark contrast to the New Richmond area was the ratio between black and mulattoes. Just two of the sixty-eight were described as mulattoes.

Seven of the sixteen households enumerated owned real estate, the highest valued at four hundred dollars. Three were farmers, nine earned their living as farm or day laborers; there were several servants, washer women, three domestics, a blacksmith, and one barber.[29]

The black community was engaged in developing its own institutions. The Felicity African Methodist Church was formed in 1859. Its early members included Perry Payne, Jacob Greason, and Benjamin Logan. A branch of the Union Association for the Advancement of the Colored Men of New Richmond was established in 1864. At some point a women's auxiliary was also formed.[30]

As with New Richmond, it appears that Felicity was a congenial, if not as prosperous, area for blacks to live. Arnold Gragston, a Mason County, Kentucky, conductor, claimed that twenty-one families he helped to freedom settled in Felicity. From his statements it is difficult to determine whether he led the families to Felicity directly or whether they settled there on their own. Since Mason County does not lie directly across the Ohio River from Felicity, it is more likely that he led them to Brown County and they made their way to Felicity.[31]

John "Highball" Watson was a fugitive who made his home in Felicity. He was originally from Norfolk, Virginia, but had been sold to the Slack family of Mason County. Watson came to Clermont County late in his life and was, therefore, known as a "has been,"—too old to be of any use to his master. Watson did, for a number of years, earn a living doing odd jobs around the village. He made many friends before dying at age 108 while living as a resident of the infirmary in Clermont County.[32]

Fig. 9.7. *John "Highball" Watson.*

Unlike many communities in which the Underground Railroad activities of the black community are largely unknown, those in Felicity can be documented. One is struck by the boldness and assertiveness of their activities, both in assisting fugitives and in resisting slave hunters. This may be seen as a testament to their mettle, but also to the character of the village's whites who supported, or at least tolerated, their activities.

Peter Stokes

The most complete narrative of a fugitive slave passing through Clermont County was that of Peter Stokes. Wilbur Siebert interviewed Peter Stokes on August 3, 1895, in Amherstburg, Canada, where Stokes had lived since his escape. The following is an excerpt from that interview:

I was born in Bracken County, Kentucky, in 1837, the 14th of October. I was born into the Everin family and when Joseph Taylor married into the family two of us was given to him and I stayed with him till I was 21. I came to this country in '52. [This is probably a transcription error as Stokes indicated he was born in 1837 and stayed with the Taylors until he was 21. This would put the date of his escape at 1858.] The idea of bein' under bondage and misusage caused me to leave him. We lived 35 miles above Cincinnati on the Ohio River on the Kentucky side. We got information from friends—one a man, Will Sleets, formerly of Kentucky, and when we started we were anxious to get to his place. Ten of us—2 sisters and 6 children—me and my brother—that makes 10, all from the same man in the fall of the year.

On Sunday night we started across the River in 2 small boats and turned 'em both adrift, and then set out for Felicity, where Sleets lived. When we got close there we left the women, and went to town to see how things were. We found the Kentuckians had surrounded the place and we couldn't get there. They weren't really in pursuit of us, but of a party that had left Augusta, 8 miles above where we lived. Our friends came out to meet us, and then we went right to a big barn on the bank of the Ohio River (the barn was called Canada) in sight of home, and stayed there two weeks then we moved to a little village called Clover, Ohio. Mrs. Eliza Woods—a sister of Taylor's wife—was an abolitionist and took care us there.[33]

The family took an unusual path from there. They went deep into eastern Ohio to Cadiz in Harrison County. There they stayed with a black man named Brown who made them pay for their passage by cutting corn. After staying with Brown for ten days, they were put in a baggage car on a train bound for Cleveland. Remarkably, Taylor, their owner, was on the same train looking for them. The baggage car was uncoupled from the train and taken into the station, enabling them to escape from Taylor. They boarded the *Morning Star*, which took them across Lake Erie to Detroit, crossing over to Windsor and freedom. Their journey took them twenty-four days.[34]

According to the Taylor family tradition, Stokes's master, Joe Taylor, owned ten slaves who escaped a short time before the Civil War. The Taylors believed that they treated their slaves well, but threatened to "sell them down the river" when they got lazy or wouldn't work.[35]

Fig. 9.8. *The home of Joe Taylor and family.*

Peter Stokes remembered things differently: "Our old master used to take us out on Saturday afternoons and whip us to keep us in training."[36]

The Taylors described the escape of the Stokes family in this way:

They got the money to escape from the woman slave who had saved a few cents now and then under a tree root. They left at night in a boat and found sympathizers in Ohio who hid them. When it was found they had left, two members of the family started out to find them. They came to a house and sought lodging for the night. When the owner of the house learned their mission, he went to the barn where he had some runaway slaves he was sheltering and told them. Some of the slaves slipped out to check their horses and recognized them as the Taylor horses; so they, with the help of the house owner escaped again.[37]

Stokes referred to his friend, Will Sleet, who took them along the road through Felicity. Sleet was a thirty-seven-year-old blacksmith at the time of the escape. He was originally from Kentucky, but had lived in Ohio for at least ten years. Sleet purchased lot no. 128 on Harrison Avenue from the Village of Felicity in 1858 for fifteen dollars, where he lived with his wife, Anna, and their three children. Fletcher Day reported that he was a prominent black operative, though we have no other direct evidence of his Underground Railroad activities.[38]

Resistance

Dr. Luther Lee, pastor of the Felicity Wesleyan Church, reported in October 1858 that there had been little to excite the "sequestered community" of Felicity since the antislavery Fourth of July.[39] On that day the Wesleyan Church "shook its longue tongue and sent forth its deep mellow peals to be heard for six miles," presumably even to slaveholding Kentucky four miles away.[40] Lee complained that the more conservative members of the community spoke glowingly of the freedoms and liberties of the republic, but overlooked millions that were still enslaved. He had the temerity to remind the community that the Bible could not be "The Palladium of Liberty" if it did not also apply to the slave. The response was immediate as people quickly left the hall. "Had they supposed," wrote Lee, "my tongue a friction match, and the air explosive gas they need not have been more excited."[41]

The sequestered community suddenly became a very exciting place one October night in 1858. A rumor swept the town that two slaves had come to the village one morning. They rested, were fed, and left the same evening. It was expected that slave hunters would be fast on their trail. This excited the black community, who were put on high alert.

Lee and his wife took a walk one evening soon thereafter and, on their return, noticed "colored citizens" standing on several street corners. The Lees retired for the evening. In the morning the town was abuzz about the events of the evening before. Lee inquired of several people and was able to put together the details.

At about 9:00 p.m., three Kentuckians on horseback came to the village in pursuit of the two fugitives who had recently been harbored the day before. Within a short time of their appearance, an unnamed "colored citizen" demanded to know what the Kentuckians were doing there. An evasive reply was given.

The resident replied, "I know what you are here after—You are hunting Negroes. You know me sir, You remember I whipped you once, and I advise you that you had better leave immediately."

A few words were exchanged between the two when the clock on the Wesleyan Church struck ten. The black man turned to his comrades and shouted to the slave hunters, "It is ten o'clock and rascals should all be home, drive them off!" Whereupon his forty supporters threw a veritable storm of rocks and bricks at the whites. The Kentuckians quickly retreated and rode out of town empty-handed.[42]

This is a remarkable story. It explodes the stereotype of the meek, unassertive antebellum free Northern black. Not only did these residents verbally confront the whites, but they physically assaulted them, driving them out of town. And there did not seem to be any repercussions from the white residents of the town. The black residents must have been confident of their position or they would not have taken the risks. The story speaks well of the status of race relations in Felicity.

It is unfortunate, but not unusual, that the names of black citizens involved in the incident described by Lee were not mentioned. Some of the citizens could have been Will Sleet, Benjamin Logan, Jefferson Alexander, and Isaac Rumsey, who are all mentioned by Fletcher Day as prominent members of the black community active in the Underground Railroad.[43]

Could the incident described by Lee be the same described by Peter Stokes? Both occurred in October of 1858. Stokes's passage through Felicity was delayed because the village was surrounded by slave hunters looking for other fugitives. The incident reported by Lee was caused by two slaves who had been sheltered in the village. The timing and the basic details are similar. It is intriguing to speculate about whether they are the same. But as a practical matter, we probably will never know for sure.

Julett Miles

Robert Fee was not the only Clermont County resident to have been indicted for slave stealing. Julett Miles, a former slave, was the other. Her story, more than any other, puts a human face on the cruelty of slavery.

Julett originally lived in Bracken County, Kentucky, just across the Ohio River from Clermont County. She was owned by John Fee, the father of the well-known Presbyterian abolitionist minister, John Gregg Fee. Fee's father, who owned thirteen slaves, was considered to be a large slaveowner for that portion of the South. It is not clear the exact nature of Reverend Fee's relationship with Julett, but it must have been close. John asked his father to free Julett. His father refused. He then asked to buy her freedom. His father agreed to do so, but only at the fair market price. John did not have that kind of money readily available. So he took ownership of a parcel of land his father owned, as an advance against his inheritance. John sold the property, bought Julett, and promptly freed her. He also tried to buy her husband from his father, but his father rejected the offer.[44]

Mr. Fee told Julett to leave his farm because "I do not intend to have a free nigger on my farm." Further, he threatened to sell her, even though he no longer owned her, if she did not leave.[45] Julett was faced with a major problem. Since she no longer had an owner or a white who would sponsor her, she had to, pursuant to Kentucky law, post a five-hundred-dollar bond to ensure "her good behavior." If a free black could not post the bond, she had to move from the state. Since Julett did not have the money for the bond, she and three of her free children moved to Felicity.[46]

Felicity was a logical choice for Julett. It was only four miles from Kentucky, making it convenient for her to visit her family. The village had a sizeable black community. And there were several members of the Fee family living there.

John's brother lived in Louisiana; he planned to return to Kentucky to sell several of Julett's children and grandchildren. After learning of this plan, Julett decided to return to Bracken County to lead her family to freedom in Ohio. One night she gathered her two sons, three daughters, and four grandchildren together and made a break for the river. They were captured at dawn on the bank of the Ohio River as they were about to cross over.

John was on a speaking tour when this happened. When he stopped in Cincinnati to speak with Levi Coffin, Coffin told him about Julett's capture. John's wife went to the jail to speak with Julett. The jailer led Mrs. Fee to a room below Julett's cell and permitted the two women to speak through a crack in the floor. Julett's family was housed in the same jail, although Mrs. Fee could not talk to them, she heard Julett's family crying.

Meanwhile, John tried to arrange bail through the help of a relative,

John Gregg. Gregg agreed to post the bond. Just as he was about to do so, an attorney from an adjoining county arrived with a writ ordering Julett's removal to that county to stand trial for slave stealing. The indictment charged her with stealing her own children and grandchildren. Apparently, her family resided in that unnamed county.[47] Julett was tried and convicted for "enticing a slave." She was sentenced to three years in the state penitentiary in Frankfort, Kentucky, and her children and grandchildren were sold to a slave trader and never heard from again.[48]

Fee and his wife, Matilda, went to Frankfort to visit with Julett. They found that she was working at the jailer's daughter's home. The Fees brought the prisoner a pair of glasses and a large print New Testament. They talked about Julett's nine children. It was the last time they saw her; she died in prison of "stomach inflamation" on August 29, 1859, at age forty-eight.[49]

White Conductors

Oliver Perry Spencer Fee, usually referred to as Perry, was the "High Priest" of the Felicity network. He was described as "intelligent, active and essentially alert." His operation was characterized as "planned, executed" showing him to be "preeminently shrewd."[50] The grandson of William Fee, the founder of Felicity, Perry was born in 1823 and lived most of his life in Felicity. He married Priscilla Sargent, of another prominent abolitionist family, in 1845.[51] Fee was engaged in the mercantile business and owned a grocery/dry goods store

Fig. 9.9. *Oliver Perry Spencer Fee.*

in Felicity. He was civic-minded, holding municipal and school board offices. He was also active in the Masons.[52]

Fig. 9.10. *Oliver Perry Spencer Fee's general store in Felicity, Ohio. He gave fugitives food and clothing from the store before sending them on to Bethel. It is located at 208 Main Street in Felicity, Ohio.*

Politically, Fee was another of the Clermont County antislavery Democrats. In 1860 he was chosen to be a delegate for Stephen Douglas at the National Democratic Convention in Charleston, South Carolina. He was the last Ohio delegate left on the floor as the National Democratic Party was splitting apart. He continued to support Douglas at the Northern Democratic Convention in Baltimore.[53]

Fig. 9.11. *The burial marker of O.P.S. Fee located in Franklin Township Cemetery in Felicity, Ohio.*

Perry publicly denounced abolitionists in order to gain the confidence of slave hunters. As a result, he was the first person that they came to for help in catching the runaways. Fee knew where the fugitives were being hidden. He led the pursuers in the opposite direction. The posse, upon realizing they were not going to catch their quarry, left town swearing "the vilest vengeance." In addition to misdirecting the slave hunters, Perry often provided food and clothing from his store to the freedom seekers.[54]

Perry was assisted by many others in Felicity. Lewis Miller also owned a store, and supplied the fugitives with food and clothing. Andrew Powell was another antislavery Democrat and a prominent businessman who used his elegant, distinctive carriage and fine team of horses to transport escapees from the river to Felicity. James Abbot learned the business of the "road" in Covington before moving to Felicity, where he continued "the good work." Salathiel Burrows, a former slaveowner, provided a safe house just outside of town on the Xenia Road between Felicity and Bethel. Arthur Fee, another cousin, maintained a safe house, hiding fugitives in his fruit cellar.[55]

Fig. 9.12. *Arthur Fee and the Arthur Fee home.*

Fig. 9.13. *The home of Andrew Powell, who transported fugitive slaves from the Ohio River in his ornate carriage with a distinctive brace of horses. It is located at 416 Union Street in Felicity, Ohio.*

Fletcher Day listed the following people as additional Felicity operatives, but did not provide details: Moses Larkin, James W. South, Rev. Smith Poage, Joseph Hayden, David House, Fred Edwards, Jack Melvin, and Deloss S. Waits.[56]

Stories of the Road

The Felicity cadre were ingenious in developing plots to foil the slave hunters. Sometime in the 1850s "a beautiful octoroon girl" escaped from her owner and found her way to Felicity. She stayed with Rev. Bruce Pettyjohn's family. A posse came to Pettyjohn's home and demanded that he turn the girl over to them. Pettyjohn asked to see their writ as was required by the Fugitive Slave Act. The slave hunters did not have the writ. Reverend Pettyjohn told them he would not turn over the girl without a writ.

The railroad operatives knew that it would take several hours for the posse to go to Batavia, procure the writ, and return to serve it. They passed the hours planning the girl's escape. The plan and its execution were flawless.

Pettyjohn came into town on horseback, leading another horse outfitted with a woman's saddle. He went to his uncle's home and asked for Mrs. Pettyjohn, saying that he needed her to help tend to his employer's wife, who was quite ill. He asked her to prepare for the trip while he went to get Dr. Matthew Gibson. "Mrs. Pettyjohn" got on the horse and, with young Pettyjohn in the lead, sped off into the darkness. The other slave hunters returned from Batavia with the writ, and demanded to search the premises for the slave girl. Pettyjohn consented. When the Kentuckians entered the sitting room they found the real Mrs. Pettyjohn in a rocking chair knitting. One can only imagine the anger and humiliation the slave hunters felt when they realized they had been duped. The girl was well on the road to Benjamin Rice's home in Bethel.[57]

Louise Abbott Fisher told a similar story of deception. Six slaves crossed the Ohio River and made their way to Felicity. Along the way, one of the fugitive's legs was severely mauled by a dog. Within one-half hour of their arrival in Felicity, a group of eight armed Kentuckians appeared in pursuit of the six escapees. They came to the home where they thought the fugitives were being harbored. A villager approached the slave hunters and offered to help them. He advised them that it would take some time to make arrangements and they might as well get something to eat. The Kentuckians ate in shifts, always posting guards. Throughout the evening, women came to the house with plates of food for those in the home.

After awhile the slave catchers were told that they could go into the home and retrieve their property. Upon entering the home they discovered six white men, not blacks, eating their suppers. Each of the white men had dressed as a woman and had given their female clothing to the fugitives, who had made good their escape.[58]

Underground Railroad activities continued in Felicity throughout the Civil War. One Sunday evening, soon after the beginning of the war, a large group of men rode into town pursuing several runaways. They rode about the town several moments with no luck. One villager posed as a "dough face," a sympathizer, and took them around town to where he said the fugitives were. Other abolitionists stood at various street corners laughing and taunting the men. The Kentuckians became increasingly frustrated and made threats against the villagers who were making fun of them, which only emboldened their tormenters. Finally, the slave hunters just rode back to Kentucky. All the while the escapees were safely hidden at the home of Salathiel Burrows in Mt. Olive.[59]

Other sites in Franklin Township were likely involved with the Underground Railroad, but their history has remained hidden. For a time, Franklin Township was the home to Augustus Wattles, one of Cincinnati's best-known abolitionists.

Augustus Wattles

Augustus Wattles came to Cincinnati from Connecticut to attend the Lane Theological Seminary. He became one of the Lane Rebels. After leaving the seminary, Wattles provided vocational training for Cincinnati's blacks. He also traveled extensively across the United States, lecturing and doing missionary work. The many trips took a toll on his health, compelling him to quit the vagabond life.

In 1848, Wattles moved to Clermont County after his brother, John, purchased the property and lands formerly owned by the Clermont Phalanx, a Christian commune. John established a spiritualist community on the site, which was destroyed by a disastrous flood in 1847. Augustus lived in his brother's home, which survived the flood, for six years. The *Clermont Sun* wrote that Augustus "was a prominent member of the Fourier Association, near Rural, and was always known as a rabid abolitionist of the Garrison school. In addition to this, he was a believer in the Free Love doctrine, and we believe opposed generally to most of the conventional rules of society."[60] There is no documentary evidence linking Wattles, the Clermont Phalanx, or the spiritual commune to the Underground Railroad, though, given their radical abolitionist sentiment and the location of the facility, it would not be surprising that they were active during the time they lived there.

Both of the Wattles brothers left Ohio for Bloomington, Kansas, where they made their home on May 7, 1855. Augustus became deeply involved in the often-violent struggle over slavery that was gripping the territory. He was elected to the Kansas legislature, but was ejected by the proslavers who took over the government.

Augustus met John Brown and, for several months, hid him from proslavers. Wattles organized an abolitionist militia, meriting a one-thousand-dollar bounty being placed upon his head. He also established an Underground Railroad station.[61]

Following John Brown's raid upon Harper's Ferry in October of 1859, Wattles and others organized a rescue party. The rescue attempt never materialized because he was ordered to appear for questioning at a U.S. Senate inquiry of the Brown raid. Cleared of any substantive involvement in Brown's activities, Wattles resumed his more prosaic work as a missionary to newly freed slaves following the Emancipation Proclamation. He died in 1876 at his home in Moundville, Kansas.[62]

NOTES

1. Rockey & Bancroft, *Clermont County, Ohio,* 345.
2. R.F.B., *Clermont Courier,* September 3, 1857.
3. Rockey & Bancroft, *Clermont County, Ohio,* 353–54; *Chronicle of the Times,* March 8, 1833; Nolie Mumey, ed., *Alexander Taylor Rankin, 1803–1885, his Diary and Letters; a Pioneer Minister who Fought Lawlessness with Religion on the Prairies of Eastern Kansas and the Frontier Settlements of Denver, Where Life was Harsh and Brutal* (Boulder, Colo.: Johnson Pub. Co., 1966) 8.

4. John Rankin to Brother Jocelyn, April 2, 1855, American Missionary Association (AMA) Archives no. 106802, Fisk University copies at the Amistad Research Center, New Orleans. The church was reunited in 1869. Rockey & Bancroft, *Clermont County, Ohio*, 354.

5. Rockey & Bancroft, *Clermont County, Ohio*, 355.

6. *True Wesleyan*, April 12, 1851.

7. Rockey & Bancroft, *Clermont County, Ohio*, 355.

8. Ibid., 356.

9. *True Wesleyan*, date unknown.

10. Ibid., June 23, 1849.

11. Ibid., September 22, 1849.

12. Ibid., September 29, 1849.

13. Ibid.

14. Ibid., November 13, 1849; December 29, 1849; February 2, 1850; December 22, 1849.

15. Ibid., December 22, 1849.

16. Ibid.

17. Ibid., April 12, 1851.

18. Ibid.

19. Rockey & Bancroft, *Clermont County, Ohio*, 355.

20. *True Wesleyan*, April 12, 1851.

21. Ibid., February 17, 1854.

22. Ibid.

23. Rockey & Bancroft, *Clermont County, Ohio*, 355. Soon after the enactment of the Thirteenth Amendment outlawing slavery, the two cousins, with nothing left to divide them, merged. The church was shut down in 1870. The Franklin Township government purchased the building and converted it to public use. From 1946 to 1951 it was the town's cinema. Many of the village's older residents still refer to it as the "Show Building." The structure is currently privately owned. The steeple was removed several years ago. The clock is still intact in storage.

24. Fletcher Day, "Its Tracks Were Clouded," *Felicity Times*, July 6, 1893.

25. J. O'Neill, *True Wesleyan*, March 12, 1856. O'Neill commented about the Garner trial which was going on at the time he wrote his letter: "Here in Cincinnati is found a woman lying in jail for the perpetration of a deed, which for the same purpose and with the same motive, would be applauded as an act of heroic daring meriting the universal commendation of mankind."

26. *True Wesleyan*, July 7, 1858.

27. Day, *Felicity Times*, July 6, 1893.

28. 1850 U.S. Census, results printed in the *Clermont Courier*, December 26, 1850; 1860 U.S. Census.

29. 1860 U.S. Census.

30. Rockey & Bancroft, *Clermont County, Ohio*, 355; Whitt, "Outstanding Black People of New Richmond," *Clermont County Bicentennial*, 17.

31. "Former Slave Ends Sojourn," *Bracken County, Chronicle*, October 6, 1938.

32. Day, *Felicity Times*, July 6, 1893; Clermont County Infirmary Records, 58.

33. Peter Stokes Narrative, interviewed by Wilbur Siebert, August 3, 1895, Wilbur Siebert Papers, OHS.

34. Ibid.

35. Taylor Family Oral Tradition as told to Mrs. Mabel Lennox, January 1999, *African American Records Bracken County Kentucky, 1797–1999*, comp. Caroline Miller (Brookesville, Ky.: Bracken County Historical Society) 2:105.

36. Peter Stokes Narrative, Wilbur Siebert

37. Taylor Family Oral Tradition

38. 1860 U.S. Census; Clermont County, Ohio, Property Records, Deed Book 68, 443; *The Felicity Times*, July 6, 1893.

39. Rockey & Bancroft, *Clermont County, Ohio*, 355; *True Wesleyan*, October 6, 1858.

40. *True Wesleyan*, July 21, 1858.

41. Ibid.

42. *True Wesleyan*, October 6, 1858.

43. Day, *Felicity Times*, July 6, 1893.

44. Fee, *Autobiography*, 62.

45. Ibid., 63.

46. *Clermont Courier*, November 4, 1858.

47. Fee, *Autobiography*, 66–68.

48. Kentucky Penitentiary, Kentucky Dept. of Library & Archives, Public Division; Fee, *Autobiography*, 67.

49. Kentucky Penitentiary Registry; Fee *Autobiography*, 142, 144–45.

50. Day, *Felicity Times*, July 6, 1893; Louise Abbott to Wilbur Siebert, November 27, 1915, Wilbur Siebert Papers, Ohio Historical Society, Columbus, Ohio.

51. Rockey & Bancroft, *Clermont County, Ohio*, 346; Oliver Fee obituary, *Felicity Times*, March 1893.

52. Ibid., 347, 352, Ibid.

53. Oliver Fee obituary, *Felicity Times*, March 1893.

54. Day, *Felicity Times*, July 6, 1893.

55. Ibid., Louise Abbott, November 27, 1915; Mary Kate Liming interview, July 17, 2001.

56. Day, *Felicity Times*, July 6, 1893.

57. Day, *Felicity Times*.

58. Louise Abbott Fisher, *History of Bethel*, Bethel Journal, 1902–3, transcribed copies at the Batavia Public Library.

59. Day, *Felicity Times*, July 6, 1893.

60. Martha J. Parker, *Angels of Freedom*, ed. Christine Reinhard (Topeka, Kans.: Chapman Publishers, 1999) 51; *Clermont Sun*, November 17, 1859; Mrs. O. E. Morse, "Sketch of the Life and Work of Augustus Wattles," Kansas State Historical Society 1926–1928, 17 (1928), 293, 294; *Clermont Sun* article was written after Wattles had been implicated in John Brown's raid at Harper's Ferry.

61. Parker, *Angels of Freedom*, 59.

62. Ibid., 59–60.

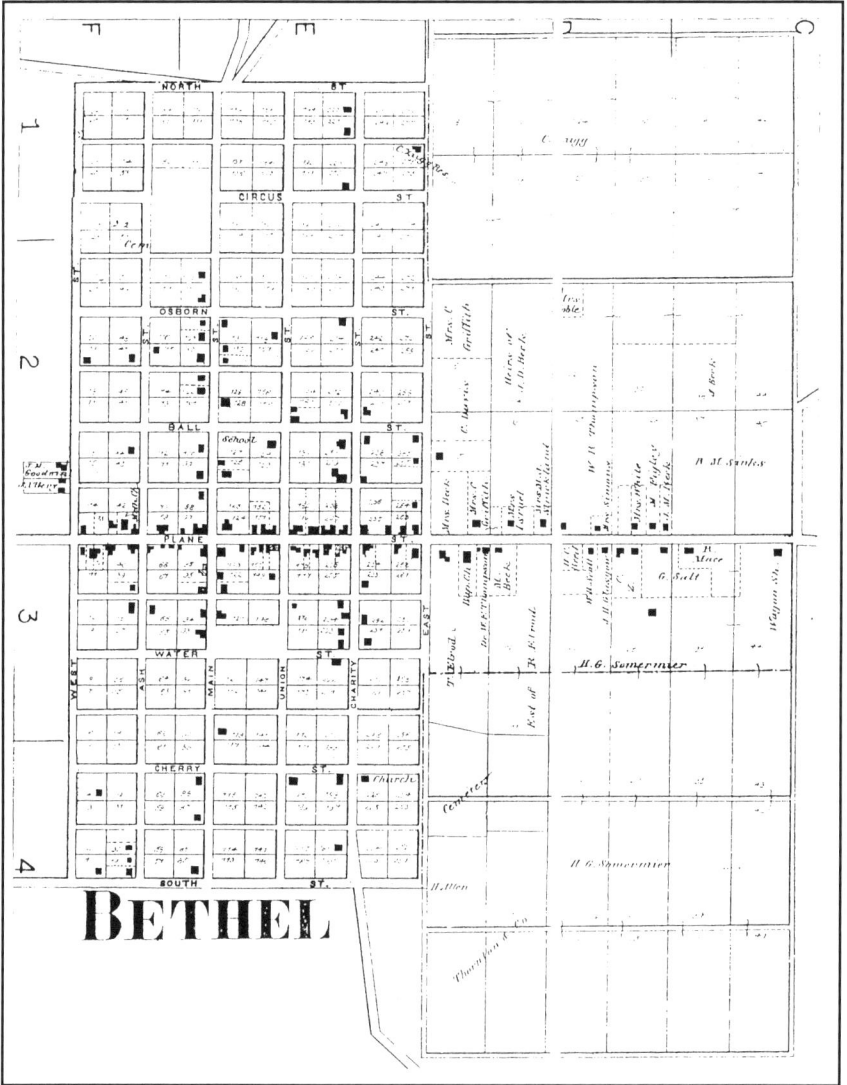

Fig. 10.1. *Plat map for Bethel, Ohio.*

CHAPTER 10

The Bethel Area

Bethel, originally known as Plainfield and later as Denhamstown, was founded in 1798 as an abolitionist colony on land purchased by Obed Denham. The Becks, Burkes, and later, others of a like mind, came to the new settlement. Denham, a Virginia-born Kentuckian, donated two lots to the village "for the use of the Regular Baptist Church, who do not hold slaves or commune at the Lord's table with those that do practice such tyranny over their fellow creatures." This declaration, according to historian Byron Williams, constituted the formation of the "first legally organized practical emancipation society west of the Alleghenies."[1]

Bethel, because of the influence of Denham's brand of practical abolitionism, became the seed bed of activists in eastern Clermont County and the northern line of the Brown County Underground Railroad network. John Mahan, Dr. Isaac Beck, the Huggins family, and the Mungers of Brown County either were born in Bethel or spent a considerable portion of the formative years of their lives in the village.

Fig. 10.1. *Burial marker for Obed Denham.*

Thomas Morris

The influence of Thomas Morris was national in scope, and he was the man most clearly identified with the antislavery movement in Clermont County. Morris reflected the dream of a new nation. Born into poverty, through native intelligence and hard work, he rose from obscurity to become a United States senator and candidate for vice president of the country.

Morris was born on January 3, 1776. His father, Isaac, was a Baptist minister. His mother, Ruth Henton Morris, was the daughter of a slave-owner. The two rejected slavery and, as a result, Mrs. Morris lost her birthright. Because of this, they moved to the free state of Pennsylvania. Morris was largely unschooled, but was taught to read from the Bible by his mother. His lack of formal education prompted one writer to rhapsodize, "the college of Thomas Morris was the mountain wilds of Virginia and there he graduated with a diploma from nature."[2]

Morris joined up with Levi Morgan's Rangers at age seventeen, chasing Indians between Marietta and Steubenville, Ohio. Two years later he left home to immigrate to Columbia, a new settlement at the mouth of the Little Miami and Ohio rivers. Here he found work as a clerk in the store owned by John Smith, a Baptist minister and later United States senator.[3]

Soon after marrying Rachel Davis, Morris and his new bride moved to Williamsburg, Ohio, where he established the first tavern in Clermont County, which he leased to the Clermont County Court of Common Pleas. It was in his own tavern that he was successfully sued

Fig. 10.2. *Thomas Morris, attorney and the country's first antislavery United States senator, was the Liberty Party candidate for vice president of the United States in 1844. This is the only likeness of Senator Thomas Morris. It was drawn in 1922, based upon the memory of Dr. William E. Thompson, by police sketch artist Richard Brand.*

by David Blew for $72.79. In order to settle the judgment, Morris had to give up his cow, but it was not enough. Blew insisted that Morris be placed in debtor's prison, as was the custom of the day for those who could not pay their debts. The court reluctantly complied with the request. Out of respect for Morris, he was not confined in the county jail, but was permitted to remain free so long as he did not leave the village.

Morris moved to Bethel soon after he completed serving his sentence because "he would rather be a king among fools than a fool among kings." He also thought that there were too many oppressive Kentuckians living in Williamsburg.[4] He began to study law. So great was his poverty that he studied "not by the light of an astral lamp, not yet by the common light of a tallow candle . . . but the light afforded by hickory bark." He was also forced, at times, to decipher the meaning of *Blackstone's Commentaries* by the flickering light of the brick kiln where he worked. After two years of study he was admitted to the practice of law, the first Clermont County resident so honored.[5]

Morris was an able and forceful advocate for his clients. He was known for his fierce cross-examinations of witnesses. On one occasion he became convinced that a witness was lying. Carefully and patiently he led the witness into a well-laid verbal trap. At just the right moment he sprung the trap, sending the witness from the courtroom in tears.[6] Morris's closing arguments were often brilliant summations, frequently laced with biblical statements. There were many times when the courtroom was filled to overflowing to hear his legal oratory. He was also determined. He asked the judge for a continuance for a trial once because a witness was stranded by a flood. The request was denied. Morris then went out and crossed the flooded stream and brought back the witness to court. He won the case.[7]

Despite his skills as a litigator, Morris, like all good lawyers, sought to avoid litigation whenever possible. "It ought to be our aim," he once stated, "to prevent litigation as far as practicable within the rules and ends of justice."[8]

James B. Swing, basing his evaluation upon the recollections of attorneys who faced Morris, wrote, "Ohio has had few lawyers more powerful before a jury than Thomas Morris. He was not a rude, uncouth lawyer, but became a clear, able, powerful reasoner—truly eloquent, not wordy, but a master of strong English."[9]

Morris drifted toward politics and was elected to the Ohio House of Representatives in 1806. He remained in the Ohio General Assembly, either in the House or the Senate, for the next twenty-four years. As a legislator he was a strong and outspoken supporter of Andrew Jackson and public education. Morris opposed canal construction, while favoring railroad development. He favored the expansion of democracy and opposed efforts to further discriminate against Ohio blacks.[10]

His proudest achievement, however, was the introduction of the bill that outlawed debtor's prison, righting an indignity he knew all too well. In his speech supporting the law he argued,

The force of moral sentiment, properly cultivated and rightly directed would be far more effectual than all the bars and cells of your prison. Abandon them, then, this relic of oppression, this appeal to force the collection of debts. People act to pay debt from a desire to preserve a good name which is more precious than gold.[11]

An incident that took place in 1827 demonstrated his physicality and determined spirit. The legislature had just adjourned. Morris wanted to leave Columbus immediately, but torrential spring rains made the roads impassable. Not to be deterred, Morris and Robert Lytle bought a canoe. Morris, then fifty-one years old, and Lytle set out on the one-hundred-mile trip down the Scioto River from Columbus to Portsmouth. There they took a river boat to New Richmond, where Morris debarked. He hired out a horse and rode the final leg of his trip to Bethel.[12]

Throughout the 1820s Morris was one of the state's chief Democratic politicos. In fact, he was considered to be "the presiding genius of the party."[13] He helped Samuel Medary of Bethel establish the fiercely Democratic newspaper, the *Ohio Sun*. By 1832 he was one of President Jackson's most trusted supporters in Ohio.[14] Morris ran for Congress that same year from the Fifth District, composed of Clermont, Brown, and Adams counties. He finished third in a four-way contest, losing out to his former protege, Thomas Hamer. There was a silver lining for Morris, however. Andrew Jackson's popularity swept the Democrats into control of the legislature. Because of his years of party service and strong support of President Jackson, the legislature chose Morris, by one vote, to be the state's next U.S. senator.[15]

Morris's six-year term began on March 4, 1833. For the first three years of his tenure Morris was very quiet. He rose but twice to speak. He concentrated his efforts on committee work and serving his constituents. By contrast, he spoke twenty times during the second half of his term, fifteen times on issues relating to slavery.[16]

Morris's first foray into antislavery politics took place on January 7, 1836, when he made a rather routine presentation of antislavery petitions from his constituents. John C. Calhoun, senator from South Carolina, known as the "Titan of the Senate," blasted Morris for his audacity and bad taste in introducing the petitions. Calhoun claimed that the South was "deeply slandered" by the mere presentation of the petitions. Other Southerners joined in denouncing Morris. Senator William King of Alabama called the antislavery activists "miserable fanatics." William Preston, Calhoun's fellow South Carolinian, was the most bombastic: "Let an abolitionist come within the borders of South Carolina; if we can catch him we will . . . hang him."[17]

Morris clashed with Calhoun again several months later. The occasion was a debate on Calhoun's bill to outlaw circulation of antislavery pamphlets in the South. Morris, by now a national antislavery celebrity, strenuously argued against the bill on constitutional grounds. He chided Calhoun when he asked him if he would have supported this bill if it had been directed against Calhoun's pet theory of nullification. But what truly stands out in this exchange is Morris's presentation of his "slave power conspiracy theory," a theory he articulated more fully over the years.[18] The bill was defeated.

Morris's "slaveocracy" theory was his most significant contribution to the antislavery movement. He set out his thoughts on this subject more fully in a letter he wrote to Alexander Campbell of Ripley.

The first solemn reflection is the arrogance of the slave holding power in their efforts to prostrate the Constitution itself, and the freedom of speech and the press, by the threats of violence; have we not seen it attempt to subject the mail of the United States to the most odious inspection, and the sacred seal of private correspondence liable to be broken by the rude hand of its power? Have we not seen it attempt to Prostrate the freedom of speech, and the liberty of the press? Have we not seen and deplored its power in the whirlwind of the mob, and in the infliction of disgraceful stripes upon the worthy and unoffending citizens? And above all, have we not seen it trampled under foot, the sacred and inherent right of petition?

Later, the slaveocracy is "a power which has for its object the prostitution of individual rights, and the establishment of the most absolute despotism and one of which the slaves of despotism itself would not permit to be executed if they knew it existed."[19]

In a private letter to a supporter, the senator underscored the stranglehold that the slave power had upon the federal government by pointing out that half of President Van Buren's cabinet, the vice president, Speaker of the House, and five of the nine justices of the U.S. Supreme Court, were from the South. With this control of the government, Morris supposed that the slaveholders would be satisfied.

But this is not so. They ask to abridge our Constitutional and undeniable rights—the liberty of speech, and the press and the right to petition on the subject of slavery . . . still they are not satisfied. Their march is *onward*.

They enter the territories of the free states, seize upon the whites as well as the black man, and convey him into their own states; sometimes under pretence of law, at others by mere personal force. They confine our citizens, who have not violated their laws, in their jails, load them with irons, and fasten them with chains. But they do not stop there.[20]

He refers to Kentucky sending a delegation to Ohio to press for an Ohio fugitive slave act, and continues, "Still like the grave, this Slave Power can not be satisfied." He writes that if these demands were made by a foreign power, "a universal burst of indignation, from the American people, would answer. NO NEVER!"

The slave holding power is

an interest, which private local, and arrogant in its nature, has united *together* more reasons for selfish purposes, and is more powerful and dangerous to the peace and prosperity of the country, than Books or any other interest that has ever existed among us.[21]

His continued outspokenness against slavery eroded support for him within his party. Eventually, the party abandoned him. In December 1838 the Ohio General Assembly selected Democrat Benjamin Tappen to replace him as senator.[22]

As if released from any remaining party fetters, Morris delivered his valedictory speech in the Senate on February 9, 1839. The speech was given in response to one made by Kentuckian Henry Clay, who urged the country to cease agitation on the slavery issue and, thereby, save the Union. Morris's speech was powerful, eloquently written, and passionately delivered.[23] In the speech he expressed his great fears that slavery would rent the country apart. He concluded,

Though our national sins are many and grievous, yet repentance, like that of ancient Nineveh, may divert from us that impending danger which seems to hang over our heads as by a single hair. That all may be safe, I conclude that

THE NEGRO WILL YET BE SET FREE.[24]

It was a remarkable speech, given that it was delivered twenty-three years before the Civil War.

Ohio Democrats were outraged by the speech. Efforts were made by some in the legislature to demand his resignation; this failed only because there was so little time before the expiration of his term. He was shouted down at the state Democratic convention. He was egged in Dayton and assaulted by mobs in Cleves.[25] But to abolitionists, he was the hero of the hour. John G. Whittier, the Quaker poet and abolitionist activist, wrote that Morris stood "confessed the Lion of the Day."[26]

After his public excommunication from the Democratic Party, Morris naturally gravitated more toward the antislavery cause. He joined the Liberty Party and became a frequent speaker at antislavery meetings. He also became a member of the Executive Committee of the American and Foreign Antislavery Society.[27]

Continuing to speak out against the slave power, he stated in the summer of 1843 that "the slave power has become omnipotent."[28] It had taken control of the nation's councils of government, the press, the pulpit, and the ballot box. "It has eaten out our substance, and brought upon us pecuniary embarrassment and public disgrace."[29] He urged the growing abolitionist community that "political action is necessary to produce Reformation in the nation."[30]

In 1843 Morris accepted the vice-presidential nomination of the Liberty Party. The campaign was plagued with the mistakes of the naive as well as the dirty tricks of its competitors. The *Ohio Sun*, the paper he helped to establish, accused Morris of having voted for Henry Clay, the Whig nominee, for president. Jesse Grant, father of Ulysses S. Grant, confirmed the allegations.[31] Morris responded that the allegations were false. He wrote,

I did not lead or attempt to lead any Whig abolitionist or any other person at the late Presidential Election in Tate Township to vote in any manner whatsoever. The ticket I voted . . . was a Liberty or Birney ticket.

He handed his ballot to an election official and said, "I vote a Liberty ticket and you are welcome to look at it.[32] To his accusers he would, if he had a chance, burn "the brand of falsehood" into his "forehead." The old war horse challenged his accusers to a duel: "they know where I live and they know their remedy."[33]

Just one week after the challenge was posted, Morris was stricken

Fig. 10.3. *This was the home of Senator Thomas Morris in Bethel, Ohio. It was later purchased by Jesse Grant, who became Bethel's first mayor. Jesse's son, West Point cadet Ulysses Grant, stayed at the home while on leave.*

with a brain hemorrhage. He entered his Bethel home, muttered "Lord have mercy on me" three times, and died. He was sixty-eight years old. Morris was buried at the Old Settlers Cemetery in Bethel. John G. Whittier wrote his epitaph, which is inscribed on his tombstone.

> Unawed by power, and uninfluenced by
> flattery
> He was, throughout life, the fearless
> advocate
> of
> Human Liberty

Salmon P. Chase said of his mentor:

He was far beyond the time he lived in. He first led me to see the character of the slave power. Few antislavery men of today, with all the light thrown on the subject saw the matter as clearly as did he.[34]

Some scholars have questioned whether Morris was a true abolitionist because he never seemed to be "filled with the deep religious indignation toward slavery nor the empathy for blacks that qualified as many of his friends as true abolitionists."[35] Perhaps the starting point would be to define the term abolitionist. Simply put, an abolitionist was one who believed in the immediate end to slavery—freedom of the slave. With this in mind, there can be little doubt that Morris was an abo-

Fig. 10.4. *The burial marker of Thomas Morris, located in the Old Settlers Cemetery in Bethel, Ohio.*

litionist. In his final speech to the Senate he declared, "Sir, if I am an abolitionist, Jefferson made me so."[36] While this may seem a curious statement, given Jefferson's personal ambiguities on the subject, it does reveal the wellspring of Morris's opposition to slavery—more political and constitutional than religious. He made the rights of "life, liberty, and the pursuit of happiness," enshrined in Jefferson's Declaration of

Independence, applicable to slaves as well.

Does this mean that Morris was less committed to the cause than the evangelical Theodore Weld? Probably not; they came to the same conclusion, but from different perspectives, and most likely entertained different means to their common end.

Morris was a politician and, as such, saw politics as the art of the possible. His theory of the slave power conspiracy found resonance in its day—the 1830s. Slavery was still on the margin of social and political consciousness at this time. Most Americans were more concerned with tarriffs and banking issues. They were not ready to accept black freedom as a "self-evident" right. But they were sensitive to political slights and the overweening arrogance of the slave power. They could identify with the infringement upon state sovereignty, the denial of First Amendment rights of freedom of speech, press, and the right to petition. Therefore, Morris's rhetoric on the subject found an audience.

Morris was a seminal figure in the antislavery movement: he was the only antislavery senator in the 1830s. He helped to transition the movement from the pulpit to the ballot box; and he brought the public to focus on the issue.

He must have known that his outspokenness on the subject would end his political career. He persisted nonetheless. He realized that he did not complete his mission: "My greatest regret is that I have not been more zealous, and done more for the cause of individual and political liberty than I have done."[37]

Morris was not forgotten by the people of Clermont County. On the eve of the 1860 presidential election, a man visited his grave. He remembered that Morris had stood "foremost in the battle and the first to face political crucifixion and martyrdom." As the man "stood over the tomb that contained his sleeping dust" he could not but help feel "how living and majestic and progressive were the principles he so nobly declared." He wished he "could penetrate the earth and reach his ear, and whisper to him that all his hopes and prophecies were on the eve of a grand national Realization," and that the "song of triumph, whose first strain was hummed from his lips in the Senate chambers was sounding through the nation."[38]

The Underground Railroad

Bethel, in addition to being a seed bed of abolitionism, was a busy center of Underground Railroad activity. The village was strategically positioned along two major routes: the Xenia Road, State Route 133, formed the south-to-north axis from the Ohio River to Williamsburg; and the Ohio Pike, State Route 125, formed the east-to-west axis running from John Rankin's station in Ripley to Levi Coffin's operation in Cincinnati.

Louise Abbott Fisher described what must have been a common view of Bethel during this time.

There were in Bethel several homes in which, if friends visiting heard voices or saw lights when everyone was supposed to be asleep, or in the morning noticed the absence of some member of the family, they said nothing about it for they knew that some poor unfortunate, had been taken on a little further toward a place of safety by a friend in the north.[39]

Isaac Holmes Brown

Isaac Holmes Brown, known locally as "Uncle Ikey," was the lay leader of the Sugar Tree Wesleyan Church. Founded in April of 1845, the church was one of the earliest Wesleyan churches in Ohio. The six charter members originally met at the Monroe Presbyterian Church in Nicholsville.[40]

Isaac Brown donated land to build a church two miles south of Bethel in the spring of 1848. The chapel was thirty-five by forty-five feet, and was described as "one of the finest in the Midwest." The church hosted a number of antislavery meetings conducted by its pastor, Rev. Gerrard P. Riley. Among the church congregation were the following members who have been identified as involved with the Underground Railroad: James Bunton, G. R. Riley, Benjamin Rice, Richard Mace, O. W. Vandosol, and Rev. Silas Chase, M.D.[41]

Brown began his work on the "Road" in 1835. He was a bold operator and soon became known as one "of the most vigilant and successful conductors in the state."[42] He brought fugitives from Felicity on wagons loaded with oats. Brown harbored the slaves in his home at Swing's Corner before arranging transportation to either "Boss" Huber's in Williamsburg or to the Huggins' farm in White Oak, Brown County.[43]

Fig. 10.5. *The burial marker of Isaac "Uncle Ikey" Holmes Brown, located at the Sugar Tree Wesleyan Church Cemetery on Crane Schoolhouse Road in Tate Township. Holmes donated the land for the church, one of the first Wesleyan churches established in Ohio.*

Fig. 10.6. *The burial marker of Richard Mace in the Tate Township Cemetery in Bethel, Ohio. Mace and Benjamin Rice transported fugitives in a wagon with a false bottom from Felicity to Bethel.*

Benjamin Rice

Benjamin Rice lived in a small settlement south of Bethel, along State Route 232, known as Rice town. He was one of the founding members of the Bethel Wesleyan Church.[44] Rice was a carpenter whose skills were used to modify a wagon to construct a false bottom. He and Isaac Brown placed fugitives into the compartment and put sacks of oats into the bed to conceal its true cargo. He and Brown picked up the freedom seekers in Felicity and conveyed them to their homes in Bethel, and from there to Williamsburg. Rice told Louise Abbott's grandfather that he helped one hundred slaves from one farm in Kentucky to escape.[45]

Fig. 10.7. *The burial marker of Benjamin Rice in the Tate Township Cemetery in Bethel, Ohio. Rice was an Underground Railroad operative. His son, John obtained a "slave banjo" from a black classmate. The banjo was the subject of an episode of the Public Broadcasting Service (PBS) television show,* The History Detectives, *in 2005.*

Dr. William E. Thompson

William Eberly Thompson was born in Bethel, Ohio, on July 6, 1835. His father, Dr. William Thompson, died in 1840. After graduating from the Cincinnati Medical College, he opened his office on March 1, 1860. He received an appointment as assistant surgeon in the Seventh Ohio Volunteer Infantry at the outbreak of the Civil War; however, he was forced to resign his commission because of a serious medical problem. He was very active in his community, serving as a member of the Bethel Village Council, the school board, and the Masons. Politically, Dr. Thompson was a Republican,

Fig. 10.8. *Dr. William E. Thompson was, in 1940, the country's oldest practicing doctor. He was involved in the Underground Railroad as a teenager.*

casting his first vote for John C. Fremont for president in 1856. He continued practicing medicine past his 100th birthday. He died on February 19, 1940, at age 105.[46]

Fig. 10.9. *The boyhood home of Dr. William E. Thompson located at 137 Main Street, Bethel, Ohio*

Dr. Thompson signed an affidavit on January 23, 1930, recounting his life experiences. Among other things, the affidavit states,

I also desire to state that Bethel, Ohio was one of the places of refuge, depot, on what was known as the Underground Railroad over which fleeing slaves passed from Kentucky onto Canada and that I am one of the persons who aided them in their escape.[47]

There are no dates associated with Dr. Thompson's involvement with the Underground Railroad. With a birth date of 1835, it is safe to say that he was one of the youngest conductors in the Clermont network. Thompson probably was a teenager when he began his career as a conductor.

Thompson apparently was quite skilled with a rifle. He hid in waiting for slave hunters with their "nigger hounds" pursuing escaping slaves. When they appeared, he shot the dogs.[48] As a young man, he probably knew the trails and hiding places of the area quite well. One evening he was asked, with no advance warning, to conduct a party of fugitives to the home of Oakley E. Vandosol near Williamsburg. This involved following a path through the Elklick Valley, what is today covered over by Harsha Lake.

He arrived at midnight. The Vandosols had no prior notice of his mission, but were probably warned by the fierce guard dogs who were described as being as "big as wolves." Despite the late hour, Mrs. Vandosol put together a spread for the fugitives consisting of ginger cookies, pumpkin pie, and coffee.[49]

Fig. 10.10. *The adult home and medical office of Dr. William E. Thompson located at 213 E. Plane Street, Bethel, Ohio.*

Thompson, Silas Chase, Benjamin Rice, and Matthew Gibson attempted to persuade a young slave girl to leave her master in August of 1849. A family from Maysville, Kentucky, brought the young girl with them while visiting with a Mr. Blake of Bethel. Silas Chase, the pastor of the Wesleyan Church, asked the fourteen-year-old Thompson to come back to the church after the Sunday service. Thompson did so. He was joined by the others in the church's reading room. The room overlooked the Blakes' yard. The four men asked Thompson, who was closer to the girl's age than they were, to talk her into leaving her master. Thompson talked to the girl, but he could not convince her to leave; she quickly darted back into the house.[50]

Rev. Silas Chase, M.D.

Rev. Silas Chase was the quintessential evangelical Christian abolitionist. He fervently believed that slavery was a sin, one that required all Christians to actively work for its extinction. This belief led him to reject the Methodist Church because the church was too lukewarm in its opposition of the institution. Leaving the church was a difficult decision for Chase; nevertheless, he did so in 1843 and joined the Wesleyans. His conversion experience was an emotional one as reported by the *True Wesleyan*: "He wept, for he was breaking the threads of attachment which had bound him to the old church. He wept for joy, for he felt like a prisoner released from his confinement."[51] His wife, Mary, followed him into the Wesleyan Church.

Chase organized the Sugar Tree Wesleyan Church and served at the Bethel and Felicity churches as well as one in Brown County. He also traveled extensively throughout the Midwest and East speaking about abolitionism and organizing other Wesleyan churches. He was a member, along with Levi Coffin, of the organizing committee of the great antislavery convention of 1850 held in Cincinnati.[52] In October of 1851 Chase was elected president of the Wesleyan Church's Miami Circuit. Glimpses of Chase's beliefs about slavery can be found in the frequent letters he wrote to the *True Wesleyan*.

I go for the overthrow and final extinction of slavery, not only in this country, throughout the world.[53]

If I have not mistaken the character and spirit of antislavery men, who from principle have set their face against slavery (and have suffered much for the truth), nothing will satisfy them but putting slaveholders and their apologists out of the church.[54]

He was confirmed in his opinion

that antislavery preaching does not retard the work of saving souls . . . more over. I am satisfied that the day is not distant when this kind of preaching will be called for, for Christianity without humanity is of little importance to the world or those who profess it.[55]

Documentation, other than the attempt to entice the young slave girl to escape, is scarce. However, Fisher wrote that Chase was a member of the Bethel network.[56] Reverend Chase died in 1864 and is buried in the Tate Township Cemetery. His epitaph reads as follows: "Talented, noble and generous. He was a true Christian Minister and a loyal citizen. He died in the service of his country."

Fig. 10.11. *The burial marker of Rev. Silas Chase, M.D., an outspoken critic of slavery, is located at the Tate Township Cemetery in Bethel, Ohio.*

Rev. Gerrard Polycarp Riley

Fig. 10.12. *Reverend Riley was a crusading antislavery Wesleyan minister and underground Railroad conductor who became the chaplain of the Fiftieth Ohio Volunteer Infantry and captain of the Sixth United States Colored Troop.*

The first thing that stands out about Gerrard Riley is his middle name—Polycarp. It forces the question: Why did his parents choose that name? Was it a family name? In fact, it seems that his parents tried to set the course of his life by giving him this name. Polycarp was an early Christian martyr—a saint.[57]

Riley was born near Bethel, Ohio, on November 17, 1821. His early education was limited; however, a fortuitous accident, cutting his foot while splitting wood, opened up the world of learning to him. After the accident, his grandfather brought books for him to read during his long period of recuperation.

He attended the Clermont Academy. Sarah Parker described him as an "interesting student" who always had to get "to the bottom of a question."[58] The Roman Catholic baptismal ritual of sprinkling fascinated him; he asked why the church adopted this practice rather than the Protestant one of full immersion. His teacher could not answer the question, but suggested that Riley ask Bishop John Purcell of Cincinnati. One day, after going to the city to sell lumber from his father's mill, the young man went to see the bishop. "The accomplished young Irishman," as Riley referred to Purcell, met him in his library. Purcell answered Riley's question by saying that the Catholic Church simply decided to make the change, period. There were no theological explanations. This answer probably did not satisfy the inquisitive Riley.[59]

The experience at Parker's Academy whetted Riley's appetite for more education. His father said that young Riley "had learning enough," and refused to give him financial support. Riley was not deterred. He attended Granville College. Riley paid for not only the tuition, but his room and board as well, by working at odd jobs, cobbling shoes or making brooms. Even so, he lived at a near subsistence level, at times having nothing more to eat than beans. Despite these handicaps, Riley maintained a high academic standing. His father paid him a surprise visit one day and was shocked at the conditions under which his son was living. From that time forward, he fully supported his son's endeavors. After graduating from Granville, he returned to Clermont County to work. In 1844 he married Sarah Blair.[60]

Riley had absorbed the abolitionist fervor of his hometown. He became the intimate of Thomas Morris. They met often to discuss slavery and the other great issues of the day. Riley recalled a prediction that the senator made one day: "Young man if you live to be my age you will see this government all torn to pieces, an international war perhaps; all on account of this great evil slavery."[61] By the early 1840s Riley had become known throughout Clermont County as a radical abolitionist.

On one occasion, Riley squared off with his cousin, the Honorable Marcus Clark, a large slaveowner from Kentucky, to debate the question: "Does the Bible justify American Slavery?" The verbal duel drew large crowds. The arguments raged on for two days and nights. At length, Riley posed this question: "If the Bible justifies slavery *who* is to be the slave in America?" His opponent was stumped, and after an uncomfortable moment answered, "No man can under heaven answer that question?" That ended the debate. The audience answered that the Bible did not justify American slavery.[62]

Riley was disgusted with what he considered to be his generation's lack of commitment to ending slavery. Some simply wanted "to stand still and do nothing. Any suggestion to defer till tomorrow," he wrote, "that which can be done today ought to be regarded as a temptation from the wicked one." He stated that the others

were once for a short time zealous in the cause of reform; they read or heard a stirring appeal in behalf of the poor slave, and with awakened sympathy forthwith broke loose from their pro-slavery organization, sounded the alarm, ran fast, hollowed loud and made a great fuss.[63]

These "reformers" backed off when they heard the first words of criticism from the proslavery lobby. And they "timely put their necks in the galling yoke of proslavery prescription and now they are tugging and sweating and pulling with no other excuse or comfort than that our hope is in the next generation."

If we are to put our hope in the next generation, he advised that "A large amount of this work devolves upon Christian parents and teachers." His prescription was to

teach your children to covenant with Jehovah that they will never be at peace with sin at home or abroad in high or low places but will 'wage an uncompromising war of extermination with every part and parcel of American slavery' . . . [until] the south shall resound with the Jubilee of the Slave's redemption; teach them that wealth, talent, life, all, is to be sacrificed until the bright banner of liberty and salvation shall be seen floating over every province of revolted man.[64]

Riley was raised a Methodist and, like others radicalized by slavery, left the church to join with the Wesleyans. He succeeded Silas Chase as the pastor of the Sugar Tree Wesleyan Church at age twenty-three. Based upon the significant percentage of the church's membership identified as Underground Railroad operatives, it seems logical to conclude that this congregation was a node in the Bethel Underground Railroad network.

In addition to his pastoral duties, Riley taught school. About one year after the beginning of the Civil War, a student asked him why, if the war was a war to liberate the slaves, he was not fighting. The student must have made a good point because soon after, Riley shut down his school and became the chaplain of the Fiftieth Ohio Volunteer Infantry, then organizing at nearby Camp Dennison. When asked why he, who was generally opposed to war, enlisted, he answered, "It was God's War." He entered the war as a soldier "as if called of God."[65]

Riley set up a regimental church and held regular services. Once the regiment went into winter quarters in Kentucky, he built a log church and held services there for three months before the regiment was called back into the field.[66]

At the Battle of Perryville, fought in October of 1862, he earned the admiration and respect of all in the regiment. Both armies, in search of water, clashed along the banks of the Chaplin River. The battle quickly escalated into a nasty, brutal, and bloody affair. The men of the Fiftieth soon drained their canteens in the sweltering sun. Chaplain Riley grabbed two fistfuls of canteens, mounted a horse, and rode off in search of water. He was a conspicuous target. The rebels sent dozens of balls buzzing past him. Still, he found water and brought the filled canteens back to his regiment. For this he was called "the fighting Chaplain." After the battle he spent many hours tending to the wounded and praying with the dying.[67]

Soon after the battle, the Fiftieth went into winter quarters near Louisville, Kentucky. There were many "contraband," slaves who attached themselves to the Union Army, seeking protection at the Fiftieth's camp. Reverend Riley hired Dave, one of the contraband, to be his personal servant. One day he left Dave holding his horse. When he came back, he found Dave struggling with two slave hunters. Riley told the men to release his servant. They claimed that Dave belonged to a man in Georgia and they planned to take him back with them. A military tribunal was convened to decide the issue of Dave's freedom. Riley suggested that Dave be sent to Riley's farm in Bethel and the judge agreed. Riley took Dave to the wharf and escorted him to a boat bound for Cincinnati. Riley left Dave for a moment. When he came back, he found the two slave hunters trying to kidnap him again. The reverend physically resisted the men and they finally relented. Riley escorted Dave to the boat.

To Dave, Riley said, "You will soon be a free man. Now Dave remember your promises to be faithful to our family. I will help and fight this war out, and then, Thank God there will be no more slavery."

At this time, the kidnapers walked away. Riley heard one of them say, "He deserves to beat us; such grit as that will make the Yankees win in the end."

Dave arrived safely at Riley's farm and remained there for the duration of the war. Dave was thankful for Riley's actions and said of the fighting chaplain, "He saved me from bondage and delivered me from the debil."[68]

Riley made it his calling to work with the contraband, many of whom were jailed upon reaching the Union lines. Kentucky law required that they be incarcerated for a period of eight months so that their masters could make a claim. If they were not claimed they could be sold. The conditions in the jails were miserable, with as many as one hundred slaves dying daily.[69] Riley worked to get their release. Others were hired by the army to dig fortifications. Riley was impressed with their work ethic. "They work faithfully 10 hours a day," he wrote to John Gregg Fee, "one will do more digging in one day than five of our white boys."[70]

At night the chaplain met with the black men—teaching, talking, and praying.

I took a seat on a box prepared for me in the middle of their quarters. All seated around I would question them about slavery, and they me about freedom, Canada, Underground Railroad, abolitionism. We have sometimes continued these interviews till midnight and it would be hard for me to say which learned the most teacher or pupil. Oh I just wish you could have been here last night and had them tell you their experiences. Oh such visions, dreams, signs, sights.[71]

He began to think about raising a regiment from among his contraband, despite the fact that Ohio's governor still did not want to recruit black soldiers. He was sure that they wanted to enlist. "They want to fight," he enthused, "and are quite willing to enlist for three years. They say 'life' is nothing to them unless they maintain their freedom. . . . They talk with great enthusiasm about fighting their way to their families in the south."[72]

Realizing that his knowledge of the military art was deficient, Riley began taking lessons in drill and tactics. So busy was he that he could not leave to secure his appointment to command a regiment or to recruit. He asked his friends, Lewis Pettyjohn and Silas Chase, to help him recruit. He also petitioned John Fee to intervene on his behalf with Gen. Ambrose Burnside, then commanding the Military District of Cincinnati, and to recruit among the blacks of New Richmond.[73]

For some reason, Riley was not successful in organizing a regiment. He did apply for an officer's commission in a black regiment. All whites applying for an officer position with a black regiment had to undergo a rigorous examination. The candidate's service record and background were scrutinized. They were given written exams testing both general and military knowledge. Riley's test results reveal him to have superior general knowledge and below average scores on the military sections. A note was written on his test indicating that he had recruited 180 black men for the service, enough for two companies, or nearly 20 percent of a regiment. It seems certain that this accomplishment secured his appointment as captain in Company K in the Sixth United States Colored Troops on October 6, 1863.[74]

Riley left his old regiment for his new command in Virginia, but he did not leave his concern for exploited blacks in Kentucky. When he learned about two slave children who were being treated badly by their master, he went to the plantation. There, he learned that the children had been accused of giving food to Union soldiers. For this they had been beaten and starved. Riley took the children from their master and placed them in a Quaker orphanage in Philadelphia. He named the boy Frederick Douglass White. Near the end of the war he accepted a position with the Freedman's Bureau in Washington.[75]

Following the war, Riley returned to Bethel. After a fire consumed his mill, he moved to Marion, Indiana. He continued his work as a minister. Riley died on October 14, 1914.[76]

The Mulatto

Not everyone in Bethel favored helping slaves to escape. Ephriam M. Cain and an unnamed black man were two such men. In October of 1852 they gave assistance to slave catchers. They took "part with the blood hounds in giving chase in favor of oppression, and against God and Humanity."[77]

At times there were men who, like Stowe's Senator Bird, proclaimed loudly that they would not assist a runaway, but who had a change of heart when forced to look upon "the imploring eye." There was one such man in Bethel. He was a mulatto who lived just outside of the village. He told everyone that he would not assist any runaways if they came to him for help. He felt that to help them would only encourage others to escape.

One early morning this man's sister-in-law came to the home of

Zekiel South, a conductor. The woman told South that two fugitives came to the mulatto's home and asked for shelter. The man not only fed them, but carried them to the next stop. South was incredulous, knowing of the mulatto's previous statements. So, South went out to the man's place to talk with him. The mulatto confirmed the story. He said that he never thought he would become involved, but when asked, he could not refuse. The escapees stayed at his home for a while until the mulatto could learn where the next stop was. He then took them on to Williamsburg.[78]

NOTES

1. Williams, *Clermont and Brown Counties*, 1:214; Rockey & Bancroft, *Clermont County, Ohio*, 324.

2. Rockey & Bancroft, *Clermont County, Ohio*, 193; G. L. Knepp, *Nine Who Made a Difference*, 18.

3. Smith later fell from grace when he was wrongly implicated in the Aaron Burr conspiracy. He died in poverty and obscurity. Rockey & Bancroft, *Clermont County, Ohio*, 194.

4. Benjamin Franklin Morris, ed., *The Life of Thomas Morris: Pioneer and Long a Legislator of Ohio and U.S. Senator from 1833 to 1839* . . . (Cincinnati: printed by Moore, Wilstach, Keys & Overend, 1856) 24.

5. Ibid., 25; George Marvin, "Clermont's Senator," *Ohio State Journal*, reprinted in the *Clermont Courier*, May 25, 1858; Knepp, *Nine Who Made a Difference*, 18.

6. James B. Swing, "Thomas Morris, Clermont's Brilliant Statesman," *Clermont Sun*, March 3, 1879.

7. Morris, *Life of Thomas Morris*, 27.

8. Ibid., 26–27.

9. Swing, "Thomas Morris, Clermont's Brilliant Statesman."

10. Rockey & Bancroft, *Clermont County, Ohio*, 195; Morris, *Life of Thomas Morris*, 31.

11. Morris, *Life of Thomas Morris*, 37.

12. Rockey & Bancroft, *Clermont County, Ohio*, 195.

13. Morris, *Life of Thomas Morris*, 60.

14. John A. Neuenschwander, "Senator Thomas Morris: Antagonist of the South: 1836–39," *Cincinnati Historical Society Bulletin* 32 (Fall 1974): 127.

15. The four candidates were Whig Owen Fishback; Morris, as the Regular Democrat; Thomas Hamer, an Independent Democrat; and William Russell, Anti-Mason. Morris carried Clermont County while Hamer took Brown and Adams counties. The two defining issues of the day were nullification and the national bank. Rockey & Bancroft, *Clermont County, Ohio*, 126,196; Neuenschwander, "Thomas Morris: Antagonist of the South," 127.

16. James W. Crocker-Lakness, "The Antislavery Rhetoric of Senator Thomas Morris: Freedom of Speech and Compensation for Failure," *Ohio Speech Journal*, 39

(2001), table 1, 81–82.

17. Morris, *Life of Thomas Morris*, 78.

18. Neuenschwander, "Thomas Morris: Antagonist of the South." 129–130.

19. Morris to Alexander Campbell, November 13, 1837, printed in the *Philanthropist*, December 26, 1837.

20. Morris to an unknown supporter, January 15, 1839, Morris, *The Life of Thomas Morris*, 26.

21. Ibid.

22. Neuenschwander, "Thomas Morris: Antagonist of the South," 133.

23. So important did the abolitionists think his speech was that the American Antislavery Society printed twenty pages of the speech and distributed it widely. Crocker-Lakness, "The Antislavery Rhetoric of Senator Thomas Morris," 91.

24. Morris, *Life of Thomas Morris*, 165.

25. Swing, "Thomas Morris, Clermont's Brilliant Statesman."

26. Rockey & Bancroft, *History of Clermont County, Ohio*, 196.

27. Crocker-Lakness, "The Antislavery Rhetoric of Senator Thomas Morris," 94.

28. Morris, *Life of Thomas Morris*, 226.

29. Ibid., 227.

30. Ibid., 229.

31. *Ohio Sun*, November 30, 1844.

32. Ibid., December 6, 1844.

33. Ibid.

34. Rockey & Bancroft, *Clermont County, Ohio*, 134; Morris, *Life of Thomas Morris*, xi.

35. Neuenschwander, "Thomas Morris: Antagonist of the South," 139n49.

36. Morris, *Life of Thomas Morris*, 175.

37. Ibid., 164–65.

38. "Alquis," *Clermont Courier*, November 7, 1860.

39. Fisher, *History of Bethel*, 1798–1902.

40. Games, *The Underground Railroad in Ohio*, 71n5; Rockey & Bancroft, *Clermont County, Ohio*, 331.

41. Rockey & Bancroft, *Clermont County, Ohio*, 333; *True Wesleyan*, February 17, 1849; Siebert, *The Mysteries of the Underground Railroad*, 65; *Felicity Times*, July 6, 1893.

42. Games, *The Underground Railroad in Ohio*, 71n5, 70.

43. Louise Abbott Fisher to W. Siebert, November 27, 1915, Siebert Papers; Rockey & Bancroft, *Clermont County, Ohio*, 195; Williams, *Clermont & Brown Counties, Ohio*, 1:401.

44. Rockey & Bancroft, *Clermont County, Ohio*, 333.

45. Williams, *Clermont and Brown Counties, Ohio*, 1:402; Ibid., 135; Fisher, *History of Bethel*, 1798–1802; Fisher to Siebert, November 27, 1915, Siebert Papers; *The New College Life Paper*, April 10, 1936. This paper interviewed Benjamin Rice's son, John, who moved to Emporia, Kansas. John donated a "slave banjo" given to his father by a black schoolmate of his. The article also mentioned that Benjamin was a conductor. The story was depicted in an episode of the PBS television show *History Detectives* in July 2005 in which the author was a guest historian.

46. *Bethel Journal*, February 23, 1940; Williams, *Clermont and Brown Counties, Ohio*, 2:53.

47. William E. Thompson, M.D. Affidavit, January 22, 1930, Bethel Historical Society.

48. *Bethel, 1748–1998* (Bethel, Ohio: Bethel Historical Society, 1998), 81.

49. Games, *The History of the Underground Railroad in Ohio*, 48–49, 71.

50. Ibid., 97. Games dedicated the book to Dr. Thompson who, at the time, was 102. She claimed he was the only living conductor in Ohio. Another Dr. Thompson story has surfaced in the papers of Dr. P. F. Greene of New Richmond. In an entry dated July 21, 1961, he noted a conversation he had with Sam Ausman, Director of Aid for the Aged in Clermont County. Ausman sold vegetables to Dr. Thompson. According to the story, Dr. Thompson pointed out one of his shotguns: "See this shotgun, I carried that over my shoulder when I was helping the underground. I was about 18 years old, three runaway slaves from New Richmond were hidden under a load of hay. I walked way behind the load with my gun on my shoulder. If any suspicious people came following up the road I was to fire my gun. This was the signal the negroes would be hustled out from under the hay into the woods so that when the slavers came to investigate they would find only a load of hay. Actually, no one came behind on that trip and I delivered the fugitives safely to Dr. Pease in Williamstown." Dr. Pease lived in Williamsburg not Williamstown. Dr. Greene's papers are in the possession of Historic New Richmond.

51. *True Wesleyan*, October 17, 1843.

52. Rockey & Bancroft, *Clermont County, Ohio*, 333, 335; *True Wesleyan*, October 20, 1849, December 29, 1849.

53. *True Wesleyan*, November 3, 1849.

54. Ibid., December 21, 1841.

55. Ibid., March 1, 1845.

56. Fisher to Siebert, November 17, 1915, Siebert Papers; Games, *The Underground Railroad in Ohio*, 97.

57. Polycarp was the bishop of Smyrna. Around 101 A.D., he was threatened with death by wild animals in the local arena if he did not denounce Christ. The Roman governor ordered him to be burned at the stake. According to the legend, the flames did not destroy his body. The executioner stabbed him. In the process, a dove flew out from the cut. So much blood flowed out of the wound that the flames were put out. Bart D. Ehrman, *Lost Christianities: The Battle for Scripture and the Faiths we Never Knew* (New York: Oxford University Press, 2003) 138–139.

58. SPBP, *History of the Clermont Academy*, 14.

59. Ibid.

60. *Bowen's Biographical Memoirs*, 601.

61. Ibid., 602.

62. Ibid.

63. *True Wesleyan*, February 2, 1850.

64. Ibid.

65. *Bowen's Biographical Memoirs*, 602.; Reid, *Ohio in the Civil War*, 1:305.

66. *Bowen's Biographical Memoirs*, 602.

67. Ibid., 603. Erastus Winters, *Serving with Uncle Sam in the 50th Ohio* (Cincinnati: 1905) 21.

68. *Bowen's Biographical Memoirs*, 604–05.

69. Riley to John Gregg Fee, June 23, 1863, American Missionary Association Archives at Amistad Research Center, Louisiana State University, New Orleans.

70. Ibid.

71. Ibid.

72. Ibid., undated; Ibid., June 17, 1863.

73. Ibid., undated.

74. G. P. Riley: Officer Examinations for Colored Regiments, Ohio Adjutant General Records, Ohio Historical Society; Reid, *Ohio in the Civil War*, 2:305.

75. *Bowen's Biographical Memoirs*, 605–07; The 30th Annual Report of the Association for the Care of Colored Orphans (Philadelphia: 1866) 5–9.

76. *The Marion Leader Tribune*, October 15, 1914.

77. "WXY," *The Herald of Freedom*, October 22, 1852. The reporter claimed that there were between forty and fifty slaves within the boundaries of Clermont and Brown counties. He also reported that two slaves were captured in Fincastle, Brown County, in September; betrayed by a Methodist class leader. W.X.Y. asked whether this Judas received his thirty pieces of silver.

78. Fisher, *The Bethel Journal*, February 23, 1940.

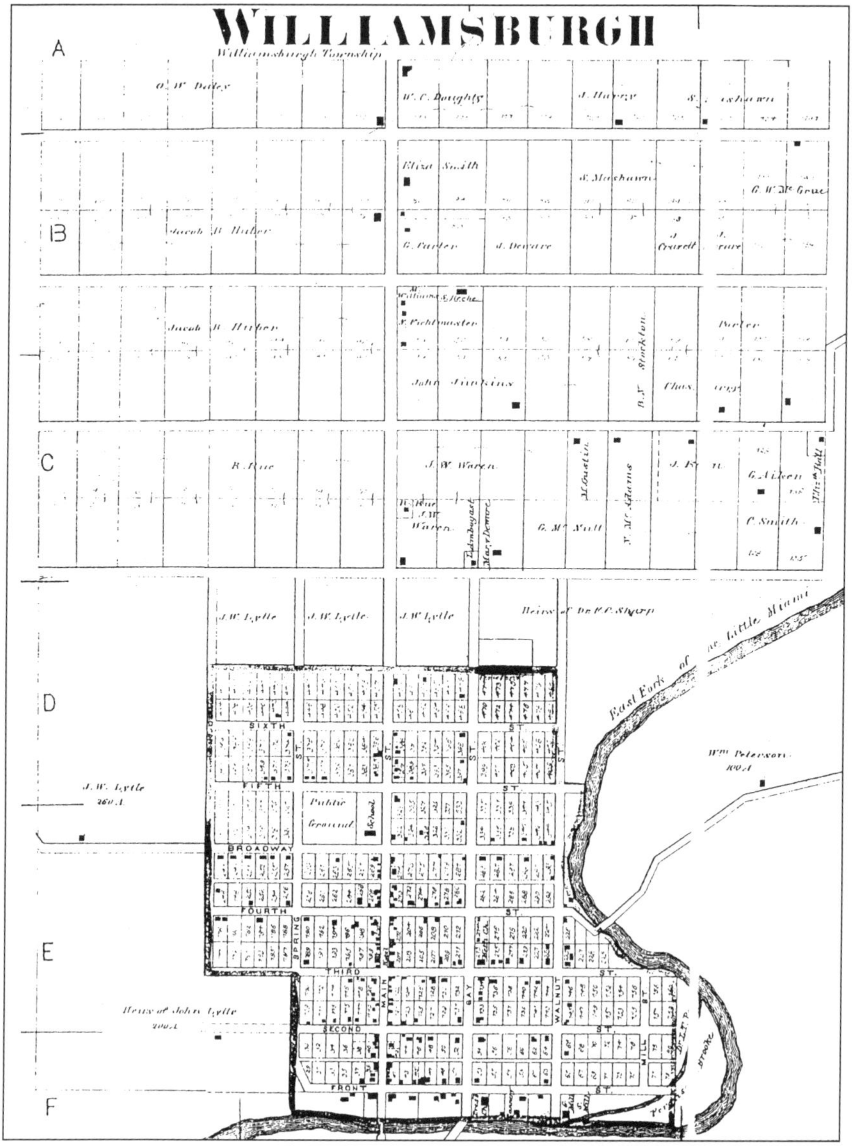

Fig. 11.1. *Williamsburg, Clermont County's first village, was the northernmost terminus of Clermont County's Underground Railroad network.*

CHAPTER 11

Williamsburg

WILLIAMSBURG WAS THE NORTHERNMOST "DEPOT" on the Clermont County Underground Railroad line. The village was founded by William Lytle in 1795 on a large bend of the East Fork of the Little Miami River. He originally named the village Lytlestown, but later changed it to Williamsburgh. Lytle supported Arthur St. Clair, governor of the Northwest Territory, in a number of political battles. Later, the governor's son married into the Lytle family. As a reward for his support, St. Clair named Williamsburg the county seat of Clermont County. Lytle's new town profited immeasurably as a result. St. Clair also chose Lytle to serve as the county's clerk of courts, giving him insider information about land trades in the county. Land became the basis of Lytle's wealth. By 1810, Lytle owned 38,998 acres of land in Ohio, making him the state's second-largest landowner. In addition to land speculation, Lytle constructed two mills, planted a large orchard, opened a distillery, and traded horses.[1]

Born in Pennsylvania, Lytle was raised in Kentucky. In many respects he remained a Kentuckian, having strong family and business ties to that state. His sister, Agnes, married John Rowan, owner of the Federal Hill mansion, better known as "My Old Kentucky Home." Rowan was a large slaveowner who built the well-known home with slave labor.[2]

Lytle's position on slavery is unclear. However, both his son, Robert, and grandson, William Haynes, were prominent attorneys who defended slaveholding interests. Other family members in Kentucky also held slaves.

Fugitive slaves began passing through Williamsburg over the Bull Skin Trace, which ran through the heart of the village in the early days of the nineteenth century, as indicated by the following letter addressed to Lytle:

Major Wagnon will please to make Enquiry relative to a Negro man belonging to Mr. Lynch who has been a runaway perhaps about Three months and supposed to have crossed the Ohio for the North Western Territory & probably pass there as a freeman. He is a fellow of low stature compact made and Remarkable black he has always been called by the name Humphry but is presumeable he has changed it.[3]

Newspapers frequently published advertisements for runaway slaves. These advertisements were usually very specific as to physical descriptions, clothing worn, occupations, and mannerisms. The papers of early Williamsburg, while not containing advertisements for slaves, did publish them for runaway white apprentices.

In March of 1835, Lemuel W. Slade of Batavia offered "ONE CHEW OF TOBACCO" for the return of his apprentice. He gave the following description of the lad:

STRANGE HUNT about 18 years of age of a light complexion, and a sneaking look! . . . Remarkable for indolence and lying. I hereby forewarn all persons from employing, harboring, or trusting him on my account. . . . The above Reward will be given on his return; but no thanks nor charges paid.[4]

Charles "Boss" Huber

There is no greater figure in the history of the Clermont County abolitionist movement and the Underground Railroad than that of Charles Boestler "Boss" Huber. Charles Huber's parents, Jacob and Anna Marie Boestler, came to Williamsburg from Pennsylvania in 1806, the same year in which Charles was born. Jacob Huber owned a mill and tannery in Williamsburg for many years. Educated and well read, Jacob Huber possessed "a fine library" that he made available to everyone in the community. Huber was an abolitionist and was well acquainted with everyone in the county's abolitionist establishment.[5]

Young Huber learned the tanning trade from his father. Like many young men, he wanted to strike out on his own, so he traveled by flatboat down the Mississippi River to answer a job posting in a New Orleans newspaper. When he reached the tannery he was told by the proprietor that the job was no longer available because he had "just bought one," meaning a slave. That experience had a profound impact

Fig. 11.2. *The home of Charles B. Huber, located at 160 Gay Street in Williamsburg, Ohio.*

upon Huber as he learned first-hand about the wide-ranging implications of slavery. He returned to Williamsburg as a practical abolitionist, vowing to do whatever he could to destroy the institution.[6]

Upon Jacob's death, Charles Huber inherited his father's business interests and the home located at 160 Gay Street. Huber was a talented businessman who succeeded in owning a significant portion of Williamsburg, as well as a cattle farm on the outskirts of the village.[7]

Huber had a commanding presence. He was, according to his nephew, "perfectly fearless," having the "head of a lion in courage" and "a woman's heart in point of tenderness." Huber had a "powerful frame" and "could throw a yearling and castrate him without help."[8]

Huber was quite open about his abolitionist sentiments. He was a leader in the Clermont County Antislavery Society and ran for state office several times as an abolitionist candidate. In 1837, he collected twenty signatures on a petition to abolish slavery in the District of Columbia. He sent the petition to Senator Thomas Morris with the following inscription: "Williamsburgh, Decem six—I send these petitions to you with the firmest confidence in your zeal for Human Rights and love of Country."[9]

Huber took every opportunity to convert others to the cause, whether publicly or in private. He went to political gatherings, carrying a soap box with him. He typically set his box in the street because many of the merchants would not allow him to speak on their property. He stood atop the box and harangued the crowd, calling them Southern sympathizers or—worse—dough faces for supporting slavery. For his trouble he was egged or pushed around by those he offended.[10]

Nephew George Fishback recalls a time when Huber's enthusiasm for his crusade outran his good sense. A large number of citizens was gathered in Batavia for a rally for William Henry Harrison for president in 1840. Young Fishback was walking among the crowd when he heard a loud voice proclaim, "All Whigs were damned abolitionists." He saw his uncle reaching for the speaker. Several citizens stepped in to restrain Huber. Fishback heard Huber yell, "hog killing would not begin until the opening of the winter season."[11] He had no idea what he meant by that, though the crowd immediately broke up.

Later he saw two attorneys, who were political rivals, engaging in an entertaining round of fisticuffs. He then saw his uncle, the "abatois orator," standing on a horse block. Huber was "pouring forth to the excited people on the subject of slavery and Emancipation." This exercise, just after the pugilists had concluded their exhibition, "was scarcely a prudent thing to do, but it showed him to be a man of undaunted courage." The crowd erupted, forcing him to shut down.[12]

Huber proselytized in private as well. He often wore "a snuff colored box coat with outsize pockets stuffed with copies of the *National Era*, and other incendiary literature" that he passed out to a promising mind.[13] Professor David Swing accidently met Huber in the woods one day and was subjected to an antislavery lecture. The chance encounter gave birth to a young abolitionist.

Huber took W. P. Fishback to see the former president John Quincy Adams in Cincinnati. Adams, who was a U.S. congressman at he time, came to Cincinnati to dedicate the city's new astronomic observatory on Mount Ida. As Fishback describes it,

There was an immense crowd in the street; the rain was pouring as the procession went by. Uncle Charlie elbowed his way to the carriage, took Adams by the hand, and said, 'I come to take you by the hand, not because you were President of the United States, but for your manly defense of the right to petition.[14]

No one knows precisely how many fugitives Huber helped to

escape. Byron Williams, Williamsburg's historian, places the estimate between three and five hundred. Huber harbored his "cargo" at his home at 160 Gay Street, his cattle farm on the outskirts of the village, and, at least on one occasion, in the woods.[15]

Professor David Swing described one such encounter in the summer of 1849. Young Swing knew Huber as "one of those fearful creatures called Abolitionists" to whom his family looked upon with "abhorrence." One day he was on his way to the village to buy sugar and molasses. In a ravine he saw Boss shaking hands with a large black man. It appeared that Huber was giving the man money and directions to a town further north.

To my young and altogether verdant soul it seemed that the Boss was sending a colored man on some errand to some distant town or state, for the fact and manner of the Underground Railroad had not fully penetrated my soul.[16]

Huber calmly walked with Swing out of the ravine to the village, talking to him about "all the wrongs and sufferings of the black men in the South." Huber pulled one of those *National Era* newspapers from his coat and gave it to the young man to read. Swing recalled a passage that particularly affected him: "We must in this country fear a temple of liberty whose shaft will pierce the skies." He quoted that statement in a debate he participated in some time later. The chance meeting with Huber that morning was a life-altering event. Swing wrote, "To-day, among things to be glad of, I am rather glad that I saw a slave make a summer morning sacred to him and to me tripping along through dense woods away from the Ohio and toward freedom."[17]

Dr. Isaac Beck of Brown County remembered one incident involving Huber. One night, while he was away, twelve fugitives arrived at his home. They were sent there by Huber. His wife entertained them throughout the night until they were safely conveyed to the next stop.[18]

W. P. Fishback recalled several of his uncle's experiences.

Many a night he stood guard about his house in Williamsburg while the slave hunters surrounded it an kept it in a state of siege. It would have cost them their lives if they would have crossed his threshold. He sometimes kept a shame guard at his house while the runaways were at the farm, in the hayloft, at corn shocks in the field. He told me a story once of a large company concealed in the corn shocks. The slave-hunters were looking for them. A baby had been sick and crying all night, but when the hunters came it quieted down and remained peacefully still until the search was over. The whole company were landed safe in Canada in less than a week.[19]

Another nephew remembered his uncle's stories of the "road." He also wrote that Huber concealed fugitives at both his farm and home. At the farm "they were secreted in the barns or in a straw stack on his farm near the village." Fishback recalled on one occasion that he had hidden seventeen slaves in the cornfield on his farm. Slave hunters came within several yards of discovering the fugitives.[20]

Others reported Huber's Underground Railroad activities. Philip Chatterton of Williamsburg wrote, "I was well acquainted with Mr. Huber who was station agent here. He with the assistance of a colored man hid and ran through quite a number to the land of freedom. Sardinia was the next station."[21] Byron Williams reported that a "truthful man" told him that "he helped Huber take food to seventeen at one time who had come in both lines and had been detained by a storm."[22] Louise Abbott also mentions the prominence of Huber in the operations of the Underground Railroad in Clermont County in her account to Wilbur Siebert.[23]

The location of Huber's farm was a mystery. Both of Huber's nephews describe activities occurring at the farm, but do not provide a location. Louise Abbott stated that the farm was located a couple of miles outside of Williamsburg on the Deerfield Road.[24] Early maps of the area were consulted, but none showed a Deerfield Road. Long-time inhabitants of the area were asked about the road, but none had ever heard of it.

Huber placed an advertisement in an August 1837 issue of the *Clermont Courier* announcing a cattle sale at his farm on the outskirts of the village.[25] Using 1837 as a base line, Williamsburg tax duplicates were examined from 1837 through 1854, the year Huber died. Each parcel of property was platted on a map of Williamsburg, revealing that Huber had, over time, purchased many individual outlots adjoining the village. These lots were located along the course of a road now known as State Route 276 running between Williamsburg and Owensville.

The final piece of evidence identifying the location of Huber's farm came from the Byron Williams's *History of Clermont and Brown Counties, Ohio*. Williams uses Deerfield Road as a landmark to locate an early cabin site. He wrote specifically that the site was two hundred yards south of Deerfield Road "and west of Kain Run."[26] Kain Run still bisects the road now known as State Route 276. This process took approximately six months to complete. The exact location of this

Fig. 11.3. *The field owned by Charles Huber on the outskirts of Williamsburg, Ohio, where Huber hid fugitives before transporting them to either Clinton or Brown County.*

Fig. 11.4. *The burial marker of Charles B. Huber, located at the Williamsburg Township Cemetery in Williamsburg, Ohio.*

important site was certainly worth the effort.

Huber did not live to see the emancipation; his death in 1854 was described as a "great loss" to the movement. To his nephew, "it has always been a matter of deep regret . . . that he did not live to see the day of triumph."[27] Huber is buried in the Williamsburg Cemetery.

Samuel Peterson

Williamsburg resident Samuel Peterson served several terms on the village council with Charles Huber. Peterson worked in conjunction with Huber. Known in the Underground Railroad parlance as an "engineer," an individual who conveyed "passengers" from one "station" to the next, Peterson took escapees by wagon from Huber's to Isaac Brown's farm in Sardinia. He also carried food baskets to the runaways staying at Huber's. Each of the baskets contained a small bottle of paregoric to quiet the children.[28]

Marcus Simms

Marcus Simms, described as a mulatto, was born in Virginia in 1820. He was employed by Charles Huber. He was so well thought of that Huber gave Simms a home. At night he worked for Huber as an "engineer," driving freedom-seekers either northward to the Quaker community of Martinsville in Clinton County or eastward to Sardinia in Brown County.[29]

Simms enlisted as a forty-three-year-old private in Company B of the Fifth United States Colored Troop (USCT) in Williamsburg on June 27, 1863. The regiment originally mustered in as the 127th Ohio Volunteer Infantry prior to the order from the War Department calling "colored men" to the service. At first, recruiting proceeded slowly. With the appointment of G. W. Shurtlef of Oberlin, a well-known abolitionist who had seen service with the highly regarded Seventh Ohio Volunteer Infantry, the regiment filled rapidly. The unit, organized at Camp Delaware, became the first black regiment recruited in Ohio. The Fifth USCT was ordered to Virginia.[30]

On September 29, 1864, the Fifth, Thirty-sixth, and Thirty-eighth

USCT were ordered to charge across a stream choked with thick brush at Chaffin's Farm, Virginia. They passed through the obstruction only to face "a thorny abates." A "murderous fire" of small arms exploded upon the colored troops. The men of the Fifth fell "by the scores." Among the twenty-eight of the regiment killed that day was Private Simms.[31]

Dr. Leavitt Thaxter Pease

Fig. 11.5. *Dr. Leavitt Thaxter Pease, the Williamsburg station-master after Charles Huber died.*

Leavitt Thaxter Pease was born on April 20, 1809, at Martha's Vineyard, Massachusetts. His father was the captain of a whaling ship. The Pease family moved to Amelia, Ohio, in 1814.

Pease studied medicine with Dr. William Thompson, the father of conductor Dr. William E. Thompson of Bethel. He began his medical practice in 1832 and graduated from the Ohio Medical College in the same year. On May 8, 1834, he married Nancy Fee, the sister of Robert Fee of Moscow. The couple moved to Williamsburg the next year and settled next door to Charles Huber. He, along with fellow conductor Samuel Peterson, became members of the Williamsburg Methodist Church in 1844. Dr. Pease was an antislavery Whig who served on the Williamsburg Village Council in 1849.[32]

Fig. 11.6. *The home of Dr. Leavitt Thaxter Pease, located at 180 Gay Street in Williamsburg, Ohio.*

Several sources mention Pease's involvement with the enterprise; however, they provide few details. Louise Abbott records a conversation she had with Samuel Peterson in which he spoke of Pease's involvement. No other details were provided. Rockey and Bancroft wrote of Huber and Pease in the same sentence: "Charles Boestler and Dr. L. T. Pease were always ready to help fugitives in Williamsburg." Byron Williams wrote, "After Huber's death the burden of the movement fell upon Dr. L. T. Pease for some five or six years." Mary Harrison Games explained, "While Huber lived, Dr. Pease acted as his assistant; but after Huber's death in 1854, the doctor took charge and carried on the work in much the same way." Games also wrote that

Marcus Simms continued his contribution to the work by helping Pease after Huber's death.[33]

Byron Williams, who lived down the street from both Huber and Pease, wrote that the "last excursion over the road" occurred in the summer of 1860 when he saw four "stalwart young men" carrying "fine double-barreled shotguns" passing through the village.[34]

Fig. 11.7. *The burial marker of Dr. L. T. Pease in Williamsburg Cemetery located in Williamsburg, Ohio.*

NOTES

1. Knepp, *Nine Who Made a Difference*, 14.

2. Virginius Hall, *From Tomahawk to High Finance, The Life of Gen. Wm. Lytle* (1770–1831), (Cincinnati: privately published, 1957) 36; Lindsay Apple (professor of history, Georgetown College), interview, December 17, 2000.

3. Magor Wagner to William Lytle, undated, Hall, *From Tomahawk to High Finance*, 59–60.

4. *Western American*, March 18, 1835.

5. Rockey & Bancroft, *Clermont County, Ohio*, 288, 430A.

6. Ibid., 288; Rockey & Bancroft state that his destination was Mississippi. Byron Williams reports it was New Orleans. Williams, *Clermont and Brown Counties, Ohio*, 1:399.

7. Clermont County, Ohio, Tax Duplicates, 1838.

8. W. P. Fishback to W. Siebert, May 23, 1897, Ohio Historical Society, Columbus, Ohio.

9. C. B. Huber , Records and Memorials, SEN 25A-H1, 25th Congress; Records of U.S. Senate, Record Group 46; National Archives, Washington, D.C., January 22, 1838.

10. W. P. Fishback to W. Siebert, May 23, 1892.

11. *Clermont Courier*, September 15, 1909.

12. Ibid.

13. W. P. Fishback to W. Siebert, May 23, 1892

14. Ibid. Mt. Ida's name was changed that day to Mt. Adams in honor of the former president. Huber was referring to Adams's heroic stand in the U.S. House of Representatives against the "Gag rule" which prohibited acceptance of antislavery petitions. See William Lee Miller, *Arguing About Slavery: The Great Battle in the United States Congress* (New York: A. A. Knopf, 1996).

15. Byron Williams, "History of Clermont County," *Enclyopedic Directory and History of Clermont County, Ohio*, eds. Thirey and Mitchel, Ohio, 1902, (Evansville, Ind.: Unigraphic, 1977) 119.

16. David Swing, *New York Independent*, December 1979, as quoted in Rockey & Bancroft, *Clermont County, Ohio*, 135.

17. Ibid.

18. Isaac Beck, *Beers History*, 284; Siebert.

19. W. P. Fishback to Siebert, May 23, 1892.

20. W. S. Fishback to Siebert, September 30, 1898.

21. Philip Chatterton to W. Siebert, Sept. 10, 1894.

22. Huber does not say who that "truthful man" was. Both lines refers to the Bull Skin Trace line from Bethel and from Sardinia. This account sounds very similar to the episode recounted earlier by Dr. Beck. Williams, *Clermont and Brown Counties*, 1:402.

23. Louise Abbott to Wilbur Siebert, November 27, 1915.

24. Ibid.

25. *Clermont Courier*, August 26, 1837.

26. Williams, *Clermont and Brown Counties, Ohio*, 193.

27. W. P. Fishback to Siebert, May 23, 1892, Siebert Papers.

28. Rockey & Bancroft, *Clermont County, Ohio*, 298; Louise Abbott to W. Siebert, November 27, 1915.

29. U.S. Census, 1860; W. P. Fishback to Siebert, May 23, 1892; W. S. Fishback to Siebert, September 30, 1898; Louise Abbott to Siebert, November 27, 1915; Philip Chatterton to Siebert, September 10, 1894; Williams, *Clermont & Brown Counties, Ohio*, 1:402.

30. National Park Service (NPS). "Civil War Soldiers and Sailors System," www.itd.nps.gov/cwss/soldiers.cfm; Reid, *Ohio in the Civil War*, 2:916–17.

31. Reid, *Ohio in the Civil War*, 916–17; Noah Andre Trudeau, *Like Men of War: Black Troops in the Civil War, 1862–1865* (Boston: Little, Brown, 1998) 291–293.

32. Rockey & Bancroft, *Clermont County, Ohio*, 308A, 298.

33. Abbott to Siebert, November 27, 1915; Ibid., 135; Williams, *Clermont & Brown Counties, Ohio*, 1:402; Games, *Underground Railroad*, 72, 73n6.

34. Williams, *Clermont and Brown Counties, Ohio*, 1:402.

Conclusion

SOUTHERN EXTREMISTS THREATENED DISUNION if Abraham Lincoln was elected president of the United States. Shortly after the election, these "fire eaters" made good on their threat. South Carolina left the Union on December 20, 1860. Within weeks, Texas, Louisiana, Mississippi, Florida, Alabama, and Georgia, all states within the deep South, followed. The states of the upper South, where slavery's hold was more tenuous, delayed. These states indicated that they would remain in the Union if the North would promise not to retaliate against the seceding Southern states. Northerners resented the hint of blackmail in the proposal.[1]

Northerners tried to pull back from the brink. President Lincoln wrote a conciliatory letter to Alexander Stephens, the vice president of the newly formed Confederacy, explaining his position on slavery. Lincoln thought slavery was wrong and would work to prevent its expansion. He would not, however, force its abolition within the states.[2]

Last-ditch efforts at compromise were made in Congress. Ohio's conservative Republican senator, Thomas Corwin, introduced a constitutional amendment that would have prohibited Congress from abolishing slavery within the states. With Lincoln's support, the measure passed both Houses. John Crittenden, senator from Kentucky, submitted several proposed amendments that would have, among other things, re-instituted provisions of the Missouri Compromise, permitting slavery to expand.[3]

Some in the North were content to let the South go. The *Chicago Tribune* advised the country to let South Carolina go "like a limb lopped from a healthy trunk, wilt and rot where she falls." Horace Greely proclaimed, "We hope never to live in a republic where one section is pinned to the residue by bayonets."[4] The North refused to provide assurances the holdout states demanded. Thus, Virginia, North Carolina, Tennessee, and Arkansas followed their sister states out of the Union and into the Confederacy. The stage was set.

The firing on Fort Sumter galvanized the North. Any remaining ambivalence toward the South disappeared. Thousands of men in the North rallied to the colors. Most enlisted in the army to fight for their country, not to free the slaves. As one Indiana private put it, "I came out pure to do my Duty and to fight the rebes and poot Down rebelyon."[5]

And so it was in Clermont County as well. Hundreds rushed to recruiting centers in Batavia and New Richmond. Dozens more formed Home Guard units. The *Clermont Courier* captured the county's mood.

Friends of Freedom! Lovers of our noble Union! That banner which has so long waved in triumph over the proudest nation in the world has been trampled upon by those who had sworn to defend it! . . .

The destruction of the Union is the only issue, and they have forced that issue upon us. . . . If a million of Union soldiers are needed, they will be forthcoming! Our cause is just, and must prevail. We have the trust in the God of battles and keep our powder dry.[6]

Few, especially in the days immediately following the fall of Fort Sumter, would have subscribed to Frederick Douglass's vision of the War.

The American people and the Government at Washington may refuse to recognize it for a time; but the 'inexorable logic of events' will force it upon them in the end; that the War now being waged in this land for and against slavery; and that it can never be effectively put down till one or the other of these vital forces is completely destroyed.[7]

President Lincoln was pressured by radical Republicans to convert the war from one of restoration of the Union to one of liberation of the slaves. Conservatives warned of the dire consequences this action would have upon the loyalty of border state slaveholders. Lincoln debated.

The president floated a plan of gradual, compensated emancipation to border-state congressmen in March of 1862. They rejected it out of hand. Thereafter, Lincoln tilted towards the radical Republicans.[8]

Lincoln had never liked slavery. He had held to a widely accepted belief that the Constitution restrained the national government from abolishing slavery within the states. The war, however, had changed all of that. The Southern states were in rebellion; the very life of the Union was at stake. Lincoln was the commander-in-chief. Did he not have certain "war powers" that he could exercise, among them the abolition of slavery within the states in rebellion?

He concluded that the current emergency justified the act. But what about the timing? It could not appear to be the act of a desperate man. He had to wait for a Union victory, but in 1862 Union victories were rare. The army provided that victory in September of 1862 at Antietam. The president, in freeing the slaves, did so in his capacity as commander-in-chief. He proclaimed that the act was a "fit and necessary war measure." Underscoring his limited constitutional powers, he freed only those slaves in areas still in "rebellion against the United States."[9]

What about the men of the nation's armed forces? Would they support this "necessary and fit" war measure? Some approved. Urich Parmele of Connecticut left college at Yale for the service specifically "to free the slave." His devotion to the cause was redoubled with the announcement, "I do not intend to shirk now there is really something to fight for. I mean freedom." Others, who were not abolitionists, saw a practical outcome in the policy. One soldier was for "putting away any institution if by doing it will help put down the rebellion, for I hold that nothing should stand in the way of the Union—niggers or anything else."[10]

But there were many who were outraged: "I came out to fight for the restoration of the Union and to keep slavery as it is without going into the territories and not to free the niggers." Gen. George McClellan heard enough of this sentiment within his Army of the Potomac that he felt compelled to issue an order prohibiting such talk.[11]

On occasion, the dissenters went too far. Col. Joseph D. Hatfield, commander of the hapless Eighty-ninth Ohio Volunteer Infantry, complained that he went to war to "fight for his country and not to free the damned nigger." He was court-martialed and cashiered from the army for his "disloyal sentiments." He returned to Clermont County to resume his mercantile interest and to establish a short-lived proslavery Baptist Association. The most famous of the army dissenters was Brig. Gen. Fitz John Porter. He expressed his opposition to the proclamation in a series of letters to the *New York World*. He wrote that the proclamation was "absurd" and that President Lincoln was a "political coward" for having issued it. Porter was subsequently reminded of the superiority of civilian authority and was removed from command.[12]

The Emancipation Proclamation also announced that the United States would accept blacks in the armed forces of the country. Frederick Douglass remarked about the profound consequences of blacks fighting for their freedom when he said, "Once the black man get upon his person the brass letters U.S; let him get an eagle on his button and a musket on his shoulder, and bullets for his pocket, and there is no power on earth . . . which can deny that he has earned the right of citizenship in the United States."[13] Nearly 180,000 black men volunteered for the service.

Many whites doubted that blacks would make good soldiers. They could be servants or laborers, but soldiers, no. The doubts were settled on the battlefield. Gen. George Thomas, a loyal Virginian, surveyed the frozen battleground before Nashville with the bodies of black soldiers strewn about. He noted, "The question is settled; negro soldiers will fight."[14] Douglass was right.

Freedom did not come for the slaves with the Emancipation Proclamation. Nor did it come with the end of the Civil War. The Thirteenth Amendment to the U.S. Constitution, which freed four million slaves, was not ratified until December of 1865. America's Second Revolution had finally ended.

NOTES

1. Levine, *Half Slave and Half Free*, 224; James McPherson, *Battle Cry of Freedom* (New York: Oxford University Press, 1988), 251.
2. Levine, 228–29.
3. Ibid, 229–230.
4. Quoted in James M. McPherson, *The Illustrated Battle Cry of Freedom: The Civil War Era* (Oxford, [U.K.]; New York: Oxford University Press, 2003) 251–52.
5. Quoted in James I. Robertson, Jr., *Soldiers: Blue and Gray* (New York: Warner Books, 1991) 10.
6. *Clermont Courier*, April 17, 1861.
7. Frederick Douglas quoted in Levine, *Half Slave and Half Free*, 239.
8. McPherson, *Battle Cry of Freedom*, 302.
9. Allen C. Guelzo, *Lincoln's Emancipation Proclamation: The End of Slavery in America* (New York: Simon & Schuster, 2004) 93; Ibid, 504.
10. Guelzo, *Lincoln's Emancipation Proclamation*, 114.
11. Quoted in Bell Irvin Wiley, *The Life of Billy Yank* (Baton Rouge: Louisiana State University, 1978) 42; McPherson, *Battle Cry of Freedom*, 559. Court-martial of Joseph D. Hatfield.
12. Ibid; McPherson, *Battle Cry of Freedom*, 559.

13. James M. Perry, *Touched with Fire: Five Presidents and the Civil War Battles That Made Them* (New York: Public Affairs, 2003) 103–04. James Garfield, the future twentieth United States president from Ohio, was a member of the court-martial board. Porter was restored to the army's active roll in 1886 by Congress.

14. Frederick Douglass quoted in Noah A. Trudeau, *Like Men of War: Black Troops in the Civil War, 1862–1865* (Boston: Little Brown, 1998) 19; Thomas quoted, Ibid, 349.

Vote Totals for
Clermont County, Ohio

Governor

Township	Shannon	Corwin	King
Batavia	209	256	4
Williamsburg	110	193	3
Tate	228	249	4
Franklin	208	193	13
Washington	252	178	2
Monroe	193	115	4
Ohio	375	184	21
Union	227	47	
Miami	252	157	1
Goshen	161	145	1
Wayne	142	47	
Stonelick	147	116	1
Jackson	54	87	1
Totals	**2,511**	**1,969**	**55**

(*Clermont Courier*, October 12, 1842)

President—1848

Township	Cass	Taylor	Van Buren	Total
Batavia	252	296	7	555
Williamsburg	132	231	19	385
Tate	206	272	32	504
Franklin	262	216	45	523
Washington	278	195	15	488
Monroe	199	115	27	341
Ohio	392	107	183	682
Union	226	71	20	317
Miami	272	329	22	523
Goshen	183	147	25	355
Stonelick	178	133	7	318
Wayne	159	67	9	235
Jackson	87	126	1	214
Totals	**2,826**	**2,205**	**417**	**5,448**

(*Clermont Courier,* November 9, 1848)

President—1856

Township	Buchanan	Fremont	Fillmore
Batavia	229	252	45
Williamsburg	170	188	87
Tate	256	231	40
Franklin	279	212	87
Washington, 1st precinct	156	111	31
Washington, 2nd precinct	108	62	18
Ohio	178	254	58
Union	190	89	33
Miami	281	132	118
Goshen	149	145	30
Wayne	169	68	59
Jackson	127	85	72
Pierce	176	121	11
Monroe	172	142	36
Totals	**2,754**	**2,188**	**795**

(*Clermont Sun,* November 6, 1856)

U.S. Census 1860
Clermont's Black Communities of New
Richmond and Ohio Township

Occupations of New Richmond Blacks: 1860

Occupation	Number		Occupation	Number
River men	14		Barber	1
Laborers	14		Cooper	1
Farmer	10		Teacher	1
Washerwoman	8		Whitewasher	1
Cook	2		Plasterer	1
Blacksmith	2		Gardner	1
Drayman	1			

Top States of Origin of
New Richmond Blacks: 1860

State	Number
Ohio	59
Mississippi	42
Virginia	40
Kentucky	33

Occupations of Ohio Township Blacks: 1860

Occupation	Number		Occupation	Number
Laborer	34		Huckster	1
Farmer	5		Blacksmith	1
River man	4		Seamstress	1
Washer woman	2		Barber	1
Minister	1		House Servant	1
Carpenter	1			

State of Origin of
Ohio Township Blacks: 1860

State	Number
Ohio	79
Virginia	58
Kentucky	53
Mississippi	27

Index